Foreign Policy Analysis

MERRILL POLITICAL SCIENCE SERIES
Under the Editorship of
John C. Wahlke
Department of Political Science
University of Iowa

Foreign Policy Analysis

A Comparative and Conceptual Approach

Howard H. Lentner

Baruch College
The City University of New York

Charles E. Merrill Publishing Company
A *Bell & Howell Company*
Columbus, Ohio 43216

Published by
Charles E. Merrill Publishing Company
A *Bell & Howell Company*
Columbus, Ohio 43216

Copyright ©, 1974, by Bell & Howell Company. All rights reserved. No part of this book may be reproduced in any form, electronic or mechanical, including photocopy, recording, or any information storage or retrieval system, without permission in writing from the publisher.

Library of Congress Catalog Card Number: 73-85554

ISBN: 0-675-08884-4

1 2 3 4 5 6 7 8—80 79 78 77 76 75 74

Printed in the United States of America

Preface

One of my favorite activities on rainy Sunday afternoons is baking bread with my children. The homely example of baking bread strikes me as a useful "model" to employ in explaining foreign policy, perhaps more adequate than many of the mechanistic "models" which most of us political scientists carry in our heads.

Mechanical metaphors such as the balance of power do not convey an image of a process of ripening and growth that so often seems to characterize political affairs. Computer programs which relate variables convey a mechanical sense that gives no flavor of process. They do not portray the impact of marginally changing and interacting ingredients.

Of course, no model or metaphor captures entirely the substance and process of social and political life. Since all of us employ them, however, I prefer the baking of bread to mechanics. Bread results not simply from the concurrent existence of the ingredients (or variables if you like) but from their mixture in particular amounts and from their interaction, fermentation, growth, kneading, and the application of heat. Homely though it is, the model of bread conveys something of the complexity and especially of the process of political life.

Though the reader will not be faced in subsequent pages with a laboring of the bread image, I ask you now to seriously consider replacing mechanistic images of political life with this one. Together, let us consider variables, but let us consider them as interacting through time in a set of processes.

I have tried to write in a style which encourages the reader to join in a common exploration of the subject of foreign policy. Too little is known and too much is tentative for this to be a written lecture. It might be regarded rather as my contribution to a seminar in which the reader is challenged to consider, to criticize, to contemplate, and to add to the effort at thought in this book.

My debts are many. Misses Shirley Pell and Pushpa Rathor and Messrs. Anthony Gaughan, Howard Levitt, and Daniel Kislenko have provided research assistance at different times. Students in my seminar in foreign policy at McMaster University in 1971-72 have made helpful comments on an earlier version of the manuscript. Professors Gordon P. Means and Gilbert R. Winham of McMaster University and Robert B. Cunningham of the University of Tennessee read parts of the manuscript and made helpful critical comments. Professors Keith R. Legg of the University of Florida, Roy Licklider of Rutgers University, and Edwin H. Fedder of the University of Missouri-St. Louis reviewed the entire manuscript and made many helpful suggestions. They may not fully approve of the finished product, but it is better because of their efforts. My wife, M. Nancy Lentner, gave me many helpful editorial criticisms. I am grateful to each of these people, will gladly share any praise the work may receive, and absolve them from any blame for errors that may be pointed out.

I am very grateful to my efficient and loyal secretary, Mrs. Edna Colclough, who typed and helped in other ways beyond the call of duty. I am also appreciative of the typing done by Misses Inger Mortensen and Elvia Horvath and Mrs. Linda Gardner.

The Arts Division Research Council of McMaster University awarded me summer research stipends in 1969, 1970, 1971, and 1972. For these awards which provided not only sustenance but also encouragement, I am most grateful.

My appreciation also goes to Roger Ratliff for his interest and encouragement over the years as an idea matured and for his help in bringing my manuscript to the publication stage. I am also grateful to Susan Ziegler for her skillful editing and smooth management of the production of this book.

Contents

1	Introduction	1

Units of Analysis

2	Actors	17
3	The International Environment	51
4	Situations	67

Determinants and Processes

5	Foreign Determinants	105
6	Domestic Determinants	135

Acts

7	Decisions	173
8	Mobilization of Resources	199
9	Application of Instruments and Techniques	215

Policies and Consequences

10	Policies: Insulation, Engagement, Expansion	247
11	Consequences	265
	Selected Readings	279
	Index	285

1

Introduction

The basic condition of international political life is the "security dilemma."[1] Countries constantly attempt to increase their power and security because they fear that other countries will develop the power to overwhelm them and kill their citizens. Yet no country can achieve a position of absolute security, either alone or in concert with others.

The Soviet Union and the United States—with spacious and rich geographical areas, large populations, major industrial bases, impressive intellectual resources, and resourceful leadership—have engaged for many years in a weapons race. Despite the major efforts that have been expended and despite the sophistication of their military technology, they remain in fundamentally the same condition of existence as they did at any time since the establishment of American independence in 1783.

---

1. The "security dilemma" or "power and security dilemma" is described and analyzed in John Herz, *Political Realism and Political Idealism: A Study in Theories and Realities* (Chicago and London: The University of Chicago Press, 1951). Its meaning in the contemporary age is analyzed in his *International Politics in the Atomic Age* (New York: Columbia University Press, 1959).

Israel and Egypt, without the resource base of the superpowers, have bought arms to provide themselves with security. After three wars, they continue to exist in the same fundamental condition.

Some countries, in an attempt to preserve what they have, opt out of the active seeking of a resolution to the security dilemma by insulating themselves from the harsh conflicts of international life. Burma today, Cambodia yesterday, and the United States in the mid-1930s are all examples.

Nazi Germany tried to resolve its security dilemma by eliminating all potential threats to its security. Its obvious lack of success seems to confirm the existence of the security dilemma, but an opposite course of historical events would not have disconfirmed it, for even a successful conqueror would not have been spared the security dilemma. It is impossible to be alone in the world.

The achievement of many values requires cooperation with others. Higher standards of living rely upon international trade. Better health and longevity depend upon the transfer of medical technology among countries. Increased safety can sometimes be achieved by alliances and other forms of political cooperation.

The security dilemma, then, is mitigated by interdependence for the achievement of values, by idealism, and by striving for the common good. This dual aspect of international political life is not unlike the basic characteristics of political life in a domestic political system. Just as individuals and groups in a society make demands upon and give support to their society, states in the international community seek to achieve their values vis-à-vis other states. Similar to domestic politics, international politics contains elements of cooperation and conflict, demands and supports, disruption and regulating. States make distinctions between friends and enemies.

There are, on the other hand, differences between domestic and international politics. The mechanisms in international society for aggregating interests and for regulating conflict are more primitive than in well-developed political systems. War is a more common threat. The structure of the international system is achieved more informally. The crucial distinction is the absence of an overarching authority. These characteristics make the struggling aspects of politics more apparent in the international realm. Although the security dilemma is basic to all human existence, it is normally obscured in domestic politics because of the presence of a governmental authority which provides order and protects individuals from one another. The protection can never be absolute, but a domestic political system more nearly approaches the absolute because of the monopoly of power and authority which govern-

Introduction 3

ments claim and hold. This same function is attempted by states in the international realm even though they do not have a monopoly of power and authority there.

In international politics, states compete for control of situations which threaten them or which might impinge on their security. There are different ways of seeking such control, and there are several perspectives from which to view such situations. The result of the varied actions of states is the formation of international structures and processes for conducting relations among states. Some of these, like a balance of power structure and the use of threats, are informal. Others, like the United Nations and diplomatic practices, are more formal.

The study of international politics may focus either on the structure and process of interactions or on the processes of foreign policy formation and execution.[2] The focus chosen in this book is the latter.

The Study of Foreign Policy

Foreign policy lies at the intersection of the domestic and international aspects of a country's life. The focus we have chosen for study cannot entirely exclude the structure and process of either the international system or domestic political systems. To clarify our focus, however, we need to lay out criteria of what is to be included in and excluded from our study. These criteria may be found in the definition and discussion of some key concepts.

Policy is a form of action which involves (1) selection of objectives, (2) mobilization of means for achieving those objectives, and (3) implementation, or the actual expenditure of efforts and resources in pursuit of the selected objectives. Although a common misconception of policy includes only the *statement of objectives* or decision making, a comprehensive study of policy recognizes that it includes all three of the types of action mentioned in this definition.[3]

It is possible for a government to decide that it wants to rule the world. Without the *means* to accomplish this, however, such a decision

---

2. See Fred A. Sondermann, "The Linkage Between Foreign Policy and International Politics," in *International Politics and Foreign Policy: A Reader in Research and Theory*, ed. James N. Rosenau (New York: The Free Press of Glencoe, Inc., 1961), for a good discussion of the distinction between international politics and foreign policy and the different implications of the two foci.

3. Whatever its merits and other flaws, the decision-making approach to the study of foreign policy is incomplete because it does not include analysis of the implementation of policy and of the mobilization of resources.

is the expression of a sentiment rather than a policy. The United States' slogan concerning the "rollback of Communism" in the middle 1950s remained simply a slogan rather than a policy. This became starkly evident during the Soviet invasion of Hungary in 1956.

The mobilization of means most often occurs within the boundaries of a country, but sometimes it may include acquiring resources from other countries or entering into alliances. An underdeveloped country pursuing a policy of raising the standard of living of its people, for example, may require the importation of capital and technology. A country pursuing a policy of providing for its security against a larger neighboring country may enter into an alliance with a third country, thus putting the resources of that third country at the disposal of its objectives.

The crucial test of policy comes in the third type of act: *implementation*. A country may have decided to go to war with a neighbor. It may even have mobilized its army and amassed it on the common border, poised for attack. Not until the army has actually crossed the border and begun fighting, however, can we say that the country has put its policy into effect.

Although policy necessarily includes all three types of acts which have been discussed, there are circumstances in which one can legitimately speak of policy even though it does not conform to the neat model implied by this analysis. Actions which cope with the environment of the actor are policies, but they may not be so coherent and purposeful as the phrase "selection of objectives" may suggest. When Japan attacked the United States in 1941, one American response was to incarcerate Americans of Japanese ancestry residing on the west coast. Hindsight has made it clear that the policy was an axiomatic response to ill-founded fears and prejudices. It did not represent a well-considered selection of objectives.

Sometimes those who formulate policy are presented with a problem and simply feel the need to "do something." They decide; they garner the means; and they act to implement their decision. Despite the absence of cool calculation, the careful weighing of alternatives, and an image of rationality, the actions associated with such undertakings conform to the definition of policy given above.

The component actions of policy need not occur in the sequence in which they have been noted. In particular, the mobilization of resources most often precedes decision making. Indeed, decision making is often constrained by the means that are available.

Obviously, in studying foreign policy, the scholar is concerned only with that policy which is foreign. The specific definition of foreign depends on the viewpoint of any particular country and refers to all that is outside that country. A distinction needs to be drawn between a country and its environment. Foreign policy refers to that portion of a country's life which copes with its environment. Insofar as the policy of a country is addressed to problems exclusively within its jurisdiction and does not affect other countries, it can be defined as domestic. Insofar as policies are directed to other countries or have an impact on other countries, they fall within the meaning of foreign.

Although this distinction may be clear conceptually, it is sometimes difficult to apply in practice. For example, the Soviet Union in 1972 passed a law requiring citizens who wished to emigrate to compensate the state for the money it had spent on their education. The law had a particular, though not exclusive, impact upon Jews who wished to emigrate to Israel. While the law applied only to Soviet citizens within Soviet jurisdiction, it nevertheless had an effect on Israel by depriving that country of valuable, skilled human resources. It also had an impact on the prestige of the Soviet Union in other countries. This example suggests that in some cases the distinction between foreign and domestic policy is a difficult one to make. Still, the foreign and domestic aspects of a policy may be distinguished.

The way in which one can separate these aspects is by defining "environment," for foreign policy is that policy which is directed toward or which responds to the environment of a territorial state and its government, referred to as an actor. (The definition of "actor" will be broadened in chapter 2.)

The environment of the actor consists of all other states.[4] To describe the environment in a manageable fashion, however, two concepts will be employed in analyzing it.

The first is the *international system*, or the pattern of interaction among states shaped by the structure of interaction between or among the most powerful actors. (Thus, in the post–1945 period, the notion of bipolarity will be used to describe the environment.)

Second, the concept of *situation* will be used to identify patterns of interaction that do not encompass the entire international system. The pattern of relationships among the western European countries which have involved the development of the Common Market and other communities would be treated as a situation, for example. Although it is not isolated from the international system, neither is it explained by

---

4. This restricted definition of environment is useful for analytical purposes. In reality, however, the environment of an actor encompasses components, some of which are discussed in chapter 3, which are not under the control of states.

the international system. Moreover, through the situation unit of analysis one can more readily account for the interactions of actors with their environments.

The main focus will be on the actors, but it is not possible entirely to neglect the environment, given the definition of foreign policy as the interaction of an actor with its environment. This basic framework of interaction leads us to inquire into basic patterns of interaction and to a classification of foreign policy. Classification is based upon the fundamental relationship of the actor and a situation, from the point of view of the actor. That is, the existence of situations is assumed.

The actor may choose to *insulate* itself from a situation, or it may lack the capacity to engage in a situation. This means that, although a country has an interest in a situation, it does not attempt to control it. At the same time, it does attempt to prevent other actors in the situation from gaining control over its own domain. The clearest examples of policies of insulation are provided by neutral countries.

The second type of policy is *engagement*. That is, a country becomes involved in a situation and shares control over the situation with other actors who participate in it. This type of policy is most common, although countries vary substantially in the number of situations in which they are engaged. There are several reasons for this variation, but the most important is the capacity of the actors. Capacity will be defined later.

Third, actors may *expand*. That is, they may seek to extend their control beyond the domain that they controlled before embarking on policies of expansion. They do not share control over situations in their external environments: they attempt to monopolize control of situations.

Many different actions occur within each of these types of policies. The policy types, however, vary according to the amount of control and with whom it is shared. All political acts involve the question of control, and all fall into the types of policy given.

There are three essential features of this approach to foreign policy. First, the central problem to be analyzed is control, whether over the actor or the environment. Second, foreign policy involves interaction with the environment. No country can achieve its values alone, and every country is dependent upon the response of other countries. Third, the actions and interactions shape situations, and situations in turn influence the actors. Ultimately, however, change occurs within the actors themselves. Despite the constant interaction and adjustment process, one looks for independent variables within countries and dependent variables in the environment. Because of the interaction and adjustment process, on the other hand, it will be useful later to examine these phenomena the other way around; that is, to regard situations as the independent variables and the actors as the dependent variables.

Foreign policy involves constant adjustments, both within states and between states and the situations in which they are interested. Part of the problem in analyzing foreign policy is to define those factors which preserve continuity and to explain how they operate, but also there is a need to identify which factors tend to produce change and to explain how they function.

Adjustments within states are made through processes which operate upon a set of determinants. For example, the foreign policy of a country is determined in part by its economic system and its productive resources. The foreign policy of the country may aim at increasing trade in order to foster economic growth. Should its major trading partner impose new restrictions such as tariffs or quotas on its most important products, the economic system would not continue to grow at the same rate. This would require further adjustments both within the country and in its foreign policy. For example, the government might be replaced because of its failure to maintain the rate of economic growth, and the new government might seek new trading partners to replace the old. Insofar as the impact of such processes on the ability of a country to function effectively in coping with its environment is concerned, the effects of foreign policy on the domestic determinants will be referred to as *adaptation*.

Constant adjustments also occur in the interactions of a country with its environment. For example, if a country initiates a policy, it may find that the reaction of other states requires it to make additional decisions which modify, change drastically, or reverse the original initiative. Long-term policies may be cast in very broad terms followed by constant shifting and specification of more precise goals and means as opportunities arise.

Broadly speaking, countries have continuing and constant policies for given situations. The process of change is normally slow for most countries with respect to most situations most of the time. Although adjustments are continuously made in situations, they tend to persist in their essential qualities and characteristics. Under certain conditions, however, situations are transformed. *Transformation* means one or more of the essential features of the situation changes. For example, if one of the essential features of the balance of power system is oligopolistic—involving more than two major states—control over the international system, and the major states are reduced to two, there is a transformation to a bipolar system. The essential features of situations will be specified in a subsequent chapter.

Because situations are the result of the foreign policies of the actors interested in them, transformation must occur as the result of changes in the foreign policies of the actors whose actions produce the situation. For this reason, the factors which produce continuity and change within the actors also need to be identified.

A set of domestic determinants will be specified, and a distinction among those which tend to reinforce continuity and those which tend to induce change will be drawn. Actors vary substantially in domestic determinants, so the domestic determinants can be analyzed comparatively. The means by which changes in foreign policy come about can, however, be specified, for they are the same in any political system. There are four such means.

The first is a change in the personnel who make decisions. Elections, *coups d'etat,* or other processes may bring different people into authoritative positions who most probably vary in significant ways from the persons they replace. The second channel of bringing change in foreign policy is a change in the perceptions, goals, fears, etc., of those who remain as authoritative decision makers. Such changes require new experiences, and sometimes these can be decisive. For example, an intense international crisis may introduce a major transformation in the thinking of a decision-making elite.

Foreign policy making, like other forms of politics, involves a struggle. It is possible, then, as the third way of introducing change in foreign policy, for a struggle between two coalitions which are competing for control of a government to result in a shift in the political coalition which dominates a given policy-making process. That is, in any government there are fissures and disagreements. It is quite possible, under given conditions, for a predominant coalition in a decision-making process to give way to another coalition with different preferences. Although similar to the first channel, it does not require a complete changeover in government. The winning coalition, in this case, will simply win on a given issue or set of issues, but it will not necessarily gain control on all issues.

The final channel for bringing change in foreign policy is the development of new structures in the government. For example, a democratic political system might be transformed into an authoritarian one in which legislative controls give way to increased executive autonomy. The impact of such a constitutional change would not be limited to the domestic political system but would also extend to foreign policy.

However it comes about, change involves choice. By identifying the determinants within actors and in the environment, we can understand the limits of choice. Foreign policy analysis cannot, however, predict the

Introduction 9

precise choices that particular countries' leaders will make, but we can understand the factors which constrain and facilitate certain choices.

We cannot, for example, predict that Libya and Egypt will either remain allied, merge in a federation, or go to war. We can, though, understand the factors that make it more probable that any country would do so. Perhaps we can even state that one or the other of these specific alternatives for these specific countries is more or less likely. Additionally, we can understand the processes which operate under each of the alternatives, and we can seek to understand why.

We should also be conscious of the fact that every choice has costs attached to it. If a country decides to embark on a foreign aid program, for example, it will have to spend some of its resources, both human and material. On the other hand, should the same country choose not to embark on such a program, it would have to forego the benefits of increased influence and economic payoffs.

Every choice involves the rejection of alternatives. For example, when a country enters an alliance, it rejects friendlier relations with the adversaries of that alliance. Such a course of action also diminishes the freedom of choice of the country which aligns. This is not to say that there are not benefits to such courses of action, but it is to say that in international politics, as in other human affairs, countries cannot gain benefits without giving up something in return.

Sometimes choices may be deferred. Depending on conditions, though, the cost of deferred choice may be a loss of effectiveness. However, choices made too soon may result in option foreclosure and a loss of effectiveness. This suggests one way in which time has an impact on foreign policy.

Time is an important consideration in the analysis of foreign policy in a number of ways. With respect to decisional outcomes, there are long- and short-term policies. The time dimension here affects the kinds of supports that are necessary domestically for implementation of the policy, the resolve and persistence necessary for carrying it out (and here we may find differences among, say, democracies and authoritarian states), expected responses of other states, and the time needed for assessment of success which may become a factor in making further adjutments in foreign policy making.

Time is a factor in learning and change. Policies may be promoted in an untimely fashion in the sense that the situation is not ripe for exploitation in the manner that the policy envisages. The policy could also come too late.

In addition, it takes time to do the things necessary to conduct foreign policy. Studies and decision making both require time. Among other factors in an international crisis, time creates pressures on the decision-making elite. Moreover, in the short time period of a crisis, events may move past the capability of a government to cope adequately. The consequences that may flow from this problem may be either the necessity to capitulate to an adversary's acts and be confronted with a new situation or a decision to go to war because of the unacceptability of an adversary's actions. As we will see in a later chapter, time is an important variable affecting the legitimacy of regimes and the acceptance of situations. Since time cuts across many of the dimensions of foreign policy, we need to keep it in mind throughout our analysis. In the first instance, it needs to be considered as a cost.

Another cost of foreign policy results from the limited ability of men and organizations to keep more than a few problems at the forefront of attention.[5] Because only a few matters can be focused on at a time, a cost of focusing on one situation entails the neglect of another. This point is sharply illustrated by American policy during the Vietnam war which made it difficult for authorities to focus on other situations.

The very act of engaging in intellectual analysis tends to impose an order and meaning on the phenomenon of that segment of the world which one is studying. Although it is useful to do this, analysis should not ignore the disorder and irrationality that often exists in foreign policy. The actors we study are human organizations. They are subject to the same frailties, doubts, fears, wisdom, meannesses, stupidities, visions, and other human characteristics that other areas of human activity are. As Charles Burton Marshall has written, "The state . . . remains, in Plato's phrase, man written large. It is only man."[6]

Scheme of Analysis

The study of foreign policy has advanced considerably in recent years, both in the development of concepts and in the use of empirical data.[7] Despite the advances, however, there is no single theoretical scheme of analysis, nor is there a standard methodology. In short, the study of foreign policy is not a mature science.

---

5. See, for example, James G. Miller, "The Individual as an Information Processing System," in *Human Behavior and International Politics: Contributions from the Social-Psychological Sciences* ed. J. David Singer (Chicago: Rand McNally and Company, 1965).

6. *The Limits of Foreign Policy* (New York: Henry Holt and Company, 1954), pp. 14–15.

7. See the suggested readings list for this chapter which includes the major works which have advanced the discipline.

Introduction 11

In this book, there is some attempt to draw on work that has been done by others, both in the field of foreign policy itself and in other fields. Although not every useful concept has been incorporated, this approach attempts to be comprehensive. It does, moreover, build upon and sometimes depart from other work. In an immature science, it is often difficult to find areas of agreement and accumulation of knowledge.

Although different scholars assign different weights to them, there is some agreement that both the character of a country's internal life and the international environment have an impact on foreign policy.[8] The scheme of analysis of this book is based on the central conception that both sets of influences interact to shape foreign policies. Moreover, where possible, an attempt is made to assess which set is more important under what conditions. For example, it is argued that revolutionary regimes tend to spread their revolutions into neighboring countries for a time after they have come to power. This is clearly a case of the internal characteristics of the country having the dominant influence. After a time, however, the resistance of other countries tends to diminish such revolutionary activity. This is a case of the external environment of a country becoming predominant over the internal characteristics.

The very nature of foreign policy in this scheme, however, is that both sets of influences are always active, for no actor exists apart from its environment, yet every actor copes with that environment in ways that are shaped by its internal characteristics. Among other things, this means that the subject matter requires us to move among different levels of analysis. The basic thesis of this book is that it is important to analyze not only particular states but also relevant environments.

This approach includes the treatment of many variables, all of which are related to all of the others. It requires the use of a variety of modes of analysis. The book attempts overall to be conceptual and comparative. When empirical data are available and useful, they are referred to, but there is no reference to empirical data without a theoretical reason for employing them. On the other hand, where empirical data are not available, the theoretical analysis proceeds without reference to data.

Where possible, concepts are operationalized, although the reader will see that some of these operations do not give us entirely satisfactory definitions of the concepts in question. In such cases, the limits of the operational definitions are probed. The rule that rough measures are

---

8. Some scholars—Charles McClelland is a prominent example—do not agree on the grounds that it is impossible to gain reliable knowledge about the internal workings of a decision-making system.

better than no measures has been followed, and sometimes suggestions of possible other measures are given. However, concern for rigorous measurement has not allowed triviality to triumph over significance.

We begin by defining and analyzing the major units of analysis: actors, the international system, and situations. After some discussion and classification of international organizations and transnational actors, states—which are the most important actors—are analyzed. Two major concepts, capacity and predisposition, are used to classify states. Through tabular material, data are presented on all of the states in the world of over one million population. These data and the accompanying analysis give us the means of knowing some of the more important characteristics of most countries.

The international environment is then analyzed as a set of constraining and facilitating forces upon the foreign policies of states. To come closer to understanding the way in which the international environment helps to shape foreign policy, the concept of situation is developed. This is a unit of analysis that lies between the individual state and the international system and is an analytical device intended to relate specific environments to foreign policies. Normally, specifics can be examined only in particular cases, and some brief case studies are included, but the device of situation attempts to provide a framework for the comparative analysis of cases.

Having defined the major units of analysis, the book then turns to an examination of determinants and processes. In conformity with the basic thesis, two sets of determinants—foreign and domestic—are treated and the ways in which they operate are analyzed. The chapter on foreign determinants is an extension of the previous discussion on the international environment. By elaboration and through an illustrative case study, a dynamic dimension is added to the prior analysis. In a similar fashion, the chapter on domestic determinants elaborates on the concepts of capacity and predisposition but also includes a discussion of the process by which the factors comprising these concepts operate to produce policies.

Foreign policy actions are then discussed. As indicated above, these are of three types: decisions, mobilization of resources, and implementation. The chapter on decisions includes a rough classification of decisions, a discussion of the conditions under which decisions are made, and an analysis of the political process associated with decision making. In the chapter on mobilization of resources, the meaning of resources and the political process associated with mobilization as well as the factors hindering mobilization are discussed. The chapter on implementation classifies the various instruments of foreign policy and discusses how

Introduction 13

they are used. Included is some discussion of the political process associated with foreign policy implementation, and there is an attempt to analyze the problem of effectiveness.

Running through foreign policy actions is a political process, or a relationship between leaders and led. The chief executive who remains in the leadership position in any country has relations with different constituencies with respect to each kind of foreign policy act. Although there are complexities which are treated in these chapters, basically decisions involve relations of the chief executive with political elites; mobilization of resources, with mass publics and nongovernmental groups; and implementation, with bureaucracies. These relationships vary among different types of political systems, but they are characteristic of any political system.

Finally, policies and consequences are examined. The concept for analyzing policies is control, and there is an elaboration on the three basic types of policy: insulation, engagement, and expansion. Through use of the concepts of adjustment, transformation, and adaptation, the analysis concludes by examining the effects of actions and policies on the units of analysis. Thus, the book completes a circle of examining the effect of each of the selected variables on all the others.

The scheme of the book treats foreign policy as a whole system. This implies that, when a change occurs in one segment, there are adjustments to be made throughout.[9] When a state takes an action in its environment, then the environment will respond, and the state will have to adjust to the response. These responses are by no means automatic but rather represent political decisions and other acts. Thus, the portrait to be painted is that of political struggle, both within the state and among states, including sometimes the struggle between the environment and the internal political processes of the actors.

Although this book does not constitute a general theory of foreign policy because there are too many conceptual and empirical loose ends, it does constitute a comprehensive approach to the study of foreign policy and a complete framework for analysis.

---

9. For a theoretical treatment of this adjustment process, see George Modelski, *A Theory of Foreign Policy* (New York: Frederick A. Praeger, Publisher, for the Center of International Studies, Princeton University, 1962).

I

Units of Analysis

2

Actors

An actor is an organized entity which is capable of making all three foreign policy acts: decisions with respect to its environment outside a state political system, mobilization of resources to carry out those decisions, and the application of instruments and techniques to other actors. If an entity is incapable of any of these three acts, it is not an actor in the sense in which the term is used in this book. Also excluded are individuals who are acting autonomously; that is, outside of organized enterprises. Organized entities which operate only within the confines of a single state are also excluded.

States, of course, are the most apparent actors, although not all states are actors within the meaning of the term as it is used here, and other organized entities which are not states are actors. Some actors are relatively permanent, while others are ephemeral. Some make decisions with respect to only a narrowly circumscribed, single situation while others make decisions with respect to many situations of broad scope. There are vast differences in the resources which various actors command, and some actors have more instruments and techniques available than others. The skills and level of sophistication of the instruments and techniques also vary immensely. Consequently, one needs to make distinctions among actors along all these dimensions insofar as they are relevant to any given situation.

One also needs to distinguish between organized entities which operate across national boundaries but do not seek control of a situation and those which do contend for control, or, short of that, influence. International humanitarian enterprises which provide relief for refugees, for example, do not normally seek control of situations although they do make decisions with respect to the environment of the state in which they operate; they mobilize resources; and they apply instruments and techniques, if not to other actors, at least to personnel in other countries. On occasion, such an enterprise may seek control, and, when it does, it would need to be taken into account. On the whole, however, such entities can be excluded from consideration.

The same is not true for other nonstate entities. The National Liberation Front (Viet Cong) in South Vietnam, for example, cannot be excluded, for it does seek to gain a measure of control over a situation and fulfills all of the other requirements. The Palestinian guerrilla organization, Al Fatah, needs to be considered as an actor when dealing with the Arab-Israeli dispute. The diplomacy of the Catholic Church and the international activities of the AFL-CIO need to be taken into account in analyzing particular situations, for these organizations meet all of the criteria at certain times and in certain places. Sometimes, a state or a province needs to be considered to be an actor within our meaning. The Canadian Province of Quebec, for example, conducts cultural and educational relations with France and with the French-speaking countries of Africa, although it does so within the framework of Canadian policy.

When international organizations meet all of the criteria, they need to be considered. On occasions like the intervention in the Congo in 1960, the United Nations conforms to the definition. There are also occasions when multi-national corporations may become actors within the meaning used here.

There is, then, a wide variety of actors which might contend for control of a situation. The most important actors in most situations, however, are states. On the whole, this book deals with states, but it will be useful at this point to identify and briefly describe the several different types of international actors. In treating them, it will be possible to determine their significance by keeping in mind the notion of capacity to influence and control situations through the performance of foreign policy acts. If an actor has the capacity to influence or share control over one or more situations, then it is a significant actor.

The types of actors to be discussed are (1) international organizations, (2) transnational actors, and (3) states.

International Organizations

There are many thousand international organizations which may be grouped along three dimensions. First, they may be associations of governments or associations of nongovernmental entities. The United Nations, the General Agreement on Tariffs and Trade (GATT), the International Monetary Fund, the European Economic Community, the North Atlantic Treaty Organization (NATO), the Organization of African Unity (OAU), the World Health Organization, and the International Air Transport Association are all examples of intergovernmental organizations. The English-Speaking Union, the International Federation of Trade Unions, the International Political Science Association, and the International Chamber of Commerce are examples of nongovernmental organizations. Unless there are unusual circumstances, nongovernmental international organizations tend not to have the characteristics associated with international actors as they have been defined above. For purposes of foreign policy analysis, they can generally be accommodated within a framework limited to states.

Intergovernmental organizations, on the other hand, play important roles in international politics. They are somewhat difficult to deal with conceptually, however, for they tend to be the mechanisms of member states and seldom develop a life of their own. By participating in intergovernmental organizations, however, member states' policies are in part shaped by the organizations.[1] Moreover, the mechanisms of the intergovernmental organizations often facilitate the goals of members. They also provide forums for communication among members and confer status particularly on smaller members, and are institutions for the transfer of technical assistance and funding for the less developed countries.

The World Bank, for example, has the capacity to draw on technical experts for assisting underdeveloped countries in planning the development of their economies and to make loans for economic development purposes. The other specialized agencies associated with the United

---

1. See Robert E. Riggs, "The United Nations as an Influence on United States Policy," *International Studies Quarterly* 11 (March, 1967).

Nations also have the capacity to offer technical assistance in their respective specialized fields.

Although member states in intergovernmental organizations are partly influenced by the organizations, this influence is limited by the capacities of states to determine their own policies. In the European Economic Community, the members have achieved many common policies which they regard as binding. This phenomenon was also true in the International Monetary Fund from 1944 to 1970. In the 1970s, with the development of trade imbalances, members began taking unilateral initiatives. West Germany, for example, revalued the mark, and Canada let its dollar float. The United States in 1971 unilaterally took a series of measures to improve its international economic position. Other countries responded, and the alliance between the United States and Japan was particularly shaken.

Intergovernmental organizations sometimes develop the capacity to control or influence a situation, and then they may be treated as independent international actors. In some situations, such as the Middle East crisis of 1956, the Congo crisis of 1960, and the Cyprus crisis of 1964, the United Nations has demonstrated this capacity. When this capacity occurs, of course, the United Nations develops its own goals, and its actions have consequences for other actors. Because of its ideology of peace, it tends to protect the weaker side in a conflict. As was made evident by the Soviet attack on the Secretary-General in 1960, its actions may also seriously offend member states.

The second dimension along which we can group international organizations is scope. Some organizations have a nearly universal membership and worldwide aims. This is the case with the United Nations and the specialized agencies. On the other hand, some intergovernmental organizations are considerably more restricted, both as to membership and interests. These are usually referred to as regional organizations, although the meaning of regionalism in some cases loses its connotations of compactness and contiguity. The Latin American Free Trading Area, the Arab League, and the Warsaw Pact are all examples of regional organizations.

On the whole, regional associations affect only members in their respective regions. Sometimes, considered vis-à-vis the rest of the world, they may be international actors within our meaning because they effectively exclude other actors from participating in a situation. The Organization of African Unity, for example, while not having developed the capacity to manage certain African problems, nevertheless controls them in the sense of excluding non-African countries from participating in African situations. An example of this phenomenon occurred in 1972 in Burundi where a policy of slaughter seemed to have been directed against members of the Hutu Tribe by the Tutsi Tribe. The OAU determined that the problem was entirely a domestic one, and the deference of other countries to the OAU allowed that to be the controlling interpretation of the events.

Theoretically, global organizations operate throughout the world. In fact, they do not. Where there are strong regional organizations and where the superpowers do not wish global organizations to act, they cannot. The United Nations has been excluded from dealing with political problems in the Western Hemisphere, in the Soviet Union and Eastern Europe, in Western Europe and in Indochina. Thus, the United Nations is, within the meaning used in this book, a sometimes and someplaces international actor.

The third dimension for categorizing international actors is purpose. Generally, one can distinguish general purpose and limited—usually single—purpose organizations. Whereas the previous two dimensions placed the United Nations and the specialized agencies on the same side of the dichotomous categories, in this dimension they appear on opposite sides. The United Nations is a general purpose organization, being concerned with political, security, economic, social, and humanitarian problems. Each specialized agency, to the contrary, is concerned with a single function such as agriculture and food, health, meteorology, money, trade, or communications, to cite some examples.

Usually, only the general purpose organizations attempt to achieve control over situations in the manner of states, for they are essentially coalitions of states. Functional organizations have purposes which do not lead them to seek control over immediate political situations. The theory underlying their formation aims at longer-term changes in the structure of the international system by addressing functional problems like health, food, and so forth, and in the long run undermining the state.[2] On occasion, however, a functional agency may develop the capacity to influence a situation.

This discussion has stressed the limited capacity of intergovernmental organizations as international actors within the meaning used in this book. Apart from direct participation in international situations as independent actors, however, these organizations perform another important function. Their existence and modes of operating help to form the

---

2. For the definitive statement of functionalist theory, see David Mitrany, *A Working Peace System* (London and New York: Royal Institute of International Affairs, 1946). A good critique is contained in Inis L. Claude, Jr., *Swords Into Plowshares*, 3d rev. ed. (New York: Random House, 1964).

structure of the international system. State decision makers, both because of the existence of the structure and because some intergovernmental organizations have the potential for developing a capacity to intervene in certain situations, necessarily are pressed to factor these considerations into their deliberations.

One can see this operating in the Middle East where the United Nations has been particularly active. Since the removal of the United Nations Emergency Force (UNEF) in May 1967 and the ensuing six-day war, Israel has held the United Nations in some contempt and regards the organization to be ineffective. Nevertheless, the Security Council developed a formula for a Middle East peace settlement in 1967 and has passed resolutions condemning Israel's attacks on its Arab neighbors. The Security Council does not condemn Arab attacks on Israel because of the Soviet veto. Egypt in particular favors United Nations intervention in the Middle East, while Israel resists the intervention, following a policy of attempting to insulate the Middle East situation from the international system. Thus, even though the United Nations is no longer an effective actor in the Middle East, Israel is required nonetheless to include it in policy calculations concerning the Middle East situation.

Transnational Actors

Less prominent than intergovernmental organizations are transnational actors. These are nongovernmental entities which are based in a single country but which operate across international boundaries. Despite the fact that these actors may have links to citizens, groups, or firms in host countries, they may be distinguished from nongovernmental international organizations because their decision-making structure is not based on the principle of association among equal units as is the decision-making structure of international organizations. Control of these actors remains in each actor's headquarters in the home country.

There have been transnational actors as long as the state system has existed. With the growth of communications and transportation technology in the twentieth century, however, transnational actors have become more active and more prominent. Particularly prominent in the post-World War II period are multinational corporations. These are financial, manufacturing, extractive, and commercial enterprises which do not simply engage in international exchanges but invest in countries other than their home countries and engage in business activities in a manner similar to indigenous enterprises. They are different from indigenous enterprises, however, in that they are able, by command, to draw on skills and technology from other countries.

Primary attention by publicists and scholars has been focused on American multinational corporations because there are more of them, they are larger, and their operations are more extensive than those from other countries.[3] Moreover, American government policy has fostered their spread. There are, however, many multinational firms from other countries with investments throughout the world. Most of the political problems associated with multinational enterprises, however, may be linked to the fact that they are American and to fears that in circumstances in which a choice would need to be made their loyalty would go to the United States. Moreover, there is fear in many countries that the resources and jurisdiction of the American government extend to these firms.

The basic problem of the multinational enterprise from the point of view of the state is the problem of maintaining control. The multinational corporation, often endowed with greater economic assets than most countries, has enormous flexibility by virtue of drawing on skills, technology, and capital in many different countries. Individual states, then, have difficulty gaining jurisdiction over them. As these corporations continue to operate, grow, and spread, states may develop a view which regards the existence of the multinational corporations as a problem requiring collaborative action by all of the states involved. Alternatively, states may act unilaterally to deal with the operations of multinational enterprises within their borders. Should this become the case, it is quite possible that these corporate enterprises would become more active in domestic political systems and that issues of jurisdiction might develop between countries.[4]

On the whole, multinational corporations do not have political aspirations, so that the problem tends to be a jurisdictional one rather than a political one. There are fears on the part of elites in some countries, notably Canada and many underdeveloped countries, that multinational enterprises threaten their independence and tend to undermine indigenous cultures. Although these enterprises do add different dimensions to the economic life of a country and probably shape some values

---

3. An important publicist of the impact of multinational corporations is Jean-Jacques Servan-Schreiber whose book, *The American Challenge* (New York: Atheneum, 1969) is widely known. Perhaps the foremost scholar is Raymond Vernon. See especially his *Sovereignty At Bay: The Multinational Spread of U.S. Enterprises* (New York and London: Basic Books, Inc., 1971).

4. See Neil H. Jacoby, "The Multinational Corporation," *The Center Magazine* 3 (May 1970), for a discussion of these problems.

—particularly those relating to work, skills, development and use of technology, and so forth—their absence of political aspirations and claims upon loyalty would seem to indicate that these fears are exaggerated when measured against the threat. Nevertheless, the fears themselves are part of the political problems of forming policy, an issue to which we will return in the chapter on domestic determinants.

On the whole, multinational enterprises address a different set of problems than do states. When they are addressing the same ones, however, we can consider such firms to be actors within our meaning.

Other transnational actors do address similar problems as those faced by states. For example, Communist parties to some extent now, and more so in the era of monolithic control from Moscow, are alternative elites to those in power and do seek the allegiance of citizens and aspire to take over governments. The Vatican through its diplomacy seeks to influence certain situations.

In those situations in which these types of actors are operative in conjunction or competition with states, we need to include them in our analysis.[5]

States

The primary actors in international politics—and the ones upon which this book focuses—are states. Although legally equal, states vary substantially in many ways. In order to deal with states on a comparative basis, one needs to classify them along several dimensions.

The most common way of classifying states in the international system is along the dimensions of size, wealth, and nature of political regime. Professor Rosenau has developed systematic genotypes, using these dimensions, then dichotomizing each in terms of large-small, developed-underdeveloped, and open-closed.[6] These are useful categories for distinguishing among states. They are not, however, sufficient for understanding foreign policy, and in some circumstances they may be misleading.

The premise of genotypic classification is that a substantial variation in behavior can be accounted for on the basis of the genotypes. Whether

---

5. See Joseph S. Nye and Robert Keohane, eds., *Transnational Relations and World Politics* (Cambridge, Mass.: Harvard University Press, 1972), for the most complete study available of transnational actors.

6. James N. Rosenau, "Pre-theories and Theories of Foreign Policy," in R. Barry Farrell, *Approaches to Comparative and International Politics* (Evanston: Northwestern University Press, 1966).

Actors

this is true statistically may be questioned,[7] but if we identify significant events, it is difficult to account for them on the basis of genotypic classification. For example, the United States militarily intervened in the Dominican Republic in 1965, the Soviet Union militarily intervened in Czechoslovakia in 1968, and India militarily intervened in Pakistan in 1971. With all of the different justifications and styles, the three behaviors were essentially similar. The United States is a large-developed-open system; the Soviet Union, a large-developed-closed one; and India would be classified as large-underdeveloped-open. In all three cases the countries were large and engaged in similar behavior, but each belonged to a *different* genotype.

Being human institutions, states behave in complex ways for many different purposes and because of a variety of motivations. Although the study of foreign policy has been vigorously pursued, with some results, we are not in a position wholly to account for foreign policy behavior or to predict it. We can, nevertheless, move some way in foreign policy analysis on a comparative basis by raising the questions of whether countries have the *capacity* and the *predisposition* to engage in international situations. If we can develop some sensible means of determining those two things, we can then proceed to analyze the behavior of states in situations.

Capacity

In a sense, capacity is only meaningful in the context of a situation, for a country's capacity is an ability to do something in relation to other countries.[8] On the other hand, there are several things to be said for treating capacity as analytically distinct. To take just a very obvious example, a country that has no standing army does not have the capacity to invade and conquer a larger neighboring country which has a well-equipped, well-trained, large standing army. Moreover, the capacity of a country to engage in an external situation presupposes that there is a government secure enough to make decisions and to mobilize and deploy the resources of its own society. That is, the capacity to engage in international situations grows out of a government's capacity to rule its own people. If one can compare the relative capacities of governments

---

7. See James N. Rosenau and Gary D. Hoggard, "Foreign Policy in Dyadic Relationships: Testing a Pre-Theoretical Extension," a paper prepared for presentation at the Annual Meeting of the International Studies Association, San Juan, Puerto Rico, March 17, 1971, in which the authors statistically test a set of hypotheses based on genotypic analysis.

8. See footnote 1 in chapter 4.

to govern—and one can—then one can compare the relative capacities of governments and their states to have an impact on their environments.

Because the political problems faced by states in situations are varied and often subtle and because the concept of capacity must be analyzed in gross terms, it is not possible to predict that the existence of any given level of capacity will either be appropriate to or effective upon any particular political problem. In gross terms, nevertheless, it will be useful to examine some factors that help us to understand capacity. More sophisticated and more subtle terms will be developed in subsequent chapters.[9]

To begin to get at the notion of capacity, it is suggested that relative capacities of states may be partly measured by classifying them in terms of economic wealth, size (including both population and geographical area), location, and type and characteristics of regime. The data and analysis used here do not operationally define capacity, but they will give us a useful classification of states which can be used for further analysis throughout the remainder of the book.

The Gross National Product (GNP) is not without problems of reliability of data and of comparability, but it remains the best single indicator of the relative wealth, power, and status of states. Moreover, it produces better results for the ranking of countries than do some combinations of various factors. As a first gross measure of capacity, then, countries are classified according to GNP and are ranked in five ranks according to the criteria indicated in table 1. Although the ranks are indicated by cutoff points, the countries are listed in order of their relative GNPs.

If we were to use the terminology of traditional international relations analysis, we could say that Rank 1 countries are superpowers, followed by great powers in Rank 2. The countries listed in Ranks 3 and 4 might loosely be termed middle powers, and India and Brazil for a number of reasons might be expected to have the potential of moving in the foreseeable future into Rank 2. The countries in Rank 5 might then be termed smaller powers. Thus, this ranking, despite its grossness,

---

9. There are available several standard sources of data for measuring many different characteristics of countries. In particular, see Bruce M. Russett, et al., *World Handbook of Political and Social Indicators* (New Haven: Yale University Press, 1964) and data for *World Handbook II* by Michael C. Hudson and Charles L. Taylor. The data are available from the Inter-University Consortium for Political Research at the University of Michigan. For evidence that the use of these measures is not sufficient for explaining foreign policy behavior, see Rudolph J. Rummel, "The Relationship Between National Attributes and Foreign Conflict Behavior," in J. David Singer, *Quantitative International Politics: Insights and Evidence* (New York: The Free Press, 1968).

TABLE 1
Ranks of Countries

Country	GNP (in market dollars) over	Rank
United States Soviet Union	350 billion	1
Japan West Germany France United Kingdom China	100 billion	2
Italy Canada India Brazil Australia Spain Czechoslovakia Mexico Sweden Netherlands Belgium Poland East Germany	20 billion	3
South Africa Turkey Austria Denmark Switzerland Argentina Indonesia Pakistan	10 billion	4
All Others		5

gives us as much information and conceptual apparatus as the traditional impressionistic ranking of states. It is more helpful than that, too, by providing a measure of change as countries move from one relative position to another. The major utilities of this ranking are to confirm our impressions about the relative positions of states and to suggest that higher ranking countries have a greater capacity to do those things which rely on economic resources.

Other major resources which countries rely on for their capacities are land and people. Employing only gross measures at this point, one combines elementary measures of geographical area and population to arrive at a measure of size. All other things being equal, a large or an isolated geographical area provides security because it is difficult to occupy and hold. On the other hand, if a territory is sparsely settled and has an accessible terrain, an adjacent country with a large population might attempt, and might be successful at, invasion and occupation of the "empty space." Combining the factors of population and geographical area, a "size index" is constructed. This index takes account of cases like that of Canada which has an extraordinarily large territory and a relatively small population.

To construct the index, countries are ranked by the size of their territories and the size of their productive population (the population between the ages of 15 and 65). The index is arrived at by simply adding the figures together and dividing by two. Two modifications are made on the size index to reflect variables impinging on security. In the case of countries which wholly occupy islands, the index is reduced one digit because the additional factor of surrounding water gives these countries additional security. The other modification affects those countries which have historically been invasion routes for larger neighbors. The index is increased one digit for them. The rankings, apart from these modifications, are based on the following calculations:

Territorial area	Productive Population
1. over 3 million sq. mi.	1. over 200 million
2. " 1 " " "	2. " 100 "
3. " 600 thousand " "	3. " 50 "
4. " 300 " " "	4. " 25 "
5. " 100 " " "	5. " 15 "
6. " 50 " " "	6. " 10 "
7. " 25 " " "	7. " 5 "
8. " 10 " " "	8. " 3 "
9. " 5 " " "	9. " 2 "
10. less than 5 " " "	10. less than 2 "

The location of states is another important variable which can be linked with size. For example, Poland's size changed at the beginning and end of World War II, as well as at earlier times. Although its location in general terms was not changed, its location with reference to its neighbors did. Before World War II, Poland was contiguous to two great powers, the Soviet Union and Germany. Afterwards, it was contiguous to only one great power. Should Germany become reunited and powerful, or if Western Europe were to become a politically integrated state, Poland once again would be contiguous to two great powers.

In table 2, an attempt has been made to deal with the size of countries in terms of their location. Although the table does not include data reflecting the total surrounding neighborhood of a country, the largest adjacent country is listed along with its size index. Then, by subtracting the size index of the largest adjacent country from that of the country in question, one has a location index. If the location index is two or more, the country is adjacent to a substantially larger country. This location suggests that it must find some way of accommodating to that fact. Although there are a number of alternative means of reaching such accommodation, there is no escaping it.

A country may be a deferential ally of the larger country, as Czechoslovakia is with respect to the Soviet Union or as Canada is with reference to the United States. It may join in an alliance with a larger noncontiguous power, as Turkey has done by joining the United States to assist its coping with the Soviet Union. It may secure armaments, and it may even engage in preventive war, as Israel has done with respect to Egypt. It might help to form a collective security arrangement as the Latin American countries have done. It might attempt to manipulate the overall structure of a situation in order to play larger powers off against each other, as was Britain's traditional policy with respect to the European continent. Whatever alternative a country might choose or find available, there is no escaping the problem. It is the sort of problem that is not faced by countries whose location index falls below two. They have different problems. They must, of course, cope with the policies determined by the smaller countries in their immediate vicinity.

The data for the size and location indexes of the countries of the world with a population over one million (plus Cyprus) are given in table 2 (p. 39).

With these data at hand, it is possible to move a bit further in discussing capacity. Other things being equal, the larger the size of the country, the more potential capacity it has. In the first instance, a country's size helps to provide it with security, at least against those countries which rank much below it on the size index. Second, although natural resources are spread unevenly over the globe and are not equally exploited even in areas where they do exist, the larger a country's geographical area, the more likely it is to be endowed with natural resources and the more capacity it has to do those things which require the use of natural resources for their implementation. Although much too crude, this can be a beginning point for a detailed examination of the incidence and use of natural resources.

Populations vary significantly in their skills, nutrition, morale, cohesiveness, and so forth, but, other things being equal, larger populations provide a greater capacity for states to pursue goals which require human resources for their implementation. Finally, states' capacities are facilitated or constrained by their location. Because states' environments are particularly affected by their immediate neighbors, the capacities of states are influenced by their relations with adjacent countries. There are substantial variations in relations with neighbors, but states which have a location index of 2 or more are particularly circumscribed by their larger neighbors from developing their capacities in ways inimical to the interests of the larger neighbor. This problem may be overcome in certain circumstances by aligning with the enemy of the larger neighbor.

Although the rankings and indexes used here are primarily tools for thinking about and measuring capacity, they may be used singly or in combination for analyzing particular problems. For example, one could dichotomize the location index between countries at 2 and above and those ranking below 2, and then cross-tabulate this with phenomena like invasions, membership in alliances, participation in wars, and so forth. One could also check the relative strengths of the size index and the location index against other data by developing a fourfold scheme of countries with size indexes above or below a certain level combined with a location index of 2 or above or below 2. The crucial notion, however, is capacity, and to explore it further states will be classified by type of regime.

The relationship of regime type to capacity is neither simple nor straightforward. Like Almond and Powell's analysis, this proceeds on the argument that both modern democratic and modern authoritarian regimes govern highly mobilized societies and have the general capacity to cope successfully with their problems.[10] The important distinctions that Almond and Powell make are among primitive, traditional, and modern systems based on the criteria of the degree of structural differentiation and cultural secularization.[11] For our purposes, it will suffice to deal only with modern systems. Among these, the Almond and Powell scheme makes a distinction between mobilized modern systems and premobilized modern systems, and they distinguish between democratic and authoritarian types within each of the distinctive categories.

Although this analysis will go in a somewhat different direction, it begins with these basic distinctions. Other things being equal, mobilized systems have a greater capacity to command the resources of society and have more resources to command than do premobilized systems. This

---

10. See Gabriel A. Almond and G. Bingham Powell, Jr., *Comparative Politics: A Developmental Approach* (Boston and Toronto: Little, Brown and Company, 1966).

11. Ibid., chapter IX.

basic distinction will be kept in mind and used as part of the classification of countries.

Our preoccupation, however, will be with the type of regime, and the classification system is based on the democratic-authoritarian dichotomy cross-classified with a dichotomy of chief executive types. That is, chief executives are classified into those composed of one person and those composed of a collectivity. We thus have the scheme of four types of regime shown in figure 1.

FIGURE 1
Types of Regimes in Mobilized and
Premobilized Modern Systems

POLITICAL SYSTEM	SIZE OF CHIEF EXECUTIVE	
	One-person	Collectivity
Democratic	presidential	parliamentary
Authoritarian	dictatorship	junta

The utility of this scheme will become apparent in the chapter on domestic determinants, but it can be said here that the classification scheme is related to capacity in the sense that the different types of regimes face different sorts of political problems, and their abilities to resolve the political problems associated with the particular type of regime affects the capacity of the respective countries to engage in and influence situations. Table 3 (p. 42) lists the countries we are dealing with according to the categories of mobilized and premobilized systems and regime types.

Even though a variety of gross data has been employed to help us get at the concept of capacity, it has not been operationally defined. Although it would be possible to develop a set of complex genotypes from this data, that endeavor would not encompass the meaning of capacity. As was stated above, the notion of capacity—although benefiting somewhat from isolation for analytical purposes—is related to goals and situations. That is, in considering capacity, one must always be concerned with the question, "Capacity to do what?" Additionally, there are other factors which are less susceptible to quantification and more susceptible to change than the factors represented by the data used thus far.

For example, the extent to which a society is cohesive (in general and on a given issue) will influence its capacity to decide on and pursue social goals. Strategic location, political posture, and other characteristics may affect the capacity of a state to ally itself with others.[12] Finally, capacity is related to the needs and demands of the international system. The capacity of the Republic of China (Taiwan) to align with the United States, for example, is dependent upon the existence of hostility between the United States and the People's Republic of China.

Predispositions

In addition to the functions which have been described thus far, capacity has the additional function of affecting the *predispositions* of states. The nature of international politics is such that countries are sometimes strongly coerced or even forced to participate in international situations. The most obvious example of this is an invasion which forces the invaded country to resist. Another example is the situation in which one country declares its hostility toward another country. The second country has little choice but to engage in the situation thus created. A good deal of choice remains, of course, for determining how to resist.

However, not all countries face this sort of pressure in every situation in which they become engaged. There is a greater range of choice, and different countries have different responses to situations with which they are confronted. It is more likely that some countries will become involved in certain situations than other countries, and it is more likely that they will act in certain ways rather than in others. That is, countries have predispositions to engage in certain kinds of situations, and they are likely to engage in them with particular styles. A predisposition is not a guarantee that a country will become involved and act in certain ways, and it is not a basis for unqualified prediction. It is, nevertheless, a concept that aids our understanding of foreign policy.

Predispositions grow out of the experience and development of a country. The development spoken of here is the evolution and accretion of capacity. The experience will be dealt with below under the notion of identity. First, let us briefly discuss the impact of capacity on predisposition.

---

12. Julian R. Friedman, in an unpublished paper entitled "East Africa in the Community of Nations: Coalition Capability with Special Reference to Non-Alignment and Alliance with the Non-African Powers," has developed the notion of the capability of a state to ally with others.

Certain predispositions are precluded because of lack of capacity. If a country is poor, cleaved between ethnic groups, and premodern, for example, it is most unlikely to develop a foreign aid program to assist other countries because it lacks the capacity to make such a decision and the skills, capital, and other resources necessary for carrying out such a program. However, if such a country were to develop a cohesive society, generate economic growth, train a bureaucracy, and so forth, it would have developed the capacity to project a foreign aid program. That does not insure that it will develop a predisposition to engage in situations which require such a program and it is no certainty that an actual program would be put into effect. It is, nevertheless, much more likely that a predisposition to engage in certain situations will be developed if the capacity is available than if it is not.

Because of the developmental nature of capacity, it is possible for countries to develop predispositions that outrun their capacities. This is particularly true of but not limited to revolutionary regimes. Revolutionary regimes tend to be fervid and visionary, with a tendency to be predisposed to expanding their revolutions to other countries. Acting on this predisposition, they tend to be frustrated, however, not only by the limited applicability of a revolution to different situations but also by a lack of capacity to sustain such revolutionary activity.

The experience of revolution is an example of how identity is formed and how experience shapes predispositions. Not all societies have revolutionary experiences, but all societies have some experiences which shape their identities. The concept of identity is based on the notion that a people is forged in its experiences, the origins and founding of an independent state being—for most peoples—the first and most profound experience affecting them. They do, of course, carry over traditions from their pasts, but the independence of the state stamps the peculiar cultural experience that sets any particular people apart from others. After independence, each new experience brings about a reinforcement or modification in a definition of the identity of a people by themselves, but there are long-term, persistent patterns of behavior and styles of behavior which characterize them.

There are two components of political identity. The first component is the set of beliefs, ideas, and emotions that provide the rationale for the separate existence of the country. Every country is unique, and its existence is justified on the grounds that its citizens can best achieve their goals through their own state. If the achievement of independence has been through violent struggle or a similar trauma, the country will tend to have a strong sense of identity from its origins. This is not to say there is not dissent in new countries nor to say that countries that have passed through a revolution are altogether cohesive. It is obvious that in mobilized countries like France and in premobilized countries like Ghana this is not the case. On the whole, however, cohesive identity will tend to be more well-developed shortly after independence in countries that have had their identities forged through struggle than those that have not. This component of identity may be clear and strong or fuzzy and weak, but every country has such an identity.

One of the differences between the older countries and those that have emerged from colonial rule in the middle part of this century is in the process of development of national identity. In most of the older countries, the state became an expression of and an instrument employed by national consciousness. With the withdrawal of European countries from their colonial empires, the state has been adopted universally to replace the colonial order. Very often, however, the relationship between state and nation is reversed, and the development of national consciousness becomes an aspiration of the state, for the state's territory is often occupied by people whose identity lies in relationship to groups other than the whole people living on that territory.[13] In such cases, the political identity of the country will be relatively weak insofar as it is widespread in the society. Authoritative leaders, nevertheless, are in a position to articulate their identity and face the problem of shaping the identity of their fellow citizens.

Despite the uniqueness of each country, political systems tend to be associated with major ideas that are shared more widely than among the citizens of one country. Identity is partly determined by a definition of one's place in the world. This brings us to the second component of political identity, but before defining and analyzing it, there may be some utility in considering the intellectual antecedents of the concept as used here.

The concept of identity as used in this book draws on the psychoanalytic theory of Erik H. Erikson.[14] In Erikson's theory, people form their individual identities in part by associating with selected factors in their environment. In particular, he holds that people in middle age identify themselves to a large extent in terms of their assertion of responsibility for others. Erikson's book on Gandhi, for example, provides a great deal of insight into the Mahatma's behavior by explaining that

---

13. An interesting article which draws attention to the problems of ethnic diversity and which criticizes the literature on nation-building is Walker Connor, "Nation-Building or Nation-Destroying?" *World Politics* 24 (April 1972).

14. For a good summary of Erikson's theory, see David Elkind, "Erik Erikson's Eight Ages of Man," *The New York Times Magazine*, April 5, 1970.

the Indian leader regarded himself to be responsible for the British Empire.[15] With Erikson's explanation, it is easier to understand that Gandhi loved and respected his British rulers even while he opposed them and why he developed tactics which might not have been used had he regarded himself responsible only for India.

Although one does not presume to bring psychoanalytic theory as a whole to bear, this one notion of Erikson's will prove useful for understanding the second component of identity and the further concept of predisposition. One can adapt Erikson's concept to states without doing violence to levels-of-analysis considerations. The authoritative leaders of countries—who tend to be in or beyond middle age—will largely be people who regard themselves to be responsible for their respective countries. That is, their personal identity is wrapped up in their roles as authoritative leaders. Consequently, they will reflect their country's identity because it is part of their own identity. Such leaders, additionally, possessing a sense of responsibility for the political system in which they play crucial roles, also reflect the system's collective definition of what it feels responsible for outside itself. This is not to suggest that "systems" have feelings of responsibility: an attempt is being made to avoid the anthropomorphizing of complex collectivities and organizations and the reification of abstractions. Nevertheless, the citizens of a country do have such feelings and attitudes, and the leadership of a country both articulates them and helps to shape them. These are functions of political leadership in any political system.

With this background in mind, let us proceed to examine the second component of identity which is the definition of responsibility for segments of the environment. States, through their authoritative mechanisms, associate themselves with and assert responsibility for people, ideas, and entities outside themselves. Because of different experiences and values, different countries may be associated with different things in their environments. Different countries aspire to achieve different goals in the environment.

For example, two neighboring countries in West Africa, Nigeria and Ghana, have been associated with quite different elements in their environment. Particularly under the Nkrumah regime, Ghana aspired to leadership of all of black Africa and, during the 1960s when there was a good deal of experimenting with different coalitions, Ghana was associated with the more radical groupings of states. On the other hand,

---

15. See *Gandhi's Truth: On the Origins of Militant Nonviolence* (New York: W. W. Norton & Company, Inc., 1969).

Nigeria, preoccupied with divisiveness at home, was much less ambitious than Ghana and was associated with the more conservative states in Africa.

The United States and the Soviet Union have assumed responsibility for opposing elements in the international system. On the whole, the United States has associated itself with the forces of stability and evoluionary change, whereas the Soviet Union has attempted to associate itself with the forces of rapid changes in the world. Each offers an alternative model for other societies to emulate.

Although not prepared to develop systematic categories encompassing all of the associations, aspirations, and roles of countries,[16] one can make some distinctions. The first is among countries which tend to identify themselves as responsible only for their own internal welfare, those which hold themselves responsible for a region, and finally countries which claim responsibility for the entire world. Rather than conceiving these distinctions as mutually exclusive categories, it will be more realistic to conceive them as points on a continuum, for countries may not fit neatly into the categories.

Establishing these distinctions, however, will enable us to say with some confidence whether a country has a predisposition to engage in a given situation. To cite an example, in the Congo crisis in the early 1960s a number of African countries asserted a particular responsibility for the Congo problem because it was in Africa. The United States, the Soviet Union, Britain, and France also were active because they regarded themselves to have very broad, global responsibilities. Belgium defined itself as responsible for the Congo problem because of its previous association and because of the presence of Belgian nationals in the Congo, but unlike the larger countries, it would not identify itself as responsible for other African problems. Some countries—India and Canada are examples—held themselves to be responsible for the peacekeeping activities of the United Nations and were thus prepared to supply human and material resources to the United Nations operation in the Congo. Other countries—most European and South American countries are examples—did not assume responsibility for this problem. However, when the challenge to the Secretary-General's Congo policy became a challenge to the United Nations organization itself with overtones of cold war divisiveness, many of these last countries did play a role grow-

---

16. For an imaginative analysis of the external roles of countries, see K. J. Holsti, "National Role Conceptions in the Study of Foreign Policy," *International Studies Quarterly* 14 (September 1970).

Actors   37

ing out of their identities with the world organization or with their alliances or both.

Despite an inability to systematically categorize the political identities of countries, one can list the considerations which have been discussed for a variety of countries. Table 4 (p. 45) lists information for all of the countries in Ranks 1 and 2 on the GNP table above plus selected countries from Ranks 3 through 5. The information is necessarily cryptic and suggestive, but it does provide a beginning for the analysis of those factors which help to explain why particular countries are predisposed to engage in certain situations rather than others.

The complexity of societies and political systems and the richness of experience of different peoples hopefully is not obscured by the meager information here. What the information in table 4 is intended to convey is that there is a variety of experience and identity, and the particular characteristics of a country need to be kept in mind in analyzing foreign policy. Although we do not have simple categories into which we can put the identities and experiences of different countries, we want to avoid two errors that are fairly common in the analysis of foreign policy. The first error is the assumption that all countries are alike and can be expected to behave in like fashion. Such an error can be applied across all countries or to a group of countries, such as Communist countries or underdeveloped countries or African countries. The second error is that of projecting one's own values and thought processes upon others, assuming for example that the French or the Mexicans or whomever will respond to situations in the same way as Americans.

As cryptic and meager as the information in table 4 is, it does alert the analyst to the very different experiences and ideas embodied in the histories and contemporary existences of different countries. These differences lead countries to relate to different cross-currents in the international system and to respond to international situations in different ways.

Conclusion

This chapter has defined actors as those entities which are capable of taking all three kinds of foreign policy acts. Although concentrating on the state as the primary type of actor in international politics, international organizations and transnational actors has been briefly examined, and the occasions and conditions for their becoming international actors within our meaning have been specified.

Focusing on the state, the concern has been with two major concepts: capacity and predisposition. Some data which help to measure capacity and the notion of identity which helps to understand predisposition have been given and explained. To proceed further, we now need to look at the international environment, and particularly at the concept of situation. As this analysis holds, both the state and the situation interact to produce foreign policy. We now turn to the task of examining the environment and analyzing situations.

Actors

TABLE 2
Size and Location Indexes

Country	Area Rank	Population Rank	Size Index	Largest Adjacent Country	Size Index	Location Index
Afghanistan	5	7	6	U.S.S.R.	1.5	4.5
Albania	8	10	9	Yugoslavia	6	3
Algeria	3	7	5	Libya	6.5	−1.5
Angola	4	9	6.5	Zaire	5	1.5
Argentina	2	6	4	Brazil	2.5	1.5
Australia	2	7	3.5*	—		
Austria	7	8	7.5	West Germany	5	2.5
Bangladesh	6			China	1	
Belgium	8	7	7.5	West Germany	5	3.5**
Bolivia	4	10	7	Brazil	2.5	4.5
Brazil	1	4	2.5	Argentina	4	−1.5
Bulgaria	7	7	7	Turkey	4.5	2.5
Burma	5	6	5.5	China	1	4.5
Burundi	8	10	9	Zaire	5	4
Cambodia	6	8	7	Thailand	5.5	1.5
Cameroon	5	9	7	Nigeria	4	3
Canada	1	6	3.5	United States	1.5	2
Central African Republic	5	10	7.5	Sudan	5	2.5
Chad	4	10	7	Nigeria	4	3
Chile	5	8	6.5	Argentina	4	2.5
China	1	1	1	U.S.S.R.	1.5	0.5
Colombia	4	7	5.5	Brazil	2.5	3
Costa Rica	8	10	9	Nicaragua	8	1
Cuba	7	8	6.5*	—		
Cyprus	10	10	9*	—		
Czechoslovakia	7	7	7	U.S.S.R.	1.5	5.5
Dahomey	7	10	8.5	Nigeria	4	4.5
Denmark	8	8	8	West Germany	5	4**
Dominican Rep.	8	10	9	Haiti	8.5	0.5
Ecuador	5	9	7	Peru	5.5	1.5
Egypt	4	6	5	Sudan	5	0
El Salvador	9	10	9.5	Honduras	8.5	1
Ethiopia	4	6	5	Sudan	5	0
Finland	5	9	7	U.S.S.R.	1.5	5.5
France	5	4	4.5	West Germany	5	−0.5
E. Germany	7	6	6.5	West Germany	5	1.5
W. Germany	6	4	5	France	4.5	1
Ghana	6	8	7	Ivory Coast	7.5	−0.5
Greece	6	7	6.5	Turkey	4.5	2
Guatemala	7	9	8	Mexico	4	4
Guinea	6	10	8	Mali	6.5	1.5
Haiti	8	9	8.5	Dominican Republic	9	−0.5
Honduras	7	10	8.5	Nicaragua	8	0.5
Hong Kong	10	10	10	China	1	9

Table 2—*Continued*

Country	Area Rank	Population Rank	Size Index	Largest Adjacent Country	Size Index	Location Index
Hungary	7	7	7	U.S.S.R.	1.5	5.5
India	2	1	1.5	China	1	0.5
Indonesia	3	3	2*	—		
Iran	3	6	4.5	U.S.S.R.	1.5	3
Iraq	5	8	6.5	Turkey	4.5	2
Ireland	7	10	7.5*	—		
Israel	9	10	9.5	Egypt	5	4.5
Italy	5	4	4.5	France	4.5	0
Ivory Coast	5	10	7.5	Ghana	7	0.5
Jamaica	10	10	9*	—		
Japan	5	3	3*	—		
Jordan	7	10	8.5	Egypt	5	3.5
Kenya	5	8	6.5	Ethiopia	5	1.5
N. Korea	7	7	7	China	1	6
S. Korea	7	5	6	North Korea	7	1
Laos	6	10	8	China	1	7
Lebanon	10	10	10	Syria	7.5	2.5
Liberia	7	10	8.5	Ivory Coast	7.5	1
Libya	3	10	6.5	Algeria	5	1.5
Malagasy	5	8	5.5*	—		
Malawi	7	9	8	Mozambique	6	2
Malaysia	5	8	6.5	Thailand	5.5	1
Mali	4	9	6.5	Algeria	5	1.5
Mauritania	4	10	7	Algeria	5	2
Mexico	3	5	4	United States	1.5	2.5
Mongolia	3	10	6.5	China	1	5.5
Morocco	5	7	6	Algeria	5	1
Mozambique	4	8	6	South Africa	5.5	0.5
Nepal	6	7	6.5	China	1	5.5
Netherlands	8	7	7.5	West Germany	5	3.5**
New Zealand	5	10	6.5*	—		
Nicaragua	6	10	8	Honduras	8.5	−0.5
Niger	4	9	6.5	Algeria	5	1.5
Nigeria	4	4	4	Niger	6.5	−2.5
Norway	5	9	7	U.S.S.R.	1.5	5.5
Pakistan	4			China	1	
Panama	7	10	8.5	Colombia	5.5	3
Paraguay	5	10	7.5	Brazil	2.5	5
Peru	4	7	5.5	Brazil	2.5	3
Philippines	5	5	4*	—		
Poland	5	5	5	U.S.S.R.	1.5	4.5**
Portugal	7	7	7	Spain	5	2
Rhodesia	5	9	7	South Africa	5.5	1.5
Rumania	6	6	6	U.S.S.R.	1.5	4.5
Rwanda	8	8	8	Zaire	5	3

Table 2—Continued

Country	Area Rank	Population Rank	Size Index	Largest Adjacent Country	Size Index	Location Index
Saudi Arabia	3	8	5.5	Iraq	6.5	−1
Senegal	6	10	8	Mali	6.5	1.5
Sierra Leone	7	10	8.5	Guinea	8	0.5
Singapore	10	10	10	Malaysia	6.5	3.5
Somalia	5	10	7.5	Ethiopia	5	2.5
South Africa	4	7	5.5	Mozambique	6	−0.5
Spain	5	5	5	France	4.5	0.5
Sri Lanka	7	7	6*	—		
Sudan	3	7	5	Egypt	5	0
Sweden	5	7	6	Norway	7	−1.0
Switzerland	8	8	8	France	4.5	3.5
Syria	6	9	7.5	Turkey	4.5	3.0
Taiwan	8	7	6.5*	—		
Tanzania	4	8	6	Mozambique	6	0
Thailand	5	6	5.5	Burma	5.5	0
Togo	8	10	9	Ghana	7	2
Trinidad	10	10	9*	—		
Tunisia	6	9	7.5	Algeria	5	2.5
Turkey	4	5	4.5	U.S.S.R.	1.5	3.0
Uganda	6	8	7	Zaire	5	2
U.S.S.R.	1	2	1.5	China	1	0.5
United Kingdom	6	4	4*	—		
United States	1	2	1.5	Canada	3.5	−2
Upper Volta	5	9	7	Mali	6.5	0.5
Uruguay	6	10	8	Brazil	2.5	5.5
Venezuela	4	8	6	Brazil	2.5	3.5
N. Vietnam	6	7	6.5	China	1	5.5
S. Vietnam	6	7	6.5	N. Vietnam	6.5	0
Yemen	6	9	7.5	Saudi Arabia	5.5	2
Yugoslavia	6	6	6	Italy	4.5	1.5
Zaire	3	7	5	Sudan	5	0
Zambia	5	10	7.5	Zaire	5	2.5

* reduced one digit because island
** increased one digit because historic invasion route

TABLE 3
Regime Types

Country	Size Index	Premobilized	Mobilized	Regime Type
Afghanistan	6	X		parliamentary
Albania	9		X	junta
Algeria	5	X		junta
Angola	6.5	X		colony
Argentina	4		X	dictatorship
Australia	3.5		X	parliamentary
Austria	7.5		X	parliamentary
Bangladesh		X		dictatorship
Belgium	7.5		X	parliamentary
Bolivia	7	X		junta
Brazil	2.5		X	dictatorship
Bulgaria	7		X	junta
Burma	5.5	X		junta
Burundi	9	X		junta
Cambodia	7	X		junta
Cameroon	7	X		presidential
Canada	3.5		X	parliamentary
Central African Rep.	7.5	X		dictatorship
Chad	7	X		dictatorship
Chile	6.5		X	presidential
China	1		X	junta
Colombia	5.5	X		presidential
Costa Rica	9	X		presidential
Cuba	6.5		X	dictatorship
Cyprus	9	X		presidential
Czechoslovakia	7		X	junta
Dahomey	8.5	X		junta
Denmark	8		X	parliamentary
Dominican Republic	9	X		presidential
Ecuador	7	X		presidential
Egypt	5	X		junta
El Salvadore	9.5	X		presidential
Ethiopia	5	X		traditional
Finland	7		X	presidential
France	4.5		X	presidential
East Germany	6.5		X	junta
West Germany	5		X	parliamentary
Ghana	7	X		junta
Greece	6.5		X	junta
Guatemala	8	X		presidential
Guinea	8	X		dictatorship
Haiti	8.5	X		dictatorship
Honduras	8.5	X		dictatorship
Hong Kong	10			colony
Hungary	7		X	junta
India	1.5	X		parliamentary
Indonesia	2	X		junta
Iran	4.5	X		monarchy
Iraq	6.5	X		junta
Ireland	7.5		X	parliamentary
Israel	10		X	parliamentary
Italy	4		X	parliamentary
Ivory Coast	10	X		presidential

Actors   43

Table 3—Continued

Country	Size Index	Premobilized	Mobilized	Regime Type
Jamaica	9	X		parliamentary
Japan	3		X	parliamentary
Jordan	8.5	X		monarchy
Kenya	6.5	X		parliamentary
N. Korea	7	X		junta
S. Korea	6	X		presidential
Laos	8	X		monarchy
Lebanon	10		X	parliamentary
Liberia	8.5	X		presidential
Libya	6.5	X		junta
Malagasy	5.5	X		parliamentary
Malawi	8	X		parliamentary
Malaysia	6.5	X		parliamentary
Mali	6.5	X		presidential
Mauritania	7	X		presidential
Mexico	4		X	presidential
Mongolia	6.5	X		junta
Morocco	6	X		monarchy
Mozambique	6	X		colony
Nepal	6.5			traditional
Netherlands	7.5		X	parliamentary
New Zealand	6.5		X	parliamentary
Nicaragua	8	X		presidential
Niger	6.5	X		presidential
Nigeria	4	X		junta
Norway	7		X	parliamentary
Pakistan	4	X		junta
Panama	8.5	X		presidential
Paraguay	7.5	X		dictatorship
Peru	5.5	X		presidential
Philippines	4	X		presidential
Poland	5		X	junta
Portugal	7	X		dictatorship
Rhodesia	7		X	parliamentary
Rumania	6		X	junta
Rwanda	8	X		presidential
Saudi Arabia	5.5	X		traditional
Senegal	8	X		presidential
Sierra Leone	8.5	X		parliamentary
Singapore	10		X	parliamentary
Somalia	7.5	X		parliamentary
S. Africa	5.5		X	parliamentary
Spain	5		X	dictatorship
Sri Lanka	6	X		parliamentary
Sudan	5	X		parliamentary
Sweden	6		X	parliamentary
Switzerland	8		X	parliamentary
Syria	7.5	X		junta
Taiwan	6.5		X	dictatorship
Tanzania	6	X		presidential
Thailand	5.5	X		junta
Togo	9	X		junta
Trinidad	9	X		parliamentary
Tunisia	7.5	X		presidential

Table 3—Continued

Country	Size Index	Premobilized	Mobilized	Regime Type
Turkey	4.5	X		parliamentary
Uganda	7	X		dictatorship
U.S.S.R.	1.5		X	junta
United Kingdom	4		X	parliamentary
U.S.	1.5		X	presidential
Upper Volta	7	X		junta
Uruguay	8		X	presidential
Venezuela	6		X	presidential
N. Vietnam	6.5		X	junta
S. Vietnam	6.5	X		presidential
Yemen	7.5	X		junta
Yugoslavia	6		X	dictatorship
Zaire	5	X		presidential
Zambia	7.5	X		presidential

SOURCES: These are impressionistic classifications based on Joseph E. Black and Kenneth W. Thompson, eds., *Foreign Policies in a World of Change* (New York: Harper and Row, Publishers, 1963); Walter H. Mallory, *Political Handbook and Atlas of the World: Parliaments, Parties and Press as of January 1, 1965* (New York: Harper and Row for Council on Foreign Relations, Inc., 1965); and *Background Notes on the Countries of the World* (Washington, D.C.: Bureau of Public Affairs, Department of State, n.d.).

TABLE 4
Political Identity

Country	Size Index	Date of Independence or Revolution	Method of Independence	Major Ideas Associated With	External Responsibility	Major Experience(s) of last 25 years
Algeria	5	1962	Colonial revolution & negotiation	Anti-colonialism, Socialism	Oppressed people	Revolution; Coup
Argentina	4	1810	Revolution	Sovereignty, Non-intervention	Western Hemisphere	Peron; Coup
Australia	3.5	1926	Negotiation	Anti-Communism, Liberal democracy	Defense of Western Pacific	British withdrawal from Western Pacific
Brazil	2.5	1822	Declaration by regent	Economic development, Anti-racism, Anti-colonialism, Non-intervention	Finding and protecting sources of economic assistance and trade, Western Hemisphere (OAS), World power ambitions	Shift from civilian to military regime, Development of urban revolution, Alliance for Progress
Canada	3.5	1926	Negotiation	Liberal democracy Peacekeeping	U.N. peacekeeping	Middle East, ICC
China	1	1949	Revolution	Revolutionary Communism	Asia, Third World Revolution	Korea War, Sino-Soviet rift, Cultural Revolution
Cuba	6.5	1934(I) 1959(R)	U.S. action Revolution	Revolutionary Communism	Latin-American Revolution	Castro revolution, Realignment, Bay of Pigs, Cuba missiles

45

Table 4—Continued

Country	Size Index	Date of Independence or Revolution	Method of Independence	Major Ideas Associated With	External Responsibility	Major Experience(s) of last 25 years
Czechoslovakia	7	1918 1945	World Wars I & II Settlements	Democratic Communism	Bridge between East-West	1948 Coup, 1968 "Spring," and invasion
Denmark	8	800	—	Neutrality	Developing countries, Support for U.N., Scandanavia, NATO	Movement from neutrality to alliance
Egypt	5	1922 (I) 1952 (R)		Pan-Arabism, Anti-Zionism, Economic development, Anti-imperialism, Nonalignment	Arab states, Middle East, Africa	Establishment of Israel, 1948 war, Crisis and war of 1956, 1952 coup and rise of Nasser, 1967 war, Nasser's death, Formation and demise of U.A.R.
France	4.5	1944	Defeat of occupation	"Mission Civilisatrice," National autonomy, Ending bipolarity	Europe, Countries subject to U.S. & Soviet hegemony	Suez, Cuba missiles, Indo-China, Algeria, European Community, Withdrawal from NATO, De Gaulle, nuclear weapons
West Germany	5	1949	Raising of occupation	European integration	NATO Europe	European Community, Berlin crises, Economic prosperity

Ghana	7	1957	Negotiation	Anti-Colonialism, Pan-Africanism	Africa	Independence, Congo crisis, Overthrow of Nkrumah
Guinea	8	1960	Granted	Socialist development	Africa	Congo crisis, Cut off of French aid
Hungary	7	1918	World War I settlement	Communism	self	1956 Revolution and Soviet suppression
India	1.5	1947	"Non-violent" pressure and negotiation	Non-alignment	South Asia, non-aligned countries	Partition and independence, Kashmir, 1962 war with China, 1965 war with Pakistan, Pakistan refugees, 1971 Bangladesh war
Indonesia	2	1948	Revolution, Negotiation	Anti-Colonialism, "Konfrontasi," "NEFOS"	Southeast Asia	West Irian, "Konfrontasi,.." overthrow of Sukarno
Israel	9.5	1948	War against Arabs	National independence, Zionism	self	Wars of 1948, 1956, 1967; Arab hostility
Italy	4.5	1861 (unification) 1947	Raising of occupation	Western European integration	Western Europe, Mediterranean, Access for immigrants	European communities, Unstable government, Entry into NATO and United Nations
Ivory Coast	7.5	1960	Granted	Negritude	French-speaking Africa	Independence
Japan	3	1951	Negotiated end of occupation	Pacifism	East Asia	End of occupation, Economic growth

Table 4—Continued

Country	Size Index	Date of Independence or Revolution	Method of Independence	Major Ideas Associated With	External Responsibility	Major Experience(s) of last 25 years
Jordan	8.5	1946	Negotiated end of mandate	Arab Nationalism	Middle East	Partial conquest by Israel & loss of territory, Arab refugees, British intervention in 1958
Malaysia	6.5	1957	Negotiation		Southeast Asia	Civil war, Federation with Singapore, Indonesian confrontation
Mexico	4	1821 1910	Revolution Revolution	Respect for international law, Non-intervention, Independent development	Latin America	
Nigeria	4	1960	Negotiation	Federalism, Democratic development	self	Independence, Coups, Congo crisis, Civil War 1968-69
Pakistan	4	1947	Negotiation	Islamic state "Basic Democracy"	self	Independence and partition Kashmir War with India Civil war, 1971 Loss of Bangladesh
South Africa	5.5	1926	Negotiation	Apartheid Anti-Communism	Southern Africa	International hostility

Spain	5	1936	Revolution	Catholicism	Europe, North Africa, Language and cultural rights in Spanish-speaking America	International ostracism, Admission to U.N., Denial of membership in NATO and EEC
Switzerland	8				Humanitian and other nonpolitical international enterprises, Undeveloped countries, Europe	
Tanzania	6	1961	Negotiation	Strict neutrality, unification of diverse peoples	East Africa, Mozambique, Southern Africa	Independence, Union with Zanzibar, Attempted coup, Mozambique revolt
				One-party state, non-alignment, East Africa common services		
Thailand	6.5			Anti-communism	Southeast Asia	Vietnam war
Turkey	4.5	1919	Revolution	Western alignment	Eastern Mediterranean, Collective security	Marshall Plan aid, NATO membership, Korean war, CENTO membership, Cyprus crisis
U.S.S.R.	1.5	1917	Revolution	Anti-Capitalism, Communism	Communism, Eastern Europe, Europe, Middle East, South Asia, East Asia and Western Pacific, Cuba, Southeast Asia	Berlin crises, Successions, Economic growth, Nuclear weapons acquisition, Cuba missiles, Hungary-Poland-Czechoslovakia, Sino-Soviet rift

Table 4—Continued

Country	Size Index	Date of Independence or Revolution	Method of Independence	Major Ideas Associated With	External Responsibility	Major Experience(s) of last 25 years
U.K.	4			Parliamentary democracy	English-speaking democracies, North Atlantic defense, Commonwealth, Anti-Communism	Loss of empire, Suez-Skybolt, Negotiations on EEC, Entry to EEC
U.S.	1.5	1783	Revolutionary War	Individualism, Freedom, Anti-Communism, Stability	Leader of anti-Communists, Economic development, Latin America, North Atlantic & Europe, Middle East, Southeast Asia, East Asia & Western Pacific, Africa	Korea-Vietnam, Berlin crises, Middle East crises, Alliances, Cuba missiles, Arms development and control

*In some countries, there are two relatively recent dates that are important in forging identity. For these, two dates are given.

SOURCES: These are impressionistic characterizations based on Black and Thompson, *Foreign Policies in a World of Change*; Roy C. Macridis, ed., *Foreign Policy in World Politics*, 4th ed. (Englewood Cliffs, N.J.: Prentice-Hall, Inc., 1972); *Background Notes on Countries of the World*; and several history texts dealing with discrete countries or regions. The dates have been checked against Bruce M. Russett, J. David Singer, and Melvin Small, "National Political Units in the Twentieth Century: A Standardized List," *The American Political Science Review* 62 (September 1968), although there is not complete agreement between their dates and mine.

3

The International Environment

The first chapter referred to foreign policy as the coping of a state with its environment. This chapter is devoted to the description and analysis of environment. The task is a difficult one because the world is the environment, and the world is immensely complex. This complexity is reflected in the academic study of international relations phenomena. Quincy Wright has stated that international relations is a synthetic field of study which is based on sixteen disciplines.[1] A brief analysis of a case will illustrate the difficulties.

On December 7, 1970, an election in Pakistan gave a majority in the election of the Pakistan National Assembly to the Awami League, led by Sheikh Mujibur Rahman.[2] All 151 seats won by the Awami League were in East Pakistan, an area with a population of approximately 70

---

1. Quincy Wright, *The Study of International Relations* (New York: Appleton-Century-Crofts, 1955).

2. The author has relied for the facts of this case primarily on *Keesing's Contemporary Archives*, Volume No. XVIII, 1971–1972.

million people and separated by 1000 miles of Indian territory from West Pakistan. The election was held not simply to fill parliamentary seats but to restore democracy to the country which had been ruled by the military since 1958. One of the tasks of the new assembly was to devise a new constitution under which Pakistan was to be governed in the future. Shiekh Mujibur Rahman indicated that the Awami League majority would impose a new constitution which would give autonomy to East Pakistan in all matters except defense and foreign affairs. Zulfiqar Ali Bhutto, the leader of the Pakistan People's Party which had won 81 seats, was opposed to the Awami League's proposed action, arguing that a broader consensus involving the agreement of all major parties was required in formulating a constitution.

In response to this conflict, on March 1, 1971, President Yahya Khan indefinitely postponed the opening of the Pakistan National Assembly, scheduled for March 3, "to enable the political leaders to reach a settlement on the question of framing a constitution. . . ." The president a few days later announced a new opening date of March 25, but he again postponed it on March 22. Civil war broken out on March 26 after Sheikh Mujibur Rahman declared the independence of a new state, Bangladesh. Although the civil war was "virtually ended" by April 18–19, the Indian Parliament had passed a resolution expressing "sympathy and support" for the people of East Bengal (East Pakistan) on March 31.

While guerrilla activities continued, President Yahya Khan outlawed the Awami League, although he indicated that those who had not become "traitors" could hold their seats. By-elections were held to fill the vacancies. At the end of August, a civilian governor of East Pakistan was appointed, and press censorship was eased on September 2.

Meanwhile, on August 9, India and the Soviet Union signed a 20-Year Treaty of Peace, Friendship and Co-operation. Interpretations of the impact of this treaty vary.

From August onwards guerrilla activities by the Mukti Bahini increased, and a Bangladesh governing council-in-exile was formed on September 8. A number of Pakistani diplomats declared their allegiance to Bangladesh. There followed not only increased guerrilla activity but also a massive repression including atrocities by the Pakistani army. Some ten million refugees fled this repression to India. India had limited resources to deal with the refugees, and assistance from other countries was inadequate.

By November 21, there were border clashes between Indian and Pakistani troops. Open war broke out on December 3 when Pakistan made a surprise air attack on military airfields in western India. Thereupon, Indian troops invaded East Pakistan. India extended diplomatic recognition to Bangladesh on December 6, and Pakistani troops in East Pakistan surrendered on December 16. The following day a ceasefire was implemented in the west. During the hostilities, the Soviet Union supported India, while China and the United States supported Pakistan.

Although the war issue had gone to the United Nations, Soviet vetoes prevented the Security Council from acting, and the issue went to the General Assembly which passed a ceasefire resolution. The resolution was accepted by Pakistan but rejected by India.

President Yahya Khan resigned on December 20, and the Bangladesh Government was established in Dacca, the capital, on December 22. Early in January 1972, Sheikh Mujibur Rahman was released from prison, and Indian troops withdrew from Bangladesh in March. The refugees were returned, and the Government of Bangladesh was recognized by over thirty governments by mid-February.

This brief sketch of the creation of a new state out of the disintegration of Pakistan through the military efforts of a rival state in the context of superpower maneuvering provides us with a case that reveals the great number of elements that make up the international environment. The elements can be briefly identified, but the major problem remains. That is the problem of finding an analytical scheme that will reduce the complexity to manageable proportions while avoiding the sort of oversimplification which gets in the way of understanding how foreign policy operates.

One of the elements in the Bangladesh case was the lack of legitimacy for the political order of Pakistan. The election results were not accepted by West Pakistan. This lack of legitimacy, and the accompanying cleavage between East and West Pakistan, was partly caused by ethnic differences between the two parts of the country. These differences were reinforced by governmental policies which allocated scarce resources for economic development in a discriminatory fashion. Not to be overlooked in the situation is the generalized attitude toward nationalism in which ethnic groups strive for self-determination through the creation of states under their control. The deprivation of economic goods to East Pakistan also took place in the context of population growth pressures as well as participation in the general striving of third-world peoples for modernization and economic growth. Another element is geography, for the thousand-mile space between the two parts of Pakistan compounded the incohesiveness of the country and was also an important strategic element in West Pakistan's loss and India's victory in the 1971 war. Thus far, the elements affecting the Bangladesh case are either purely "domestic" to Pakistan or they are particularly

Pakistani manifestations of more widespread phenomena. They nevertheless represent factors that would be regarded as part of the international environment of any other country involved in or affected by the Bangladesh situation.

There were also other countries and other actors that formed part of the international environment in this case. Foremost among these was India, a neighboring and for Bangladesh the decisive country. There had been long-standing antipathy between India and Pakistan. At the time of independence in 1947, British India was partitioned between India and Pakistan. Religion was the *raison d'etre* for the formation of Pakistan, and India as a secular state had an opposed rationale for its existence. Thus, religion was a factor in the antipathy of the two states, but the territorial dispute over Jammu and Kashmir, the occasion for war in 1965 and still unresolved in the early 1970s, was an added element. In 1954, Pakistan aligned itself in anti-Communist alliances encouraged by the United States and began receiving arms assistance from America. This policy represented a rejection of India's policy of non-alignment. In the late 1950s and 1960s, as the Sino-Soviet dispute grew, Pakistan developed ties with China, while India maintained its close relations with the Soviet Union. Although India and China began discussions about their territorial borders following the Bangdung Conference of Non-Aligned States in 1954, the differences over border definitions had not been resolved by 1962 when the two countries went to war and the issue was resolved, temporarily at least, by force and on China's terms. Following the war, India expanded its military capabilities.[3]

The evolution of relations between India and Pakistan, then, created predispositions in each to be opposed to the other. When the political elite in India was confronted with the intolerable burden of refugees in 1971, it was able easily to gain the support of the population for resolving the problem by conquering East Pakistan—in collaboration with Bangladesh guerrillas and irregular forces—and providing the support needed to create Bangladesh. Moreover, it had the military capability to implement its goals successfully.

In this case, decisive action was taken by India which controlled the situation, but other actors were marginally related to and affected by it. No other country, however, took action which was decisive to the situation. The Soviet Union, partial to India, and the United States and China, partial to Pakistan, were peripheral to the situation as such. Why these were peripheral rather than central, thus allowing India to be

---

3. See K. Subrahmanyam, "Five Years of Indian Defence Effort in Perspective," *International Studies Quarterly* 13 (June 1969): 159-89 for a description and analysis of India's defense capabilities.

decisive, is a question requiring further extended analysis which need not be a concern here.

The point of this narrative is simply to illustrate the complexity of factors affecting a situation in which countries formulate policy. The factors described are not simply the states involved in interrelationships but also the forces which operate within the confines of a state or which are transnational. These are factors which constrain or facilitate policy making and implementation.

In order to grasp and explain these constraining and facilitating forces, it is necessary to develop an analytical scheme which will enable us to reduce the complexity of the environment to manageable proportions. One widely used approach is systems analysis.[4]

Although the use of the concept of system varies substantially with different scholars, it has a common meaning, at least in the field of international politics. This core meaning is that the international system consists of a set of interrelated variables which are structured into an identifiable pattern. The pattern tends to be maintained as the actors in the system conform to identifiable modes of behavior. The international system is held to be an open system which is subsystem dominant. That is, the system is influenced by inputs from its environment, and it is controlled by the sovereign actors rather than by an over-arching authority.

The device of the international system helps to clarify the existence of patterns such as the balance of power and bipolarity. It also is useful for identifying gross patterns of behavior, and it helps to explain the

---

4. The foremost exponent of systems analysis in international politics is Morton A. Kaplan. See esp. his *System and Process in International Politics* (New York: John Wiley and Sons, Inc., 1957). Much of the work on systems analysis in the social sciences is indebted to the work of Talcott Parsons. For the more ambitious undertaking of placing all phenomena—physical and social—in the systems framework, see the work of Ludwig von Bertallanffy. In political science, the leading exponent of systems analysis is David Easton. Additional treatments of the international system may be found in Karl W. Deutsch and J. David Singer, "Multipolar Power Systems and International Stability," *World Politics* 16 (April 1964); F. H. Hinsley, "On the Present State and Future Development of the International System," *World Politics* 20 (July 1968); George Liska, "Continuity and Change in International Systems," *World Politics* 16 (October 1963); Roger D. Masters, "A Multi-Bloc Model of International System," *The American Political Science Review* 55 (December 1961); George Modelski, "Kautilya: Foreign Policy and International System in the Ancient Hindu World," *The American Political Science Review* 58 (September 1964); George Modelski, "Agraria and Industria: Two Models of the International System," *World Politics* 14 (October 1961); George Modelski, "Comparative International Systems," *World Politics* 14 (July 1962); Fred W. Riggs, "International Relations as a Prismatic System," *World Politics* 14 (October 1961); James N. Rosenau, "Transforming the International System: Small Increments Along a Vast Periphery," *World Politics* 18 (April 1966); and Oran R. Young, "Political Discontinuities in the International System," *World Politics* 20 (April 1968).

actions of states. With systems analysis, one can assess the state of the whole pattern of relationships of all countries in the world in terms of stability and change. Processes such as integration can be understood, and the conditions of transformation of the system from one state of equilibrium to another can be discovered. Particularly contributing to the understanding of this problem is the work of Rosecrance.[5]

The major advantage of systems analysis is that it does provide a tool for reducing complexity to manageable proportions. The total pattern of international relationships can be understood, at least at a given time, in terms of a limited set of specified behavioral patterns and a few simple processes, such as disturbance and regulation (of equilibrium). Systems analysis has the added advantage of providing insights into behavioral patterns, and it sets forth hypotheses at a high level of generalization. Relationships among nations are explained at one level of generalization. Another advantage is that systems analysis is a very useful tool in making explicit when the analyst is moving from one level of analysis to another.[6]

These are considerable advantages, and systems analysis is a powerful tool for analyzing international politics. Nevertheless, substantial criticisms have been brought to bear upon it, and one needs to be aware of the disadvantages as well.[7] In particular, systems analysis does not handle the kinds of variables which were identified in the narration of the Bangladesh situation above. Since these variables seem to be relevant to an understanding of the international environment for purposes of understanding foreign policy, systems analysis—despite its advantages—does not seem to be a sufficient tool of analysis for our purposes.

One of its major disadvantages is that it treats countries as monolithic actors. A result of this treatment is that causal factors lying within a country cannot be dealt with using systems analysis.[8] For example, in

---

5. See Richard N. Rosecrance, *Action and Reaction in World Politics: International Systems in Perspective* (Boston and Toronto: Little, Brown and Company, 1963).

6. This point is made by Charles McClelland in his book, *Theory and the International System* (New York: The Macmillan Company, 1966). For an explanation of why it is important to be clear about which level of analysis one is using, see J. David Singer, "The Level of Analysis Problem in International Relations," in *The International System: Theoretical Essays*, ed. Klaus Knorr and Sidney Verba (Princeton, N.J.: Princeton University Press, 1961).

7. See esp. Stanley Hoffmann, *Contemporary Theory in International Relations* (Englewood Cliffs, N.J.: Prentice-Hall, Inc., 1960), particularly his essay, "Theory as a set of questions," pp. 40–50.

8. The criticism leveled here does not entirely apply to Rosecrance's work which does take domestic politics into account.

the Bangladesh case, the economic and ethnic cleavages between East and West Pakistan would be ignored by systems analysis. Yet these were major causal factors in the disintegration of Pakistan, and India's policy was premised on the existence of these cleavages. India did not treat Pakistan as a monolithic actor but rather treated East and West Pakistan as two distinct entities.

Additionally, systems analysis overlooks the political dynamics of interactions. Its abstract quality and its tendency to reify "actors" prevents it from taking into account the emotional dimensions of politics, the struggles over decisions, and features of politics such as loyalty, identity, and alienation. Neither does it account for different kinds of political systems and different national cultures. All of these are factors which influence politics, whether domestic or international.

Finally, systems analysis does not address the questions of how foreign policy is formulated and executed. This is a problem that lies outside systems analysis to a large extent, yet even the internal decision-making dynamics of a country often form part of the environment for others. For example, the existence of major dissent in the United States during the Vietnam war and the fact that the American political system is characterized by an independent press and legislature were important features of the environment for all of the antagonists.

We must conclude that systems analysis is an insufficient conceptual device for treating the international environment in a book on foreign policy analysis. Before developing another scheme which can handle the complexity of the environment, however, it will be useful to set out the major factors in the environment which act as constraining and facilitating forces upon foreign policy.

Constraining and Facilitating Factors in the International Environment

The actions of states and other actors are major constraining and facilitating factors upon the foreign policies of countries. The ways in which these operate are treated below in the chapter on foreign determinants. In addition to these, however, there is a number of factors which are not under the control of political volition but which form an important part of the environment for foreign policy activity.

These factors vary over time and by circumstances. For example, technology provides a different set of constraints in an age of high-speed transportation than in a time of more primitive communications. Religion, to cite another example, is a more significant cleavage in the relations between India and Pakistan than it is, say, in the relations between France and England today. Yet religion has been an important variable in French-English relations in the past.

A brief review of the major factors in the international environment may be subsumed under three headings: (1) physical environment, human resources, and technology; (2) social cleavages and widely-shared attitudes; and (3) political and economic institutions. Although each factor can be thought of as setting limits or constraints on what countries can do in their policies, each also has an enabling or facilitating function. That is, each factor is characterized by an implementing function which helps countries to pursue their policies. International law, for example, provides some constraints on countries, but it may also be invoked as a tool for accomplishing certain purposes. Taking an obvious example, the international law of domestic jurisdiction makes it more difficult than it would be in the absence of the law for one country to intervene in the affairs of another. Simultaneously, the law of sovereignty provides a shield to a country which enables it to organize its own resources so as to accomplish the purposes it sets by its own political decision-making process. Each of the factors discussed below has this dual character, and each will be treated in terms of both the constraining function and the facilitating function.

Physical Environment, Human Resources, and Technology

The physical environment includes a number of dimensions that affect foreign policy. Geographical size and location as well as natural resources are obviously important dimensions, but weather and climate affect international behavior as well. In some cases, factors such as these can have a dramatic impact. The continental expanse of countries like the United States and the Soviet Union provide them with a security that smaller countries do not have. The plains of Poland, lying between larger countries, have provided a path for invaders. Zambia, a landlocked country which is economically dependent upon and has a common border with the Republic of South Africa, is constrained from taking militant action against its southern neighbor regardless of ideological pressures and considerations of justice.

Natural resources, like oil in the Middle East, also have constraining and facilitating functions. The dependence of Western Europe on oil helps to shape policies. The oil provides the fuel for industry, and dependence on suppliers provides constraints on policies that may be pursued. Just so, the oil-producing countries generate wealth to pursue their goals, but they are constrained by dependence on markets.

Both quantitatively and qualitatively, human resources perform constraining and facilitating functions. In the baldest sense, numbers of people provide the manpower for accomplishing a society's goals, yet an imbalance between population and economic development as has occurred in a number of poor countries in this century means that numbers of people are a burden to the accomplishment of social ambitions. Moreover, the level of education and the incidence of scientific and technical expertise affects what a country can accomplish. More consideration will be given to population as a factor in a country's capabilities in the chapter on domestic determinants.

Technology is related to and can have a considerable impact upon the physical environment and human resources and is, in turn, affected by those factors. Some examples of this mutual influence were cited above. Science and technology are so pervasive in the contemporary world that it is difficult to separate their influence from our modes of thought and from any aspect of life.[9] With respect to the study of foreign policy, however, there are several ways in which technology is particularly relevant in providing constraining and facilitating functions. Technology is responsible for the formation and evolution of the territorial state in that the state was formed as a device for protection against military weapons and the evolution of weaponry and communications technology have required adaptations of the state.[10]

Apart from providing the organizing principle for the territorial state, technology affects the international environment in two particularly important ways, both of which are important elements in the structure of the international system. The first is the industrialization process which is the application of technology to the production of economic goods and involves mastery over the factors of production: land and resources, labor, and capital. Industrialization provides the capabilities for individual countries to pursue state-directed goals, and the unequal distribution of technology and the uneven growth of economic development around the world helps to shape the structure and the pattern of the international environment. This is illustrated in the fact that the gross national product of a country is the best single indicator of the

---

9. A very interesting article, appearing after this was written, which elaborates and explores this concern is Kenneth A. Dahlberg, "The Technological Ethic and the Spirit of International Relations," *International Studies Quarterly* 17 (March 1973): 55–88.

10. See John H. Herz, *International Politics in the Atomic Age* (New York: Columbia University Press, 1959) and, by the same author, "The Territorial State Revisited: Reflections on the future of the Nation-State" in *International Politics and Foreign Policy*, ed. James N. Rosenau, rev. ed. (New York: The Free Press, 1969).

rank of that country in a world hierarchy of states. Many other factors need to be taken into account in studying a country's foreign policy, but the GNP alone gives a good rough indication of a country's power in relationship to others.

The most highly industrialized countries are also those involved in the most political situations and which have the most influence on other countries. The industrial base of the country is necessarily linked with the political aims, and the exceptional case of Japan in the post-World War II period does not disprove the generalization about the relationship of industrialization to influence. Economically, Japan has an immense influence on the world system, and that country's potential is both a source of concern for the calculations of other countries and is available for employment if the Japanese political situation were to produce leaders with more ambitious external goals.

Nuclear weapons and their delivery systems are the second particularly important manifestation of technology. Since the demonstration of their use in 1945, nuclear weapons have helped to structure the international environment. The American monopoly of nuclear weapons, combined with its invulnerability until the development of the intercontinental rocket in 1957, assured the United States of superior military power in the world. The period of duopoly, when the Soviet Union and the United States held the only effective nuclear weapons systems, was a time when these weapons reinforced the bipolar structure of the world. France and China then developed nuclear weapons which were symbols of their independence. In the 1970s, the greater sophistication and destructive power of the American and Soviet weapons systems assured the two superpowers of a continuing role of predominance in the international system. Broadly speaking, the economic and political dimensions of the international system are characterized by a greater decentralization than during the cold war years as other countries have developed the economic strength and political will to be more nearly independent. On the strategic dimension, however, the United States and the Soviet Union continue to be predominant and hold the keys—literally and figuratively —to global warfare and destruction. Neither China nor France nor any foreseeable new nuclear power is likely to have more than a capacity for regional employment of nuclear weapons, and none has the capacity to coerce either the United States or the Soviet Union.

Social Cleavages and Widespread Attitudes

The major currents of thought and attitudes in the world today are derived from western Europe, but the fundamental ideas are so rich that they have led to very different manifestations and to a condition in which there are basic disagreements in the world. The two foremost designs for ordering society—liberal democracy and communism—even though derived from European civilization, represent a basic cleavage that rends both many domestic societies (such as Chile) and the international system. The matter is further complicated because the spread of western ideas throughout the world also clashes with other civilizations and other traditions and attitudes. Many countries in Asia and Africa, for example, are torn by the clash of loyalties to the tribe, village, religion, culture, and ethnic group on the one hand and to the state and the inchoate, artificial, modern nation on the other. These divergences, like the factors discussed in the last section, perform both constraining and facilitating functions.

A commitment to the communist ordering of society, for example, facilitates the Soviet Union's control over eastern European countries. On the other hand, the Soviets were constrained to assist North Vietnam in its resistance to American attacks, just as the American resistance to communism constrained the United States to take on the liabilities and frustrations of the Vietnam war. In neither case is the belief upon which action rests an inevitable determinant, but it is a factor which operates in the situation to constrain or facilitate political judgments and actions.

The human experience is so rich and diverse that there are innumerable sets of social cleavages and attitudes which operate in politics. Only the most obvious and prominent ones can be identified here. There are others which emerge only in specific situations, and still others emerge from time to time as prominent features of the international system.

At the center of the phenomena discussed here is the divergence on the question of how to order the world. Although the sovereign territorial state has been adopted almost universally as the accepted form of political organization, the question of how the world should be ordered is far from being settled. There are prominent challenges to the sovereign state organization. The integration movement in Western Europe is one challenge, and the Soviet Union's retention of empire is another, particularly in the justification of the Brehznev "doctrine" which claimed that socialist states have the right to intervene in other socialist states. The claims of the United Nations General Assembly to intervene on behalf of individuals in South Africa despite the legal, sovereign status of the government and the subnational loyalties as manifested in the Biafran succession from Nigeria are other challenges. With the increasing awareness of the pollution consequences of industrial society, there are voices raised on behalf of using environmental criteria rather than political criteria for making production judgments.[11] The spread of the multinational corporation and the growth of the transnational student movement based on generational loyalty and linked by mass communications are other phenomena which operate without respect to the framework of sovereignty and which contradict the principle of order based on the state.

These cleavages over the question of how to order the world—whether they are explicit or implicit—represent not only the process of working out the future order of the world but also cleavages that may be exploited and which, depending on the point of view and the circumstances, may be constraining and facilitating factors in the conduct of foreign policy.

Apart from the question of world order, the most basic cleavage is over the type of regime. Liberal democracy and communism are the two most prominent regime types over which there are differences of view. Military and civilian rule provides another cleavage which is prominent in the world. The history of Latin America is characterized by this cleavage, and the countries of Asia and Africa have featured changes from civilian to military rule very often, with the reverse occurring less frequently. Not long ago, fascism was an accepted form in many countries. Monarchical rule continues in several countries—Jordan, Iran, and Ethiopia being examples—and this form is opposed by groups in each country.

The world is generally characterized as being in a revolutionary situation, particularly in this century and more especially since 1945. This revolutionary situation is based on the widespread appeal of the dominant value in modern political thought—a value shared by Hobbes and Marx and by their adherents, liberal democrats and communists. This is the value of equality. The value of equality, however, has spread and become widely accepted in the context of inequality of condition in political, social, and economic life. Sometimes violently and sometimes peacefully, some seventy-five countries have gained formal political independence. Although these countries have gained some status and dignity, particularly through membership in the United Nations, most of them continue to lack the capacity to participate on a nearly equal basis with the wealthier and more powerful countries. Economically, they are developing more slowly than the economically advanced coun-

---

11. See, for example, the recommendation that synthetic rubber production be replaced by natural rubber in Malaysia by Barry Commoner "Motherhood in Stockholm," *Harper's Magazine*, June 1972.

tries. Within them, inequality continues to exist as they are divided between an upper class and a lower class.[12]

The cleavages are more numerous and complex than can be usefully employed in foreign policy analysis. There are cleavages between the privileged and the unprivileged, between the powerful and the powerless, between the scientific mind and the traditional mind, between the wealthy and the poor, between visionaries and pragmatists, between the satisfied and the dissatisfied, between the exploiters and the exploited, and so forth. Class is perhaps the most useful term for representing cleavages which can be analyzed as having politically potent constraining and facilitating functions.

Class is a category which assumes that groups of people, regardless of other things that divide them, are in a roughly equivalent social, economic, and political condition, and that not everyone belongs to the same class. Class will be defined here to represent any group of people who consider themselves to exist in the same condition and who view others as belonging to a class that exists in an opposite condition. When leaders of poor countries view their countries as underdeveloped and define other countries as developed, they constitute a class. Thus, the Group of 77 which was formed to deal with the rich countries at the first United Nations Conference on Trade and Development (UNCTAD) in 1964 is a class.

Within countries, a class exists when a group of citizens recognize their equality of condition and oppose another group which it sees as being in the opposite condition. For example, the Bengalis in East Pakistan saw themselves as exploited by West Pakistan prior to their achievement of independence as Bangladesh in 1971–72.

Because inequality of condition exists everywhere, there is always a potential for the development of class consciousness. When it does develop within a society, it can become significant to international politics when persons outside the country—whether officials or other actors —perceive themselves in the same class as one of the opponents or when the existing cleavage may be instrumental for their own purposes. Potential class developments can also be exploited by actors from other countries through a variety of devices, including money, training, propaganda, and direct intervention.

---

12. Although most economists, projecting Western categories on to the poor countries, speak of a middle class, I prefer the dichotomy used here which is taken from Gunnar Myrdal. See his *Asian Drama* (New York: Twentieth Century Fund and Pantheon Books, 1968) and *The Challenge of World Poverty* (New York: Pantheon Books, 1970).

Race, religion, culture, language, and ethnicity are other cleavages which act as constraints and facilitators in the international environment. The cohesion of white South Africans is supplied by race, and their opponents in bordering countries have the same basis for their cohesion. Language but little else other than a common enemy unites the Arabs. Ethnic differences made it impossible for the Federation of Malaysia to remain united. None of these cleavages is extraordinarily powerful and consistent, but all provide potential for exploitation for political purposes.

Political and Economic Institutions

The international environment constrains and facilitates states through a large number of institutional mechanisms that have been created by governments and through some nongovernmental institutions. International law—based on customs and treaties—has already been alluded to. Global and regional organizations such as the United Nations and its affiliated specialized agencies and the Organization of American States provide mechanisms for facilitating governments to achieve their purposes when their interests are in harmony and to constrain them when their purposes are in conflict.

Although the attempts in this century to extend international law to making war illegal have failed, international law nevertheless regulates many international activities which might, in its absence, lead to war. The regulation of fishing is one example of this function of international law. In addition, international law gives protection to diplomats, thus facilitating the conduct of diplomatic intercourse. Treaties provide a legal sanction to cooperative undertakings like the European Economic Community and a precise terminology and a formal status for undertakings like the Moscow agreement of 1972 on the limitation of strategic arms. Occasionally, disputes are settled through legal proceedings. The law of sovereign equality confers status on small states and even sometimes gives them some protection. International law also provides the basis for the development of intergovernmental organizations.

Intergovernmental organizations may be global or regional, and either type may be a general purpose or a limited—usually single—purpose entity. Organizations are primarily facilitating in that they provide services. The Food and Agricultural Organization and the Universal Postal Union, for instance, facilitate international cooperation and impose almost no constraints on countries. The International Bank for Reconstruction and Development and the International Monetary Fund, as contrary examples, both facilitate cooperation and constrain member states by applying criteria to loans and regulating currency flows.

The International Environment

These are not so coercive as legal constraints, but they nevertheless operate. The United Nations, on the other hand, sometimes has the capacity to set severe constraints on a country. For example, the United Nations' action in the Middle East in 1956 was effective in ending hostilities, securing an Israeli withdrawal from Egyptian territory, and maintaining a more secure border until 1967.

The way in which these many factors in the international environment operate is not predictable in any exact fashion. Neither is their potency known. Moreover, as has been indicated, there is a great variety of factors at work in the international environment which do not fit neatly into general categories of analysis. This brief discussion nevertheless points to a variety of elements in the international environment which perform constraining and facilitating functions for the foreign policies of countries.

The problem now is to develop a scheme which will enable us to accommodate the complexity of the international environment for use in studying foreign policy. Such a scheme is based on the notion of situation.

4

Situations

Phenomena associated with foreign policy occur in situations. Specific circumstances provide boundaries for making decisions and for executing policies. These circumstances place limits on what any given country can do in coping with them. Although one might attempt to isolate a country's foreign policy from its environment, that exercise would lead to a very incomplete understanding of foreign policy. The interrelationship of the country with its specific environment should not be ignored because the environment influences the foreign policy of a given country, and the country's foreign policy influences the environment.

On the other hand, to treat the environment in an undifferentiated way would also lead us to misunderstand how it influences foreign policy. Given countries engage in limited situations in their foreign policies.[1] A situation may be as simple as a two-party negotiation of a

---

1. The problem addressed in this chapter and the next is one of responding to the criticisms of much of the international politics and foreign policy literature made by Harold and Margaret Sprout. The concept of situation developed in this chapter is intended to provide an analytical device for relating foreign policy capabilities analysis

commercial treaty or it may be a global crisis which threatens a comprehensive thermonuclear exchange among several countries. It may be a problem confronting a multilateral alliance, or it may be a regional dispute.

Despite the fact that in any given instance a country confronts a specific set of circumstances, the analyst need not treat everything as unique. He can analyze patterns of interaction, and he can identify the common characteristics of situations, paths of influence and control, and the directions and rates of change in the patterns.

The international system as a whole is a pattern of interrelationships among all the countries in the world. It is not, however, a set of equal actors. There are vast differences among them, and they vary immensely in their capacity to affect the overall system. Governments even vary in their respective capacities to command the territory over which they have jurisdiction. If we limit our study to these two units of analysis—the international system and the individual state—however, we overlook the capacity of states and groups of states to control and/or manage situations which are bounded on a scale smaller than the global system.

Although such situations are linked with the global system, a combination of the capacity of those central actors in the situation to control it, on the one hand, and the restraint of linked or peripheral actors, on the other, can insulate the situation from the global system and minimize the effects of the situation on it. Situation, then, is a unit of analysis on a scale larger than the individual country and smaller than the international system as a whole. It is nevertheless linked to both.

The criterion for identifying a situation is that a pattern of interaction exists among actors seeking control over objects and events. This criterion is different from those which seek to identify subsystems which are intermediate between the state and the international system as a whole by identifying and defining regions.[2] Although situations often

---

to specific circumstances. In their "Environmental Factors in the Study of International Politics," reprinted in James N. Rosenau, ed., *International Politics and Foreign Policy* (New York: The Free Press of Glencoe, 1961), p. 117, the Sprouts state, "Failure to keep the discussion of state capabilities within some policy frame of reference is one of the reasons why a good deal that has been said about the so-called 'elements' or 'foundations' of national power is footless and unconvincing."

2. Foremost among these efforts are Louis J. Cantori and Steven J. Spiegel, *The International Politics of Regions: A Comparative Approach* (Englewood Cliffs, N.J.: Prentice-Hall Inc., 1970) and Bruce Russett, *International Regions and the International System: A Study in Political Ecology* (Chicago: Rand McNally & Company, 1967). See also Leonard Binder, "The Middle East as a Subordinate International System," *World Politics* 10 (April 1959) and Michael Brecher, "International Relations and Asian Studies: The Subordinate State System of Asia," *World Politics* 15 (January 1963).

Situations   69

have regional boundaries according to various criteria, they do not always. The notion of situation is a more inclusive concept which still has the advantage of providing a unit of analysis between the state and the global system.

The remainder of this chapter will develop the concept of a situation and the means for analyzing situations. To that end, a set of questions that an analyst might ask in determining the boundaries of a case study will be developed. In doing this, perhaps the means for achieving comparability among case studies can be found. In addition, models of a finite number of situations which can be used in analyzing specific events are developed.

Although this is an abstract enterprise, it also needs to be noted that real world situations tend to persist over time. By focusing on them, one can explain why there are regularities in foreign policies and why change occurs.

As situations persist over time, the countries involved define their own roles in the situation and develop expectations about others' roles. This leads each country's policy makers to predict the behavior of others and leads to expectations about the reliability of allies and the resolve of adversaries. We will see later how pressures for change arise and the conditions under which changes occur. We shall also see how miscalculations can occur when changes in a situation go unnoticed.

The conception of situation developed in this chapter is crucial to understanding the following analysis, for the thesis of this book is that the very meaning of foreign policy lies in the interaction of states in situations. The entire mode of analysis rests on treating the actions of a country in a situation.[3]

Not only will an understanding of situations aid us in subsequent analysis of foreign policy but it will also contribute to a broader theoretical enterprise. One of the major sets of alternative assumptions in the post-World War I period is the proposition that peace is indivisible and its alternative: peace can be preserved in limited areas. The general consciousness of the problem of escalation and the possibility of the use of thermonuclear weapons acknowledges the ultimate reality that

---

3. Cf. Richard C. Snyder, H. W. Bruck, and Burton Sapin, eds., *Foreign Policy Decision-Making: An Approach to the Study of International Politics* (New York: The Free Press of Glencoe, 1962), who take as their basic unit "the state in a situation," and who cite the "external setting" as a prominent set of influences on decision making. They do not, however, explicate the meaning of "situation" nor do they analyze the "external setting." This chapter is an attempt to elaborate those concepts in order to apply the framework of analysis which holds that "the state in a situation" is the basic unit.

the world could be engulfed in war, making peace indivisible. On the other hand, the experience of keeping the Korean war limited and the success of the United Nations operation in the Middle East in 1956 give evidence that certain situations can be isolated and that peace is divisible. What we do not know is whether these specific events can be universalized or whether the situations in which they occurred had identifiable characteristics that can be differentiated from other situations where there would be less likelihood of isolation and in which peace was not divisible.

Roles

In addition to noting distinctions among actors as developed in chapter 2, it is also necessary to note that actors play different roles in international situations. There are five such roles in this scheme of analysis.[4] Any given actor may play each of these roles at different times and different situations. It is also possible for an actor to perform two different roles in the same situation.

The first role is that of the *direct, central actor*. Direct, central actors apply instruments to one another in a roughly equivalent ratio to the application of instruments by other direct, central actors. Whether the actors are engaged in diplomatic negotiations, cultural exchange, trading relationships, or war, the relationship of instruments is the criterion used for this role. There are occasions when, in a hegemonial situation, a single actor may apply instruments at a sharply greater level than the other actors. In such a case, one would say that there is just one direct, central actor.

The second role is that of the *direct, noncentral actor*. Direct, noncentral actors apply instruments to direct actors at a sharply lower level than central actors. Direct, noncentral actors would be the smaller parties to a negotiation or smaller allies in a war. Another example of a direct, noncentral actor would be the deferent partner(s) in a hegemonial relationship.

The third role is played by *peripheral actors* who transfer resources to the central actors or are greatly affected by a situation but who do not

---

4. For an alternative and impressive treatment of roles in foreign policy behavior, see K. J. Holsti, "National Role Conception in the Study of Foreign Policy," *International Studies Quarterly* 14 (September 1970): 233–309. Holsti's treatment is closer to the treatment of identity in chapter 2, however, than to the use of role in this chapter.

Situations 71

directly apply their instruments to other actors. Arms-supplying nations would be obvious examples of this type of actor.

Target actors fulfill the fourth role. Target actors have instruments applied to them but are unable to become central actors. With respect to much of the Vietnam war, Laos was in the position of a target actor.

Finally, there are *intermediary actors* who attempt to achieve the end of conflict by assisting central actors to "realize their common interests while at the same time preventing consequences that might prove disruptive for the international system as a whole."[5]

Direct actors are distinguished from the others, particularly from peripheral and target actors, by the fact that they are those which control the instruments which are directed to the domestic determinants and the foreign policy acts of other direct actors. A peripheral actor is involved with one of the direct actors, but the instruments and resources which it controls are directed only toward its ally.

Five dimensions of situations will be discussed in the following pages. The first dimension is the boundaries of a situation. The three aspects of boundaries—arena, scope, and objects—will be discussed. The second section will treat the number and rank of actors involved in a situation. Structure of situations is the third dimension, and several schematic models will be presented. The fourth section deals with the conditions of interaction of which four types will be identified: conflict, competition, cooperation, and integration. Finally, the stability and dynamics of situations will be considered. This discussion of the dimensions of the concept of situation is followed by a section on cases which illustrate different types of situations.

Boundaries of a Situation

It is very difficult to draw precise boundaries around situations. One can, however, identify the *arena* in which the direct actors apply their instruments to one another. If two contiguous countries are involved in direct negotiations or transactions of one kind or another and this business does not include the participation of other actors, the arena would be the area of the two countries. In such a case, one would say that the arena is local.

---

5. Oran R. Young, *The Intermediaries; Third Parties in International Crisis* (Princeton: Princeton University Press, 1967), p. 45.

If the two actors are engaged in, for example, negotiations in a third country that is not contiguous to both of the participants, we would say that the arena is regional. For example, in settling the 1965 war over Kashmir, Indian and Pakistani representatives met with a Soviet representative in the Soviet city of Tashkent. The arena extended to the area of an actor—in this case, an intermediary actor—which was not contiguous to the territory of both direct actors.

When there are more than two actors, any of which is not contiguous to all of the others, the arena can be said to be regional. A useful subcategory of regional is supraregional. This can be defined as a situation in which there are subsets of actors that meet the regional test, each subset in a different region. The interaction between the Soviet Union and its Eastern European allies and the United States and its Western European allies is an example of a supraregional situation because each of the coalitions conforms to the definition of regional.

A global arena is sometimes the boundary of a situation because virtually all state actors are involved in the situation. A global arena is a rare phenomenon and is likely to occur only in a comprehensive war. If a situation has global dimensions, a large number of countries will be applying their instruments to another large number of countries.

Most of our focus will be on regional and supraregional arenas, for they are the most common in the world. Most case studies involve the complexity of more than two actors involved over a space that includes noncontiguous actors. The arena of a situation is not difficult to identify, for it is simply the area in which the direct actors apply their instruments to each other.

More difficult to identify is *scope*. Scope refers to the effects of a situation outside the boundaries of the arena through linkages with other situations. It is the link between a situation and the international system.

The Kashmir situation, for example, is a limited situation involving only India and Pakistan as direct actors. Because each of these countries is involved in other situations, however, there are sometimes ramifications from the Kashmir dispute to those other situations. For example, the war in 1965 functioned as an issue in the Sino-Soviet dispute as China backed Pakistan and the Soviet Union gave support to India. The Soviet Union continued transferring resources to India during the war, and China used its diplomatic and informational instruments to support Pakistan. Through their activities as peripheral actors in the India-Pakistan situation, their own direct relationships were affected.

The most important effect of a situation for the global system occurs if it is linked with the overall international system. The impact of a local or regional situation, then, will depend upon two factors: the capacity of the central actors in the situation to manage it and the interest or restraint of the larger countries.

This problem is perhaps best illustrated in the Middle East situation in the 1960s and 1970s. Despite the fact that the 1956 and 1967 wars were controlled, particularly by Israel, the United States and the Soviet Union were both linked to the situation. Not only were they peripheral actors in the Middle East situation itself, but that situation was to some extent a function of their strategic relationship and had the potential for drawing them in more directly should the situation have become unmanageable (as it would if there were an imminent threat that one of the Middle East states was about to be obliterated).

A global situation in today's world would have to include the superpowers, the United States and the Soviet Union. In addition, they are the only countries with the capability for engulfing the world in comprehensive war. Peace, then, is indivisible where there is a high risk of war between these two superpowers. Because they are interested in so many situations throughout the world, there is a potential for war in many of them. However, as was noted above, a situation may be insulated from superpower conflict if the direct actors have the capacity to control the situation and if the superpowers are restrained from intervening.

If they do intervene, their interests—and, thus, the global system—would tend to predominate, and there would be the tendency for the local or regional situation to become merely a function of the global situation throughout the course of the conflict. The problem for the smaller country in this kind of situation is to gain support for its policies without losing effective control over decisions in support of its objectives. As we will see in the section on conditions of interaction, a smaller partner may not only be cooperating with a larger partner in conducting a local conflict, but it would also be engaged in a competition with the larger partner for control over decisions.

In the Vietnam war, both Saigon and Hanoi faced this problem. The situation was one which interested the superpowers. Hanoi demonstrated its capacity to control its side of the situation, and the Soviet Union remained as a peripheral actor. Saigon, on the other hand, faced with the imminence of a probable defeat in 1965, was assisted by American intervention. Washington then ascended in control over the partnership as its interests tended to predominate, but the course of events showed a continuing competition between Washington and Saigon over decisions affecting not only the military activities of the war but also the related questions of operating the political system of South Vietnam.

Scope is not a definitionally precise concept, but it does raise a question that needs to be asked by the analyst who seeks to put finite boundaries around the case he intends to study. Exactly what all the effects of a situation outside its arena will be are not predictable because there is so much room for discretion. By identifying linked situations, however, we can estimate the potential for involvement by countries other than the direct actors and the possibilities for transforming a situation. Scope, then, is a useful notion even though it is imprecise.

Another consideration in defining the boundaries of a situation is the *objects* over which the actors are attempting to get control or influence. Objects may be tangible, such as territory or trading concessions, or they may be intangible, such as prestige or the commitment of an ally. Countries seek a wide variety of objects and so they are difficult to classify.[6] It is important for the analyst to identify what is at stake in a situation, however, for it is important to know who controls the object and whether goals can be achieved. It is also important to know whether all of the countries involved view the object in the same way and whether they are seeking the same object as others or something else. In identifying objects, the analyst must look to each actor, for very often different actors have very different objects in mind.[7]

It would seem, for example, that the United States and the Soviet Union approached the problem of a nuclear nonproliferation treaty in the 1960s from quite different points of view. The United States was concerned about any country developing an independent nuclear deterrent. In this context, some officials saw no incompatibility between advocating a multilateral force (MLF) for NATO which would have allowed West German participation in the handling though not the control of nuclear weapons, on the one hand, and favoring a nonproliferation treaty on the other. In contrast, the Soviets seemed not so concerned about any country's acquisition of nuclear weapons, but they were intent upon stopping Germany from either acquiring or partici-

---

6. Even such an elementary classification as tangible and intangible is very difficult to operationalize and apply. James N. Rosenau has used this classification, employing the criterion of photographability to determine whether an object is tangible or intangible. He uses the Berlin wall as an illustration of a tangible object. However, the wall was simply an instrument for achieving the intangible—using Rosenau's criterion—object of retaining East Germany's human resources within its boundaries. See his "Pre-Theories and Theories of Foreign Policy," in his *The Scientific Study of Foreign Policy* (New York: The Free Press, 1971), p. 146.

7. Analysis of situations would be much simpler if there were an agreed measure of objects such as the monetary measure in economics. In that case, it would be possible to transfer the theory of oligarchy to foreign policy analysis. Because there is no measure of the objects of foreign policies equivalent to money and profits, however, the foreign policy analyst is faced with a task that defies theoretical formulation akin to that of the economic analyst.

Situations 75

pating in any nuclear weapons program. Only after President Johnson shelved the MLF did the Soviets agree to the nonproliferation treaty.

The problem of identifying objects is further complicated by the fact that countries often pursue minimum and maximum objectives in their policies. The Soviet Union may have a maximum objective of removing American influence from western Europe, but its minimal objective is control of eastern Europe. Similarly, the United States may have the maximum objective of removing Soviet control from eastern Europe, but at a minimum it has wanted to prevent the extension of Soviet control to western Europe. States generally enter negotiations with other states with maximum and minimum objectives.

With the arena, scope, and objects discussed, we proceed to classify situations along three additional dimensions: the number and rank of the actors, the structure of the situation, and the nature of the interaction.

Number and Rank of Actors

The number of actors in a situation may be large or small and may vary over time as a result of interests and circumstances. The general principle governing the number of actors is that interested actors will attempt to seek or maintain control in as few hands as possible and will seek to expand or contract the number of actors only to that number which is necessary to gain control over the object of the situation.

The participation of a very large number of actors generally means that control is diffused and that the situation is evolving. In such a case, there will be a tendency to develop two coalitions. A coalition which feels that it is gaining or has gained control over the objects of the situation will attempt to limit or diminish the number of participants to that number which it calculates will gain or secure its control. A coalition which feels that it is losing control over the objects of a situation, in contrast, will seek to expand the number of participants to a size which it feels necessary to gain or secure control over the objects. The number of actors available for participation, of course, is limited to those which have the capacity and the predisposition to participate in the given situation.

Even when there is a small number of direct actors, there is a tendency for other actors to attempt to gain some measure of control over a situation. We can say that the preference of any actor is to have monopoly control, and, short of that, shared control with only one actor. In situations of duopoly, there is a tendency for the number of actors to increase and for the situation to be short term because other actors—seeing the possible effects on themselves and the international system—attempt to influence the direct actors or to take such unilateral actions as are designed to give them some measure of control over the further evolution of the situation.

The case of nuclear weapons provides an example of this phenomenon. As with other technological developments, there is a tendency for them to spread. Political decisions are made to acquire the technology in order to give to those making such decisions a measure of control over situations influenced by the technology. Other actors, short of developing the requisite technology and spurred by fears of the weapons, attempt to influence those who possess them by posing moral issues, requesting controls, arranging for negotiations, and so forth. During the period of American nuclear monopoly, for instance, the Soviet Union argued that it was immoral to possess the weapons. When the Soviet Union itself had developed a nuclear capability, it shared in the control and ceased that particular line in its international informational policies.[8]

Two-power control of nuclear weapons was broken in the late 1950s when the French developed their capability and in the 1960s when the Chinese entered the "nuclear club." In the absence of shared-control agreements or effective nuclear disarmament, other countries are likely to make decisions to gain nuclear weapons. The pattern will occur, situation-by-situation, with Japan, India, and Indonesia the most likely new nuclear powers.

The short-term nature of the nuclear monopoly and duopoly also illustrates another phenomenon. Just as there are tendencies to proliferate, there are also tendencies by the two major powers to collaborate to check or slow down proliferation. Thus, the Test Ban Treaty and the Nonproliferation Treaty were attempts by the Soviet Union and the United States (with British cooperation) to preserve as much of their position as they could with respect to nuclear weapons.

Stated another way, there will be two-party attempts at collaboration in a conflict situation to gain duopolistic control over the situation. The short-term nature of the collaboration is insured by two factors. The first is the attempt by others to gain a measure of influence and control. The second factor is the differing interests between the collaborators which make it difficult to hold their duopolistic coalition together. This

---

8. See William R. Frye, "Characteristics of Recent Arms-Control Proposals and Agreements," in *Arms Control, Disarmament, and National Security*, ed. Donald G. Brennan (New York: George Braziller, 1961), pp. 68–85, esp. p. 71.

Situations

hypothesis is applicable to other situations than the nuclear weapons question, as the following examples show.

In 1939, Germany and the Soviet Union signed an agreement which prepared the ground for the invasion of Poland. Before the Molotov-Ribbentrop agreement was signed, both Britain and the Soviet Union had attempted to form a dual coalition with Germany to gain control over events in Europe. After the agreement was signed and Poland was invaded, Britain continued to try to influence events by going to war over Poland when the German-Soviet pact was implemented. Further, at the time that Hitler judged that German interests would be served by attacking Russia, he did so. The coalition was transformed into an enemy relationship, and Germany aimed to replace the duopoly with a monopoly of control over the European situation.

The Cuban missile crisis of 1962 was another example of duopolistic control, this time in an acute conflict short of war. Despite attempts by others to gain influence, the situation was almost completely controlled by the two powers. Both the short duration of the conflict and the ability of the United States and the Soviet Union to collaborate on a solution which ended the crisis enabled them to retain control over the situation.

The chances for success in maintaining duopolistic control over a situation will be much greater if the two actors in question are the highest-ranking actors in the situation. When smaller actors attempt to maintain such limited control in situations in which larger actors are interested participants, the larger actors are limited primarily by self-restraint and their own calculations of advantage. Should they not be restrained, they are more likely to be able to gain some measure of control over the situation or, at least, to deprive smaller actors of exclusive control.

The number and rank of actors, then, tell us something about control patterns and probabilities of directions of further evolution of situations. Some relationships between number and rank of actors on the one hand, and the structure of situations on the other have already been hinted at. The structure of relations among actors requires a good deal more elaboration, and to this task we now address ourselves.

Structures

The reason for being concerned with structure is that patterns of control and paths of influence vary with different structures. By addressing ourselves to the structure of a situation, we can identify where control over a situation resides. We can also identify the possible paths of influence, and thereby reveal what is possible by way of affecting or gaining control over a situation.

The task of examining in detail how countries may use the paths of influence is performed in subsequent chapters. What one wishes to illustrate here are the potential patterns of control and paths of influence which foreign policy makers face when addressing themselves to a situation.

There are four basic types of situation structure that can be identified. The type depends upon the number of direct actors in the situation. The first type is the simplest: the two actor or dyadic situation. This type of situation is presented schematically in model 1. The two direct actors in

MODEL 1
Two-Actor Situation Structure

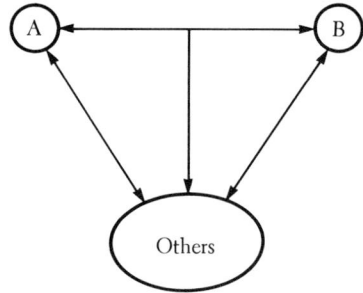

this type of situation hold control over the situation. The arrowed lines represent the paths of influence. The two direct actors influence each other, and each of them influences other countires. The situation itself also influences others. Should other countries wish to influence the situation, the only paths available to them are directly upon the two direct actors.

A minor variation on this model is the one in which there is a dyadic relationship between a single actor, on the one side, and a coalition on the other. This variation is presented in model 2 and indicates that the paths of influence are somewhat more complex. In this type of situation structure, others may deal with the coalition as a whole or with any of the partners. The problem for the coalition is to maintain its boundaries in order to hold the coalition together. Others may either attempt to penetrate and join the coalition, thus influencing it, or to reduce it by inducing one or more coalition partners to withdraw. Short of those drastic actions, others may simply attempt to influence one of the coali-

Situations 79

MODEL 2
Variation on Two-Actor Situation Structure:
One Actor-One Coalition Structure

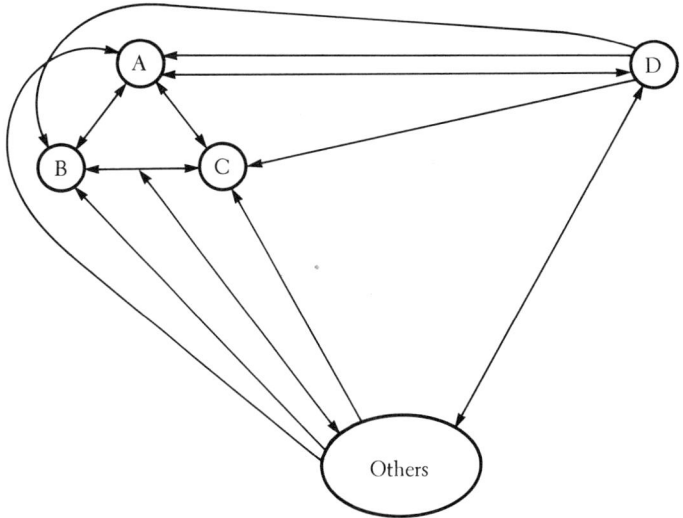

tion partners, thus hoping to achieve indirect effects on the coalition as a whole by altering one segment of the pattern of foreign policy acts.

The second basic type of structure is the several actor situation with a dominant partner. This type includes hegemonial relationships and some types of alliances. This structure is presented in model 3. The paths of influence in such a structure are largely those between the dominant partner, which controls the situation, and the deferent partners. However, the deferent partners can collaborate to oppose the dominant partner. In such a case, the dominant partner would attempt to organize as many segments of the coalition as it could to counter the opposing deferent partner coalition. This potential disintegrating function and the potential process of offsetting it are suggested by the dotted lines in the model. Others who wish to influence the situation can deal with the dominant partner, with the result of assisting in keeping the coalition together; or with the deferent partners, with the result of weakening the coalition. If successful dealings with the deferent partners is a tendency, this reflects a process of disintegration in the coalition. If the dominant partner is able to retain control of dealings with others, this reflects continued integration and dominant partner dominance.

The third basic type of structure is portrayed in model 4. It is a two-coalition situation in which there are several direct actors. In this type of

MODEL 3
Several Actor with Dominant Partner Situation Structure

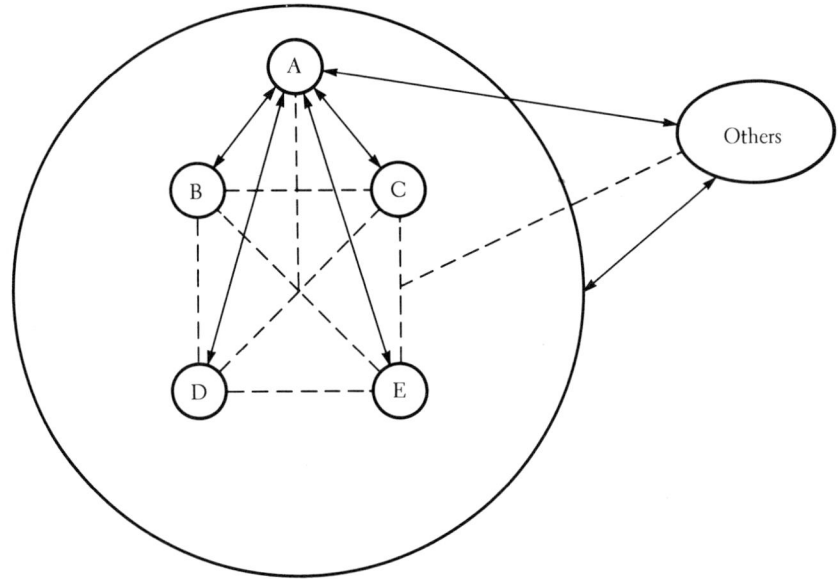

situation, we have a combination of the first and second types. That is, there are aspects of a two-actor situation in that control resides in the two coalitions, but there are also the paths of influence into each coalition that we saw in model 3. In such a situation, each coalition is interested in bringing about disintegration of the other, and each is also interested in maintaining the integration of its own coalition. The paths of influence are very complex.

The last basic type of situation structure is the one in which there are several direct actors. There are two variations on this pattern: the one in which there are two direct, central actors and the other in which there are several direct, central actors. These two variations are displayed in models 5 and 6. Control in this type of situation is much more problematical than in the other types. The paths of influence are much more complicated. The first variation, shown in model 5, is similar to the simplest type of model 1. However, the two direct actors are not isolated from others and do not maintain the same duopoly of control as in the simpler type. The paths of influence are more complicated, although the focus of all actors' efforts will be, whether direct or indirect, upon the situation as defined by the two direct, central actors.

MODEL 4
Two Coalition with Several Direct Actors Situation Structure

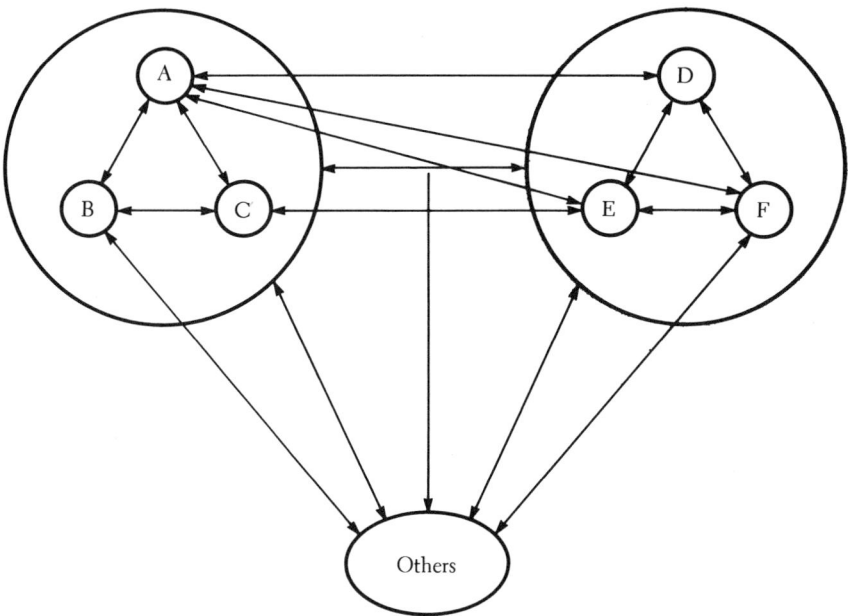

In the other variation, there will be attempts at forming coalitions, but when they are successfully formed, they will tend to be very unstable. This type is a classic balance-of-power model of interaction. The basic pattern will tend to be stable, as are the other types of structures, but it will be very difficult to transform the situation.

What do these models and the discussion of situation structure tell us, and how can this analysis be used? The answers to these questions will become more apparent as we proceed, but some preliminary answers can be given at this point.

As reiterated, the basic problem for actors in a situation is to exercise influence and to gain or maintain control of the situation. The problem for the student of foreign policy is to understand patterns of relationships and control. The proposition put forward here is that there is a limited number of patterns and that, by identifying these patterns in terms of structure, we can understand the limits of who may, with some potential for effectiveness, attempt to influence whom. We also have a criterion for criticizing the foreign policies of particular states and for illuminating possibilities for policy which may not be readily apparent.

MODEL 5
Several Actor with Two Direct Actors Situation Structure

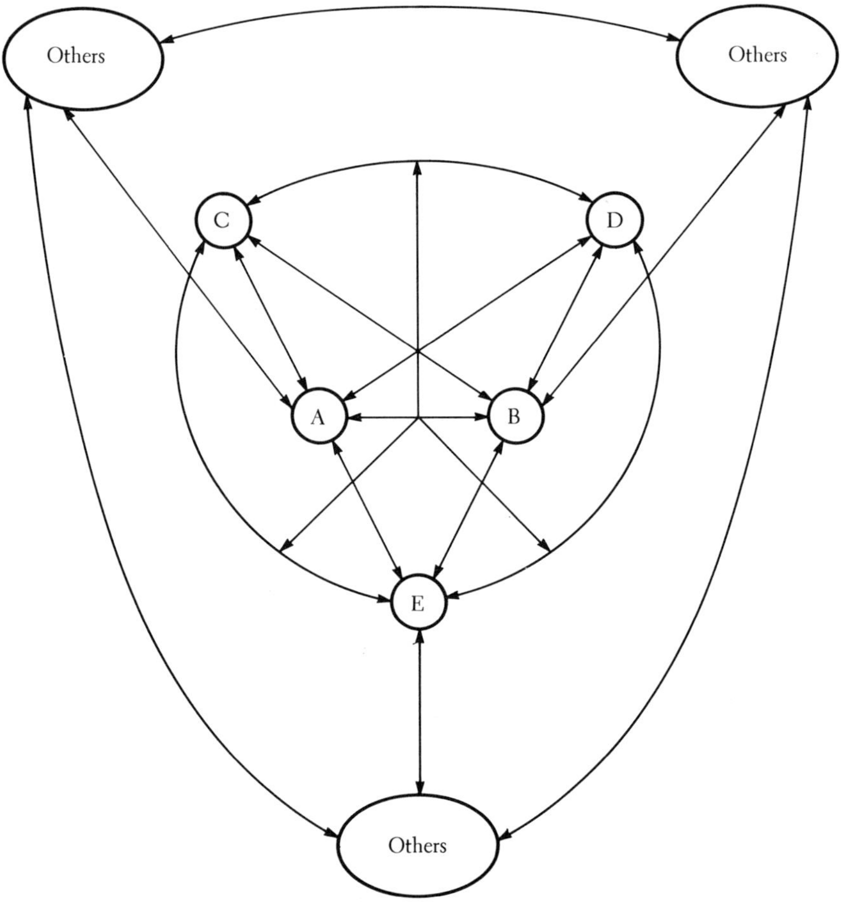

The actual exercise of influence depends upon the use of instruments by one actor and the response to that use of instruments by another. These models do not indicate the actual influence of actors, but they do indicate the directions that attempts at influence may take.

Let us, for example, examine the possibilities of exercising influence in different situation structures of two pairs of relationships, those between A and D and those between A and Z. In the discussion, let us assume that our only concern is with those relationships which affect the situation in question and that we can exclude the problem of linked situations.

MODEL 6
Several Direct Central Actors Situation

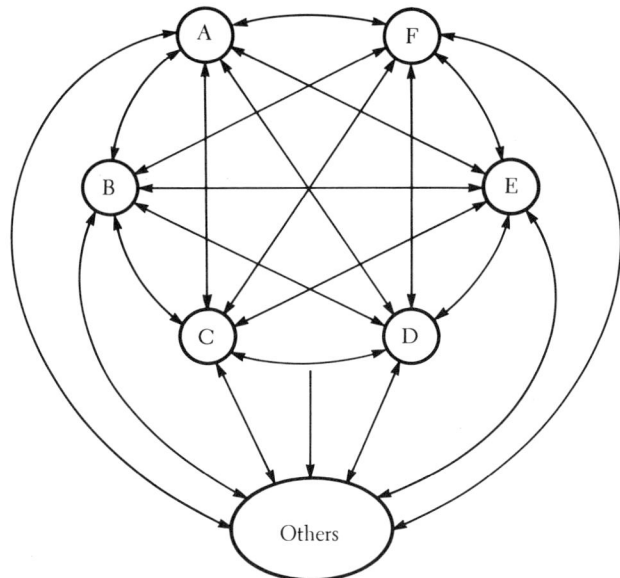

In model 1, a two-actor situation, A can attempt to influence D and Z to refrain from participating in the situation and can interact with B to maintain this state of affairs. D and Z must interact with A directly if they wish to influence its behavior with respect to the situation.

In model 2, A influences D in concert with B and C. D may attempt to influence A not only directly but also by working through B and C. A's influence on Z is through its coalition with B and C, but Z may attempt to influence A, B, and/or C directly, all aimed at influencing A.

Focusing on model 3, A's influence with D is direct as is its influence with Z. Z's influence on A is also direct, and, so long as A remains dominant, Z must deal with A, either to influence A or any of its partners in the coalition. Unlike model 2, it does not have the path from itself through B or C to A.

Model 4 illustrates a different set of paths of influence. A may treat with D directly, through a relationship of its coalition with D's coalition, or through E and/or F. A's relationships with Z may be direct, through its coalition, or indirect, through B and/or C.

In model 5, A is a direct actor, D is a peripheral actor, and Z is outside the situation. A's relationships may be directly with D or indirectly with D through other peripheral actors. D's influence on A similarly may be exercised directly or indirectly. Z's relations with A, similarly, may be direct or indirect.

Where there are several direct actors as in model 6, the possibilities for paths of influence are even more complicated, for A is not in the same clearly superior position that it was in the previous five models. Its influence upon D and D's influence on A are governed not only by their direct relations or the relations of their respective coalitions but also by the relationships of each with the several other direct actors. In such a situation, A's influence on Z is more likely to be direct and discrete.

One problem that is apparent from this discussion of situation structure in a manner isolated from the other dimensions of situations is that the relationships seem to be flattened out. Such is not the case, however, and it needs to be remembered that roles make a substantial difference in how important to the situation the attempted exercise of influence is. In all of our discussion, A has been a direct, central actor, and Z has not been a participant in the situation. D's role has varied. Control varies between models also. In terms of the discussion in the preceding section on the rank and number of actors, A's control diminishes as we move from model 1 through model 6. Hence, we need to keep that dimension in mind, too. Moreover, we have not differentiated here either the variation in instruments that may be employed in attempts to exercise influence or the variation in conditions of interaction. The richness of this variation should become more apparent at the end of this chapter when real world situations are mapped.

These models do not convey, either, the sense that judgments are made both with respect to the selection of goals and instruments and the selection of targets and paths of influence. In this area of judgment we may use the models for criticizing governmental policies. For example, if our model shows several paths of influence, we can inquire into whether the government in whose policy we are interested has been effective in exploiting the paths available or whether it has neglected potential paths of influence in a situation.

Let us now turn to the final dimension of situation in this analysis: the conditions of interaction.

Conditions of Interaction

The condition of the interaction involves the classification of situations in terms of conflict, competition, cooperation, and integration. No situation is purely one or the other of these types of interaction. There are elements of conflict in cooperative and integrative patterns of interaction, and there are elements of cooperation in very conflictful relationships. Nevertheless, there are differences between situations in terms of this dimension, and an examination of situations involves finding the conflict and other elements in the pattern of interactions. A number of hypotheses will illustrate the importance of this dimension.

The more conflictful the situation, the greater will be the tendency to form coalitions leading to a two-coalition situation structure. War, the most conflictful of interaction patterns, illustrates this tendency most clearly. Military struggle and coercive bargaining are the means by which such a pattern of interaction is carried out. When such coalitions are formed, each may be treated as a different pattern of interaction, one in which cooperation is the dominant element but in which conflict and competition are also present.

In the pattern of predominant cooperation, the interests of the dominant partner in the coalition will tend to prevail, and the common interest will be a bargaining tactic of the dominant partner against allies. Dependent partners, nevertheless, will be able to secure some of their interests as the dominant partner makes concessions in order to continue to have the fullest possible cooperation of its allies.

Depending upon the organization of forces in a conflict situation, there will be more or less integration within any given coalition. Integration suggests common decision making, while conflict suggests struggle and bargaining. There will be different mixes of these in different coalitions. Moreover, the patterns of interaction need not occur in the same manner at all levels of the coalition. This problem can most usefully be discussed by comparing cases. The coalitions of World War II, Korea, and Vietnam in which the United States was involved illustrate the problems of this analysis.

In the European theatre of World War II, the major partners in the coalition were the United States, the Soviet Union, and the United Kingdom. For our purposes, the discussion can be limited to these three and to the period of the war in which all were involved. One cannot say that the whole structure of this coalition was characterized by any one of the classifications in the condition of interaction. At the strategic and top leadership levels, cooperation was dominant until the last stages of the war. But at the level of armies, cooperation between the United States and the Soviet Union was limited to the transfer of resources from the United States to the Soviet military. This kind of cooperation continued until the end of the war when it became necessary for cooperation among American and Soviet field commanders who made arrangements to meet in Germany.

In contrast, the American and British armies had a high level of integration, with a dominant partner. There were also elements of closer cooperation at the strategic and leadership levels between the United States and Britain than between either of them and the Soviet Union. Elements of conflict and competition were also present at all levels. Churchill's spheres of influence arrangement with Stalin and General Montgomery's disagreements with Eisenhower are examples.

The situation in Korea was different, for there was integration at all levels and, thus, United States' domination of the coalition. Conflicts such as the one arising from Syngman Rhee's ambitions could be contained. In the integrative pattern, then, there is a greater tendency for the dominant partner to retain control over the conflicts which arise in the coalition. This is not to say that this control is not maintained in part by satisfying the dependent partners in some of their objectives.

The Vietnam situation exhibited different characteristics. At the tactical and military field commanders' level, there was a good deal of integration. At the strategic and leadership level, however, there was characteristically cooperation intermingled with competition and conflict. At the top level and throughout the relationship, there was a good deal of mutual manipulation and bargaining. This particular situation, as we shall see, was further complicated because of the different sets of roles played by both partners and the variety of instruments and techniques that were used.

Given the complexity which these cases illustrate, we have the task not only of defining the meaning of the four types of interaction but also of developing typologies of how these different types operate at different levels, particularly but not exclusively in coalition structures.

Conflict is a condition which meets the zero-sum condition of game theory, in which what one party gains, the other party loses. If there are more than two actors at the beginning of a conflict, the actors will form coalitions and structure a two-coalition situation. Although not all two-actor or two-coalition structures are predominantly conflictful, all conflictful interactions will have this kind of structure. The zero-sum condition also implies that the objects over which the actors seek control are the same for both sides. This implication is clearest in a situation in which the objects are concrete, as in a territorial dispute. But it is also present in situations in which the objects are somewhat less clear, as in a situation in which the object is to determine or control who will rule a country. The conflict condition also generally includes either the actual presence or a substantial risk of using military instruments. The arena of conflict may include both the adversaries and/or third areas. In contrast, competition can arise only in a third area.

Competition is a condition which may be differentiated from conflict in that it does not meet the zero-sum condition. The objects in the competition may either be different or of such a nature that the acquisition of control over its object by one actor does not require the diminution of a like amount of control by the competitive actor. Let us say that two countries are competing for influence in a third country and that influence is defined as the right to be heard upon certain questions before the government of the third country makes decisions with respect to those questions. There is no incompatibility between the gaining of this sort of influence by one party and a similar sort of influence gained by the other. Even if only one party is successful in this quest, it is still a competition rather than a conflict because nothing has been lost by the other actor. Because the gain of one party is not a loss for the other party, competition is less intense than conflict, direct clashes are less likely, and there is less at stake for any of the protagonists. There is also less likelihood of the use of military instruments. Competition is also more likely to be characterized by a greater decentralization of structure rather than by bipolarity.

Cooperation is a condition in which the interacting countries follow collusive or parallel policies in seeking common objects or mutual advantages. Consultation among the actors is likely, and there may be formal agreements and institutions for such consultation. Although cooperation is not exclusively dependent upon the existence of a mutual adversary, one often finds this to be the case. This means that in a two-coalition structure, one will find that cooperation is the dominant condition within each of the coalitions. There is likely to be, in a cooperative condition, coordination of all three sets of foreign policy acts when the condition exists within a coalition with a common adversary. Although coordination through consultation is the most common index of cooperation, it is not necessary in all cases, because at certain times two countries may pursue parallel policies which are not coordinated but which place them in a cooperative relationship.

Integration is a condition in which there is common action and an interweaving of the elements of different countries to such an extent that the decisions of a national of any of the parties is regarded as authoritative by the others. The process that occurs among the cooperative actors in this condition has many similarities to a domestic situation. There is a federator, or leader, in the integrative condition, and this will generally be the highest ranking of the partners. Military instruments are not likely to be used, although they cannot be completely ruled out if a partner acts independently and does not fulfill the expectations of other partners (particularly the federator) with respect to cooperation and conformity to the norms of the partnership.

As indicated above, the real world seldom contains a case of pure condition. There is a mixture of elements. Nevertheless, situations can be differentiated in terms of the predominant condition, and one can take account of the other elements that are present. Also noted was the observation that the same condition might not prevail at all levels of a relationship. Consequently, we now need to embark on a quest for typologies of different mixes of conditions at different levels.

Levels are used to draw a distinction between those foreign policy actions which directly involve the top-level political leadership of an actor and those which involve only lower-level participants, usually the executors of policy. The former are designated as the strategic level and the latter as the tactical level. The following four figures are suggestive of how the elements operate when there is a predominant condition of interaction.

FIGURE 2
Other Elements in a Predominantly Conflictful Condition of Interaction

	Strategic	Tactical
Competition	for influence with others	
Cooperation	on limitations on ending conflict	on limitations
Integration		

Figure 2 illustrates some of the ways in which the other elements operate when the predominant condition is conflict. The parties to the conflict compete for influence with others, attempting to line them up on one side or precluding them from the opposing coalition or persuading them to remain neutral in the conflict. There can be cooperation on keeping limitations on the conflict. For example, this sort of cooperation might extend to keeping certain weapons out of the conflict if it has already included the use of military instruments. Finally, there will be cooperation on ending the conflict, either through negotiations or through the acceptance of defeat by one side in the situation.

Figure 3 suggests some of the ways in which other elements may operate when the condition is predominantly competitive. Without the cooperation on limits to the competition, the competitive condition might move to one of the predominant conflict. This means that competition *must* include an element of cooperation for it to continue to exist. Under certain conditions there can also be elements of conflict in a competitive situation. If two countries are contending for influence in a third, for example, it is possible for one to insist on conditions which would completely exclude the other, thus meeting the condition for conflict in that what one party gains, the other party loses.

FIGURE 3
Other Elements in a Predominantly Competitive
Condition of Interaction

	Strategic	Tactical
Conflict	under certain conditions	under certain conditions
Cooperation	on limits	on limits
Integration		

In figure 4 we see that, in a predominantly cooperative condition, there can be conflict over tactics among the parties to the cooperation. There can also be competition for influence over others, and there may even be some elements of integration at the tactical level.

FIGURE 4
Other Elements in a Predominantly Cooperative
Condition of Interaction

	Strategic	Tactical
Conflict	over tactics	over tactics
Competition	for influence over others	
Integration		some possible

Figure 5 illustrates a predominantly integrative condition. Here, there may be cooperation among deferent partners which might even lead to a challenger coalition pitted against the predominant coalition. There can be competition between the dominant partner and the leading challenger partner for support for their respective positions. Elements of conflict may also enter into the relations of the dominant coalition and the challenger coalition. If this element should grow, the relationship might be transformed into two conflicting coalitions, each of which might be characterized by integration.

FIGURE 5
Other Elements in a Predominantly Integrative Condition of Interaction

	Strategic	Tactical
Conflict	between dominant coalition and challenger coalition	over goals and tactics
Competition	between dominant partner and challenger partner	
Cooperation	among deferent partners	

In addition to understanding the mixed conditions of interaction, it is important to identify the nonpredominant elements in situations because, as suggested in the last paragraph, these elements are indicators of how the conditions of interaction can be transformed. If one of the nonpredominant elements grows in significance in the relationship, it may develop into the predominant condition. The analyst, then, needs to pay particular attention to the mixture of condition elements if he wishes to predict possible transformations of situations.

We can now turn to an examination of a number of situations which have existed in the post-1945 world in order to apply the situational analysis developed in this chapter.

Cases of Specific Situations

In order to illustrate how situational analysis may be applied, seven cases will be examined briefly. Six of the cases illustrate the six models of situation structure, and one illustrates the transformation of a situation structure. Model 1 is illustrated by the Cuban missile crisis; model 2, by the Middle East; model 3 by the North Atlantic Treaty Organization (NATO); model 4, by the Vietnam war; model 5, by the Kashmir dispute; and model 6, by the emerging pattern of relationships in the Western Pacific and East Asia. Also to be examined is the

Situations 91

Sino-Soviet dispute as an example of transformation from model 3 to model 4.

Cuban Missile Crisis

The direct, central actors in this situation were the United States and the Soviet Union. Secretary-General U Thant of the United Nations was an intermediary actor, and Cuba was a peripheral actor by virtue of providing the resource of territory to the Soviet Union. American allies were peripheral actors by virtue of their diplomatic support. The arena was a regional one, for the instruments of the actors were applied directly to each other (diplomacy), and in third areas (diplomacy and information at the United Nations and military instruments in Cuba and the sea approaches to it). Diagram 1 shows the paths of influence and the instruments used in the crisis.

There were a number of linked situations, making the scope quite broad. The Sino-Soviet situation was linked, and two American alliances—NATO and OAS—were linked. In addition, the prestige of both the United States and the Soviet Union among the general membership of the United Nations was involved. The objects were fairly clear: the Soviet Union was constructing missile sites in Cuba, and the United States wanted the Soviets to stop further construction and to remove those that were already in place.

The structure of the situation was two-party. Paths of influence were limited to direct bargaining between the two direct, central actors. The solution to the crisis was achieved by introducing a new object, a pledge by the United States not to invade Cuba, thus adding to the condition of conflict an element of cooperation in which the United States traded that pledge for Soviet removal of the missiles. Coercion by the United States continued until the cooperative condition was accepted by the Soviet Union as dominant.

The crisis had a substantial impact on both the major participants and on the linked situations. An element of cooperation continued to be a condition of the relationship between the United States and the Soviet Union. The Sino-Soviet dispute was inflamed by the crisis, and President DeGaulle of France read American behavior as emphasizing the distinction between French and American national interests. We shall see in a later chapter how such dramatic experiences affect the foreign policy behavior of actors. Now, let us illustrate a model 2 structure.

The Middle East

An adequate treatment of the Middle East situation would require a much longer study than that undertaken here. Diagram 2 indicates

DIAGRAM 1
Cuban Missile Crisis

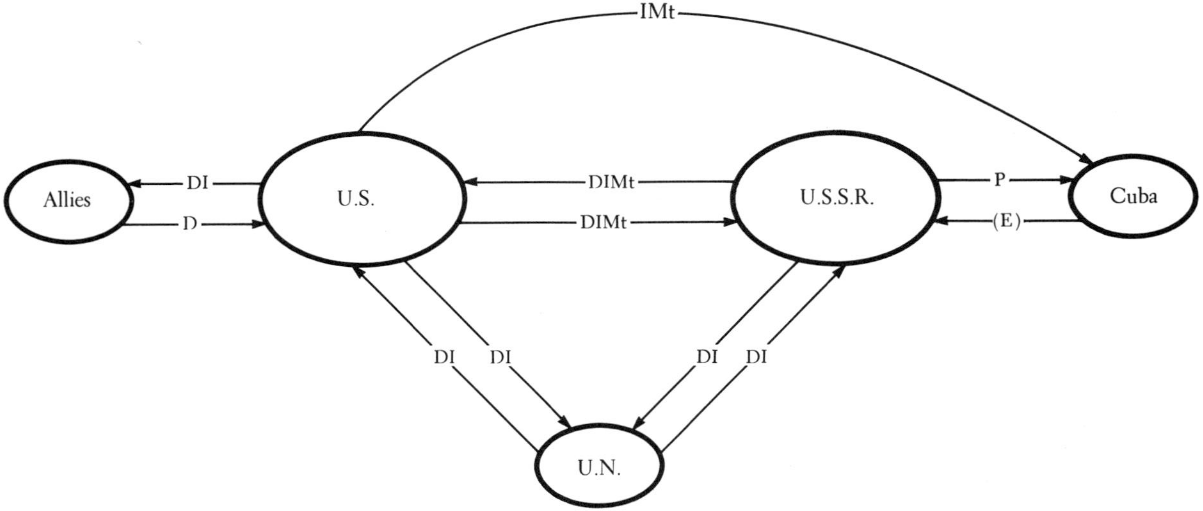

- D = diplomatic means
- M = military means
- P = political means
- I = informational means
- E = economic means
- t = threat
- ( ) = transfer of resources

Situations

that the situation (as it stood in 1971) was substantially more complicated than the previous case. There is a similarity to the previous case in that there were two sides in the situation, and in that there were peripheral actors. The fact that one side was a coalition, however, plus the fact that the peripheral actors were higher ranking than the direct actors make the paths of influence more complex. In addition, there were more roles in this situation, and, as a glance at diagram 2 reveals, all classes of instruments were in use in the Middle East situation.

The basic situation structure was a two-party one, with Israel on

DIAGRAM 2
Middle East—1971

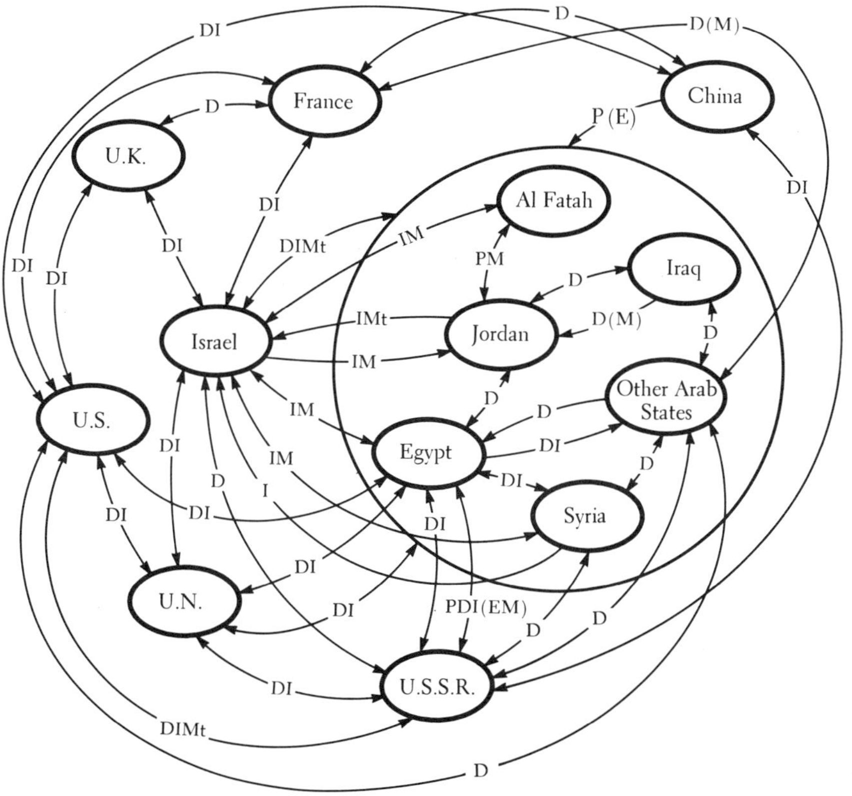

D=diplomatic means   I=informational means
M=military means   E=economic means
P=political means   t=threat
        ( )=transfer of resources

the one side and a coalition of Arab states on the other. The Arab coalition was not integrated, however, and this cooperative condition allowed for direct action upon each of them by Israel and others. Israel and Egypt were the direct, central actors. Jordan, Syria, and Al Fatah were direct, noncentral actors; and in its relationship to them, Israel was also a direct, noncentral actor. The other Arab states were largely peripheral actors, although some of them attempted to be intermediary actors or neutrals. The Soviet Union and the United States were major peripheral actors, and Britain and France were second-rank peripheral actors. The United Nations and the United States were both intermediary actors. The scope was supraregional, verging on global, because of the linkages of great power interests and the potential for direct conflict should the situation evolve in certain ways.

The object of the direct, central actors was the control of territory and population. Israel in 1967 had occupied territory belonging to Egypt, Syria, and Jordan, which these countries wished to get back. As a more maximal objective, the Arab states wished to control the territory of Israel proper. The peripheral actors had general strategic objectives in the situation which carried the potential for direct conflict.

The predominant condition of the situation was conflict. Attempts by intermediaries to transform the condition to one of cooperative settlement had been going on for several years without success. The use of military instruments was common, and a fourth round in the war between Israel and the Arabs was a constant threat.

If the situation had not been linked to American-Soviet conflict, there might have been a possibility for an imposed settlement by these two actors. Because it was, however, the situation continued to exist in a state of high tension.

NATO

Model 3 is illustrated by NATO, a several actor with dominant partner situation structure. The basic structure is simple, although the patterns of relationships among many of the partners provide potentially different groupings. The arena is supraregional, with both Western Europe and North America involved. The scope includes not only those two areas but also Eastern Europe and the Mediterranean. The object is to provide security for the members. The predominant condition is integration.

Although, on the whole, all the others are linked most directly and dependently with the United States, the situation is undergoing slow though clear change. The existence and growth of the European Economic Community (EEC) after 1958 made the European allies more

DIAGRAM 3
North Atlantic Treaty Organization

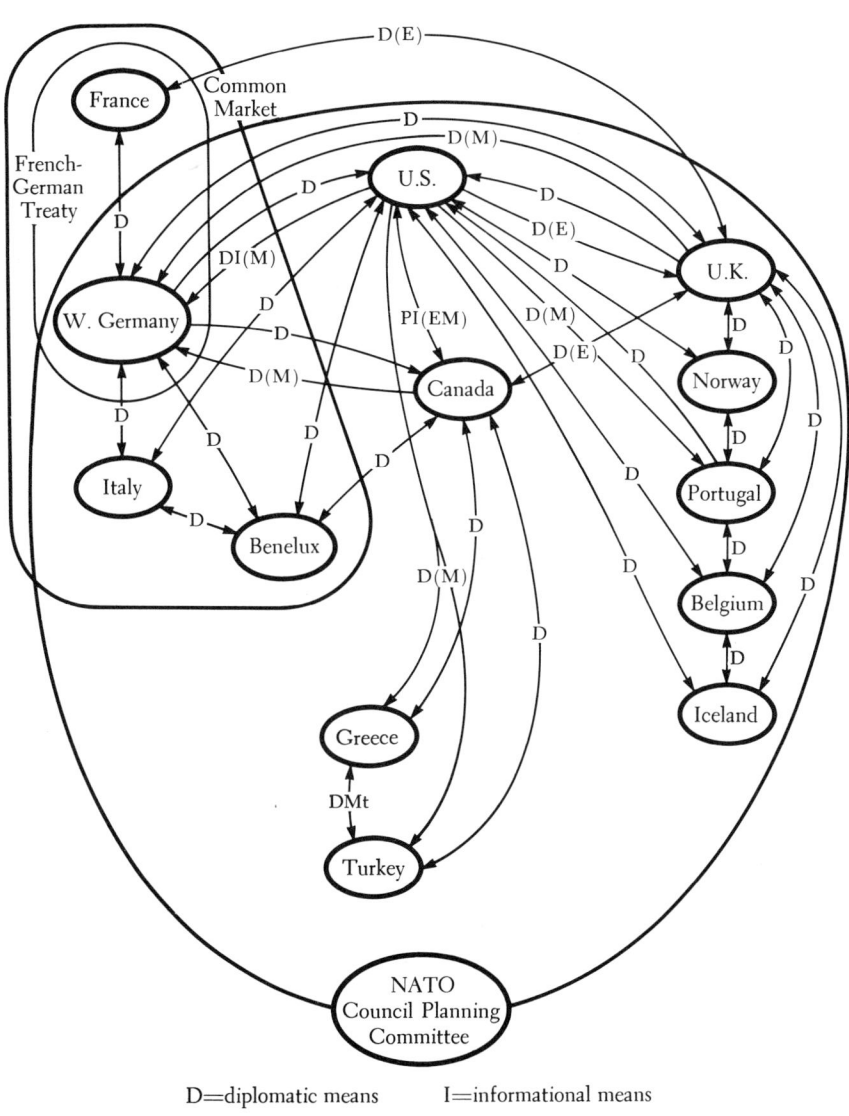

D = diplomatic means   I = informational means
M = military means   E = economic means
P = political means   t = threat
() = transfer of resources

independent. France and Germany signed a treaty of friendship in 1963, and France withdrew from all of the integrating institutions, completely severing its participation in NATO planning structures in 1969. After the Cyprus flare-up of 1964, Greece and Turkey developed a relationship that included the threat of war. Canada and the United States have a more complex relationship than most of the others, although Canada has been resisting integration whereas the Common Market countries are encouraging it. Even apart from the opportunities which other countries have for influencing each of the NATO partners, then, a number of things have changed within the situation itself which is slowly transforming it.

The Vietnam War

The Vietnam War, shown in diagram 4 in 1968, is an example of model 4, a situation structure with two coalitions in which there are several direct actors. The arena of military conflict was Vietnam, Cambodia, and Laos, but the inclusion of peripheral and intermediary actors made it supraregional. The scope was broad because of the linked situation of Chinese-Soviet-American relations. The object was the control of South Vietnam. The condition was conflict, with an element of cooperation as the direct, central actors met in Paris for peace negotiations.

The United States, the Government of South Vietnam, North Vietnam, and the Viet Cong were the direct, central actors. Thailand, South Korea, Australia, and New Zealand were direct, noncentral actors. Canada was a peripheral actor in the non-Communist coalition by virtue of its fulfillment of obligations under a defense-sharing agreement with the United States. The Soviet Union and China were peripheral actors in the Communist coalition by virtue of supplying assistance to North Vietnam. Laos and Cambodia were targets for both sides. Although largely ineffectual, the International Control Commission composed of Canada, Poland, and India was an intermediary actor. Britain was an intermediary actor, as were private persons and groups, by acting as a go-between between the United States and the Soviet Union or between North Vietnam and the United States. France was an intermediary actor, and allowed use of its territory for the negotiations.

Although the paths of influence were several, most were unsucussful as the war continued in a stalemate. Most clearly influenced were the leaders of the United States who faced deep divisions at home and frustration on the battlefield.

Situations

DIAGRAM 4
The Vietnam War—1968

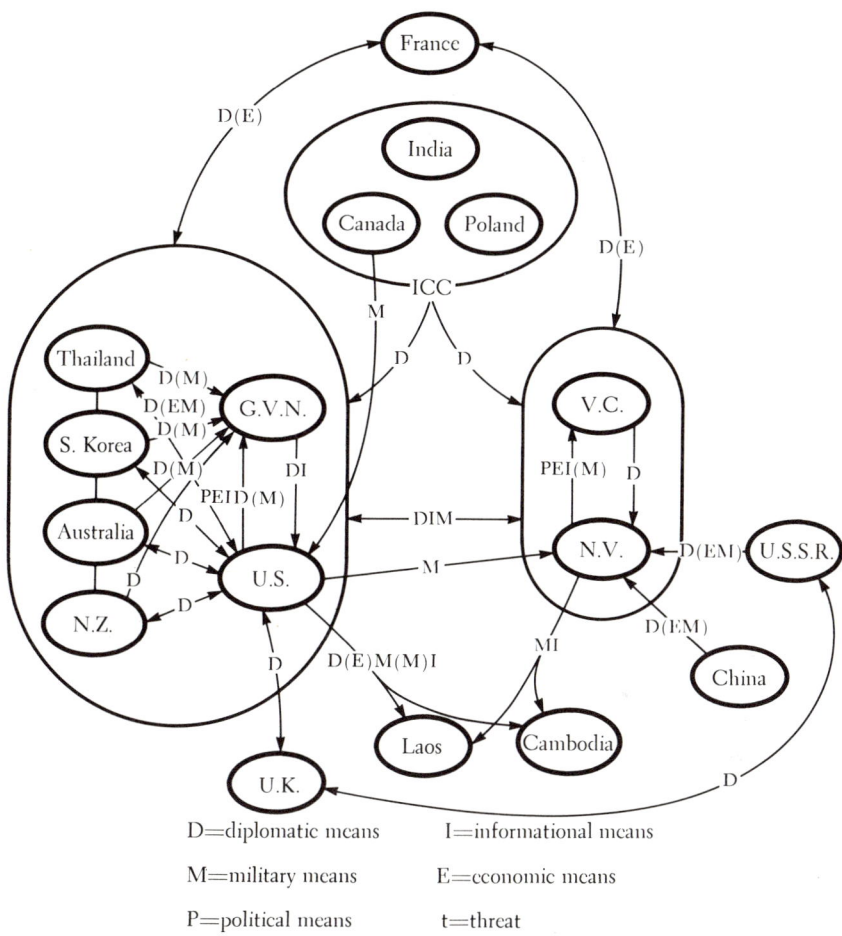

D=diplomatic means   I=informational means
M=military means   E=economic means
P=political means   t=threat
() =transfer of resources

The Kashmir Dispute

The Kashmir dispute developed after 1947 when British India was partitioned, and broke out into a war in 1965. A settlement was achieved through the mediation of the Soviet Union. Diagram 5 illustrates this situation of a several actor with two direct actor structure. India and Pakistan were the only direct actors, both central. The Soviet Union, the United States, and China were peripheral actors. The Soviet Union and the United States collaborated as mediators through the

DIAGRAM 5
The Kashmir Dispute—1965

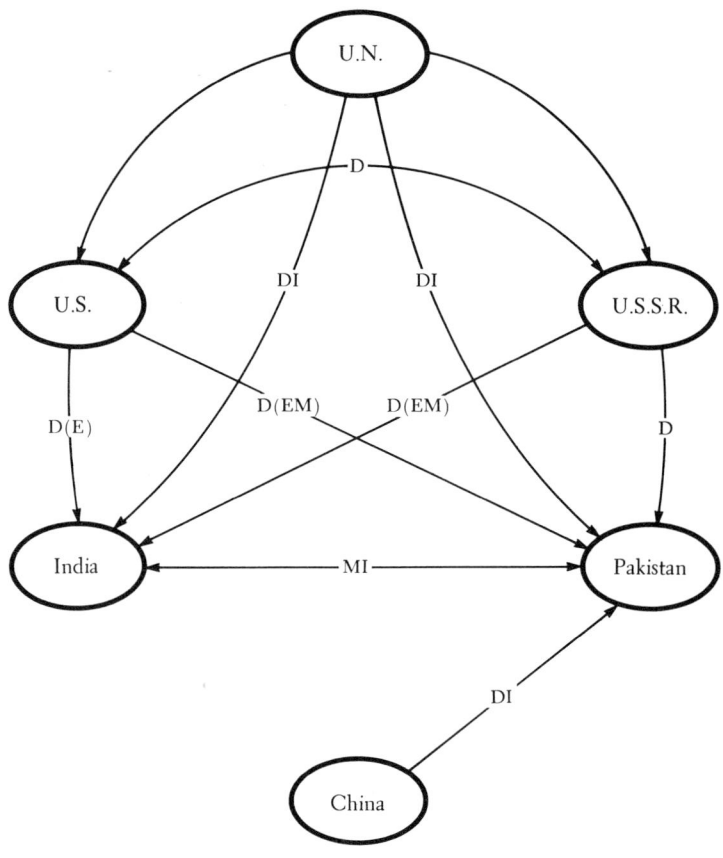

D=diplomatic means   I=informational means
M=military means   E=economic means
P=political means   t=threat
( )=transfer of resources

United Nations. The scope was broad, affecting the Chinese-Soviet and United States-Soviet Union situations. The paths of influence and the instruments used were relatively simple as compared with some of the other situations we have been dealing with. The two-actor situation did not last long as higher ranking powers acted to gain control of the situation. This situation is similar to the one which will be used as a case study in the next chapter, although there the perspective will be from the point of view of a single actor rather than the omniscient point of view of this chapter.

Western Pacific and East Asia

The example used to illustrate model 6 is one which emerged in the 1970s. It is more speculative than the others because it deals with a situation which does not have much history (from the viewpoint of the 1970s). By engaging in this exercise, however, we can perhaps see how situational analysis is useful for inquiring into the future. The situation is schematized in diagram 6.

The direct, central actors in the situation are the United States, the Soviet Union, and China. Japan has the potential for becoming another direct, central actor. The arena covers the general area defined, and the scope is supraregional because of the involvement of three major powers. The United Kingdom might withdraw completely because of joining the European Economic Community. The condition in the early 1970s was one of competition. There is substantial room for conflict to develop, but the situation is sufficiently fluid for the coalitions to take any of a variety of forms. The general balance is among the three major powers of the region. It is likely that American influence will be excluded from the Indochina peninsula, leaving that area for Chinese-Soviet competition. Any of the three major parties could play the role of the holder of the balance, as could Japan.

The major object is control and influence in the whole area. The noncentral actors wish to retain their independence. There are also trading and prestige objects. In such a fluid situation, however, objects may become more specific as the situation unfolds.

The Sino-Soviet Rift

The final case is the Sino-Soviet dispute and rift. This case illustrates how a situation may be transformed. The Soviet Union and China signed a fifty-year treaty of friendship in 1950, and they were close allies during the early part of the fifties. The Soviet Union sent economic and technical assistance to China, and China supported Soviet leadership of the Communist bloc. The arena of the situation was local, but the scope was virtually global because of the engagement of the Communist coalition with the anti-Communist coalition. The object was to provide mutual aid and assistance to achieve common goals. The condition was predominantly cooperative. China was a deferent partner, and the Soviet Union was the only direct, central actor.

DIAGRAM 6
Western Pacific and East Asia

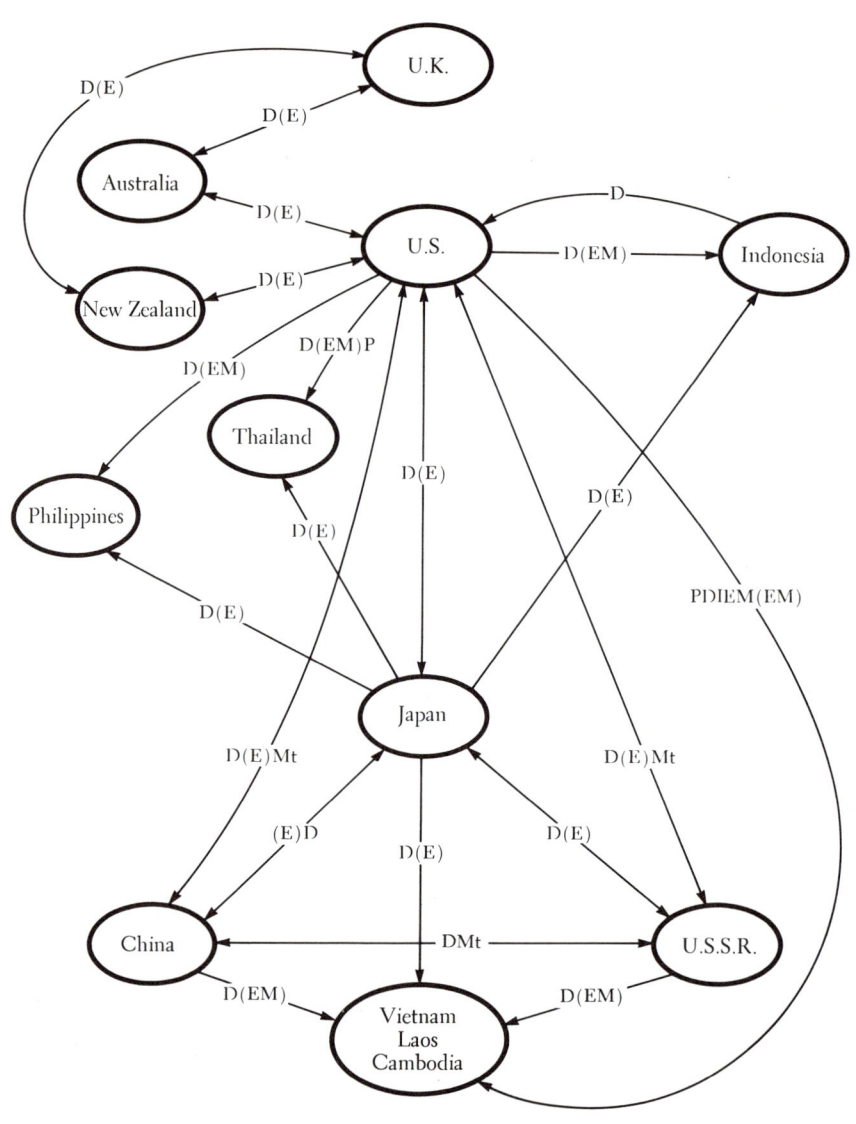

D=diplomatic means   E=economic means
I=informational means   P=political means
M=military means   t=threat
( ) =transfer of resources

The rift included many issues and events, but basically the Chinese, while deferring to the Russians, wished to be consulted on overall Communist policy. When they were ignored and they questioned the judgment of Soviet leaders, especially that of Premier Khrushchev, there began to develop a conflict over goals and tactics in the Communist movement. Once this fundamental conflict emerged, the Chinese sought to take control of their own fate at a minimum and attacked the Russians through diplomatic and informational means. At one point in 1969 there even developed some minor military skirmishes. Thus, the situation was transformed, and the global implications of this transformation were profound, for the whole structure of world politics shifted as a result. The resulting transformation is illustrated in the last case in the Western Pacific and East Asia situation.

Because the situation was local and because of the cooperative elements in the situation, it is unlikely that a supraregional conflict would have developed even if a major war had broken out between the two countries. In this case, peace was apparently divisible.

Conclusion

Situations analysis gives us a means of determining the relevant environment of foreign policy makers. As an intermediate unit of analysis, it also provides a means of linking two other units of analysis, the state and the international system. The several dimensions which have been discussed are those which help us to identify the paths of influence and the possibilities for action. In addition to the usefulness of situational analysis as an analytical tool, it is useful in dealing with the broad and important question of whether peace is divisible.

Situational analysis has also enabled us to classify in order to avoid dealing with every case study as unique. The classification system allows us to confront any single case study with a set of categories, or it may enable us to do comparative analysis by treating a number of cases along each of the dimensions.

What situations analysis does not do is explain how and why instruments are used, how countries determine their policies, the chances of success, and a host of other questions. These are questions which we will grapple with in succeeding chapters.

Many situations tend to be relatively stable for long periods of time. They do evolve, and sometimes they are transformed. When changes do occur, they are the outcomes of foreign policy acts by the actors interested in the situations, and they are reflected in the elements of the situation which this chapter has described. Countries which intend to change a situation may attempt to influence any of the elements. The dimensions which have been described also circumscribe the range of choices for countries in the situation. A given country in a given situation may, for example, take actions to limit, stabilize, or expand the arena and scope of the interaction pattern.

The situation in the Middle East following the 1967 war illustrated all of these alternatives. Israel attempted to exclude non-Middle Eastern powers by calling for direct negotiations with Arab states. Egypt, on the other hand, sought to bring in the great powers by posing the threat of a new war. The United States tried to stabilize the situation by working for a negotiated settlement either under the auspices of the United Nations or itself. The growth of Soviet influence in Egypt tended to expand the scope by making its interests more important in the Middle East struggle.

Using the Middle East situation to illustrate the point further, the Middle East is a situation of institutionalized crisis conflict, with rhythms toward and away from bipolarity as war approaches and recedes, although the basic structure is like that in model 2 above. In terms of the conditions of interaction, the choices for the actors are available for moving the situation toward or away from conflict. Through a series of mutual steps, it would be possible to go as far as integration, the dominant partner probably being Egypt.

The changes that may occur in a situation are, then, as follows. The arena may be expanded or contracted. The scope may be broadened or narrowed. The number and rank of actors may become larger or smaller. Actors may take on new roles. The structure may move toward bipolarity or toward diffusion. The condition of the relationships may be transformed from one type to another. As we examine cases, these are the changes that we will look for. Since these changes are affected by the foreign policy acts of the participants in the situation, we will have to put off consideration of how they come about until we deal with foreign policy acts in later chapters. In the following chapter, we will see how the foreign policy acts of countries in a situation interact.

We will return to the problems of this chapter and the last when we deal with outcomes later in the book. For now, outcomes are defined as the impact of policies on the three units of analysis: the international system, the situation, and the state.

II

Determinants and Processes

5

Foreign Determinants

The external environment, as we have seen, provides a set of factors which constrain and facilitate the foreign policy of any given country. These factors have been examined and some ways of ordering and thinking about them have been developed. In this chapter, the process by which these factors operate will be analyzed.

The state of the international system as a whole determines at least the broad outlines and sometimes the specifics of alignments, indicating which countries are more likely to be arrayed for and against a given policy. For example, in the bipolar state of the international system from 1947 to the late 1950s, the Soviet bloc countries were extraordinarily limited in their foreign policies. When the crunch came in Hungary in 1956, the Soviet Union insured the retention of Hungary in the Soviet alliance by an invasion. At the same time, the NATO countries were unanimously opposed to the Soviet action.

As the state of the international system became more fluid in the 1960s, Rumania was able to move into a position of "partial alignment."[1] In a more flexible state of the international system such as the classical balance of power, it might be possible for one of the eastern European countries to shift alignment completely. Only Cuba has been successful in completely shifting alignment in the bipolar state of the system, and that success may be accounted for by the structure of the American alliance system being looser than that of the Soviet system. Within the Communist part of the world, however, there has been some flexibility of alignment as the Chinese and the Russians have parted ways. Albania in particular shifted from alliance with the Soviet Union to alliance with China, and there has been some competition by the two leaders to gain the allegiance of other countries such as North Korea and North Vietnam. Such flexibility of alignment as has existed within the Communist bloc, however, has been contained within the boundaries of that bloc system and has been consistent with a fundamental bipolar division of the world.

Such patterns as do exist are determined primarily by the policies of the countries with the greatest capacities. Other countries, however, have some impact on international systematic patterns. For example, the development of NATO under the leadership of the United States grew out of the smaller European alliances under the Brussels Pact and the Western European Union. Later, the United States pressured other countries to join alliances which it either led or endorsed. Other countries such as India, Indonesia, and Egypt, on the other hand, resisted the pressures of the great powers and developed the concept and practice of nonalignment.

Being dependent upon other countries to achieve their goals, nevertheless, countries do undertake formal alliances, commitments, or postures in conformity with their calculation of long-term interests. The result of such relationships is a pattern of the international system. Sometimes such a pattern is discernibly rigid and fixed. At other times the pattern is more fluid and thus less discernible. Although not regarding these categories as confined and mutually exclusive boxes, one can characterize the fifteen years following World War II as relatively rigid and the subsequent fifteen years as relatively fluid.

Even in a rigid pattern, however, the specific actions of a particular country in a particular situation are not predictable.[2] The case study of the British involvement in the 1956 Middle East crisis will illustrate

---

1. This is the descriptive term used by Robert L. Farlow in his "Romanian Foreign Policy: A Case of Partial Alignment," *Problems of Communism* 20 (November-December 1971).

2. See the discussion of the shifting of allies even in wartime in Hans J. Morgenthau, *Politics Among Nations*, 4th ed. (New York: Alfred A. Knopf, 1967), chapter 14. For a discussion of alliances specifically in the post-World War II period, see

the unpredictability of the behavior of even close allies. On the other hand, there are overall tendencies for alliance patterns at any given time to prevail.[3]

Perceiving both aspects of the phenomenon of international system patterns, the authoritative decision makers of a country, in contemplating a foreign policy initiative, need to recognize the pattern which prevails and to calculate the probabilities that the pattern is reflected in the situation which they address. Thus, the structural pattern of the international system is a necessary but not sufficient condition to explain the pattern of alignments which affect any given situation. Moreover, a country's success is affected by its ability to calculate the limits of the pattern's appropriateness to any given situation.

In addition to the characteristics of the international system, other constraining and facilitating processes are at work in the international environment. These include the articulation of attitudes toward a country's action through forums such as the United Nations Security Council, diplomatic representations, and direct communication through the mass media. Certain norms in the international community effectively give coherence to widespread opposition when they are violated and provide some measure of deterrence against certain actions. An example is the worldwide consensus in opposition to colonialism in the post-1945 era. Such a norm gives some protection to smaller and weaker countries. It operated in the situation which will be analyzed later in this chapter.

These patterns and processes in the international environment affect any country's foreign policy undertakings, but they are implemented by and are the result of the capacities and predispositions of other countries in the context of specific situations. To analyze the process by which the international environment constrains and facilitates any country's foreign policy, then, requires us to examine the elements that comprise a situation from the point of view of a single country.

In the preceding chapters on the international environment and situations, we adopted the point of view of the omniscient analyst. As such, we attempted to circumscribe the analysis of international situations in which foreign policy operates and to develop a typology of situations. That analysis provided a framework of the environment which we need to keep in mind throughout the remainder of this book.

Herbert S. Dinerstein, "The Transformation of Alliance Systems," *The American Political Science Review* 59 (September 1965): 3.

3. See J. David Singer and Melvin Small, "Alliance Aggregation and the Onset of War, 1815–1945," in *Quantitative International Politics*, ed. J. David Singer (New York: The Free Press, 1968), p. 284.

We need now, however, to shift our focus from an overall perspective to the view of the foreign policy analyst of a particular country. This new perspective will enable us to look at a situation from a vantage point which facilitates doing case studies of particular countries' foreign policies. The framework of this chapter will give guidelines not only for analyzing particular countries' actions in a limited situation but also for comparing cases.

The theme of this chapter is that the foreign policies of any country are determined in part by the foreign policies of other countries interested in a situation. In performing the analysis of this chapter, we do not need to be concerned with the decisions and mobilization of resources of the other interested actors. We need only be concerned with the application of instruments and the transfer of resources. This is because the foreign determinants of any given country's foreign policy are the effective applications and transfers of other countries. Although each of the other actors will have made decisions and mobilized their resources, we can arbitrarily leave consideration of these aside for ease of analysis.

As we saw in chapter 1, foreign policy includes both the projection of intended actions and the actual carrying out of policy. Just so, we shall in this chapter be concerned with the intent of actions and their real consequences. Any given country makes projections of what others will do in response to its actions. Then those other countries do indeed act. We will hold this distinction between the "psychological environment" and the "operational environment."[4] Unlike decision-making analysts, however, we shall not restrict our analysis to the psychological environment, for the unanticipated consequences of action in a situation have important impacts on the outcome of the action and provide important experiences for subsequent foreign policy.

Categories of Action

Countries may take a wide variety of actions in response to the foreign policy initiative of any single country. It will be helpful to reduce this variety by developing a set of categories for classifying actions. For our purposes here, the categories need to reflect the point of view of the single country upon which we focus. Additionally, the system of cate-

---

4. This is the terminology used by Joseph Frankel in his *The Making of Foreign Policy* (New York and London: Oxford University Press, 1963). Frankel's distinction relies on the work of Harold and Margaret Sprout. See especially *The Ecological Perspective on Human Affairs With Special Reference to International Politics* (Princeton, New Jersey: Princeton University Press, 1965).

Foreign Determinants 109

gorization used refers to the intentions of the other countries in the environment taking the actions. The categories are (1) inaction, (2) supportive action, (3) oppositional action, (4) neutral action, and (5) inducive action.

Inaction is the insulation of an actor from a situation in which it is interested. Despite its interest in a situation which may affect it, a country may decide that its engagement in a situation will have no effect or will have harmful effects on itself. In the case of the Israeli-British-French invasion of Egypt in 1956, for example, Jordan took no action but rather stood aside and allowed others to participate in the actions and determine the outcome.

Supportive actions are those applications of instruments and transfers of resources which are intended to help achieve objectives of the given country upon which we focus. If we were to focus on the Soviet Union's actions in World War II, the actions of the United States would be considered to be supportive in that the United States both applied its instruments to the common enemy and transferred resources to the Soviet Union which it could apply to Germany.

Oppositional actions are those transfers and applications which are intended to prevent the achievement of the objectives of the given country. Looking at the Vietnam war from the point of view of North Vietnam, the actions of the United States would be considered to be oppositional in that it applied its instruments to North Vietnam and transferred resources to South Vietnam in order to prevent North Vietnam from achieving its objectives.

Neutral actions are those transfers and applications which are intended to stop actors from what they are doing and to help them to find solutions to their disputes. In view of the fact that neutral action often occurs in a situation which appears to be moving in the direction of greater conflict, it is also often intended to arrest a "chain of events" which seems to be leading to a loss of control over the situation by everyone. The activities of the United Nations Secretary-General in his diplomacy represent a well-known form of neutral action. The diplomatic activities of the United States following the 1967 war in the Middle East and the Soviet Union's activities with respect to the 1965 Indian-Pakisani war are examples of neutral action.[5]

Also falling into this category are the interruption of transfers of resources or the refusal to make transfers which would enable the given

---

5. Unlike the other categories developed here there is a literature which has analyzed this category of action explicitly. See Oran Young, *The Intermediaries: Third Parties in International Crisis* (Princeton: Princeton University Press, 1967).

actor to accomplish its objectives. During the 1956 Middle East war, for example, the United States refused to allow the United Kingdom to withdraw reserves from the International Monetary Fund, thus not alleviating the pressure on the British pound sterling which was weakening the British ability to carry out its objectives in Egypt and the Middle East.

Inducive actions, the last category, are those transfers and applications which are intended to get actors to do something that they would not otherwise do. The Soviet blockade of Berlin in 1948 is an example of an inducive action whereby Stalin hoped to induce the Western Allies to depart from Berlin. The actions of both the United States and the Soviet Union in the Middle East in November 1956 were inducive actions which sought to get the invaders to withdraw from Egypt.

Because these categories are based on intentions, they do not say anything about the success of the actions involved. The examples may illustrate this point, for some of them were successful while others were not. It is a test of the foresight of the authoritative foreign policy makers of a country to be able to predict with some measure of accuracy the effectiveness of their own and other countries' actions. On the other hand, it must be realized that virtually any foreign policy act is likely to have unintended consequences. There is no way of predicting accurately the extent to which intentions will be fulfilled.

The reasons for this are several. The most important is the theme of this chapter: the accomplishment of the intentions of any nation is partly dependent upon what other countries do. Second, the formulation of objectives may be defective in that the constraints of the situation cannot possibly allow their fulfillment. Third, there may be misunderstandings and misconception of the situational environment which leads to gross miscalculation. Finally, the execution of actions may be imperfect.

There is a persuasive case, nevertheless, that better understanding of how foreign policy works will lead to better prediction. At least the grossest errors of selecting objectives and of misperception may be avoided by the use of careful analysis.

Two Phases of Operation

Foreign determinants operate in two phases: the decisional phase and the execution phase. This is essentially the application of the distinction between the "psychological" and the "operational" environments.

Assuming some modicum of rationality on the part of decision makers, there is a good deal of relationship between these analytical categories. Assuming, on the other hand, that there is an inadequacy of information in any situation, particularly in predicting the actions of others, the distinction between the two is an important and useful one.

Policy makers base part of their expectations on what other countries are doing and on what they are expected to do in response to given actions. For the given country, the postures, actions, and communications of other countries will influence calculations. One of the things to accomplish in the subsequent analysis of this chapter is to chart what would be taken into consideration in any comprehensive review of a situational environment in which a given country was intending to act.

The psychological environment of decision makers does not operate in a vacuum. The decision makers of any given country will give consideration to the past behavior of other countries interested in the given situation. They will take into consideration the reliability of allies and the credibility of adversaries. They may make calculatons about the capabilities of themselves and the other pertinent actors, and they will be concerned with timing.

Since there is an obvious mix, in this phase, of what other states actually do and are calculating, on the one hand, and the perception of these actions and calculations by ego state, on the other, it is also obvious that there exist possibilities for misunderstanding, misperception, and misinterpretation. These faults may be attributed to two factors: incomplete information and unskillful interpretation by ego of the information that it does have. There is an additional source of confusion operating in this phase: alter may also be unskillful in communicating its intentions to ego. This too will cause misperception.

These sources of confusion may be compounded by deliberate attempts at inducing confusion. Alter may be attempting to mislead ego about its intentions. There are many ways of doing this, but the techniques may be categorized as the deprivation of information and the purveying of "noise," or information which may be intentionally misleading. In addition, ego itself may set a train of misperceptions into motion by engaging in this same kind of process.[6]

The nature of the decisional phase of foreign determinants analysis is such as to include many sources of confusion. One can nevertheless identify and sort out the ways in which these work. The consequence

---

6. See the excellent analysis of these factors in Roberta Wohlstetter, "Cuba and Pearl Harbor: Hindsight and Foresight," *Foreign Affairs* 43 (July 1965).

of such analysis may be to formulate a means of making more accurate predictions in foreign policy calculation.

Allies, Adversaries, and Neutrals

The responding actions of other countries may be performed by any of those interested in a situation. They may act singly or in concert. Because the calculations of statesmen include perceptions of the state of the international system and the classification of other countries as allies, adversaries, and neutrals, the analyst may find it helpful also to think in these terms, particularly as they are employed in the decisional phase. We also need to keep in mind the concepts of capacity and predisposition as examined in chapter 2. Despite the inadequacy of rank based on GNP as an index, the rank of countries will be designated simply as a gross indicator and as a reminder of the factor of capacity.

No decision maker can predict with absolute certainty that allies will support an action or that adversaries will oppose it. He will nevertheless make different kinds of calculations, depending upon whether he views another country as an ally, an adversary, or a neutral. These categories are common ones in developing an image of a situation.[7] Because they are, the analyst will want to ask, in doing a case study, how calculations about the behavior of decision makers is influenced by the image of patterns of overall ally-adversary-neutral distribution.

On the whole, one can assume that allies in a situation will give support to an undertaking and treat departures from this pattern as deviations. One of the questions for further empirical research might be to establish the probability that the pattern would be retained. In any particular case, on the other hand, this general expectation can lead to rather severe miscalculation unless careful assessments of the predispositions of allies with respect to the intended action are made.

By the use of rank attachments to any particular country, a rough calculation can be made of the importance of the responding actions. Whether a respondent state has the capacity to do injury to the initiating state can make a considerable difference in evaluating the importance of that actor's oppositional action.

---

7. See Dean G. Pruitt, "Definition of the Situation as a Determinant of International Action," in *International Behavior*, ed. Herbert C. Kelman (New York: Holt, Rinehart and Winston, 1965).

Foreign Determinants 113

Means and Targets

The final set of categories that needs to be developed before charting foreign determinants is that which identifies the means used by both the initiating and responding actors and the targets to which those means are directed. These are introduced only briefly at this point and will be developed at length in subsequent chapters, particularly in the chapter analyzing the applications of instruments and techniques.

As we shall see, the instruments and techniques—that is, the means—of foreign policy are usually employed in combination. It may nevertheless be useful for analytical purposes to distinguish between different types of means. Although there are alternative ways of classifying them, a system of categorization will be used here that is generally accepted in the literature of international politics. The means employed in foreign policy actions may be classified as political, diplomatic, international, economic, and military. Each of these classes of means may be used to influence or control a political system other than the one which is using the instruments and techniques. Each, however, operates in a different way than the others, and each usually involves a different and specialized personnel. Despite the similarity of end results toward which they all are used, each tends to operate upon different intermediary targets than the others.

Political Means

Political means are those actions performed by personnel whose loyalty is to State A but who are present in State B. Because the activity takes place entirely within a single political system, the distinction between foreign operatives and indigenous personnel may at times be blurred. If we had perfect information, however, it would be clear that political means were being employed on behalf of the objectives of State A within the political system of State B. For example, political personnel attached to the embassy of a large country in an underdeveloped country might advise the leader of an opposition party on tactics and might provide him with funds, skills, and equipment. Another example might involve the government rather than an opposition receiving the same kind of assistance.

Linkage between political personnel and an opposition may be either supportive or subversive of the regime, but linkage with the government would nearly always be supportive.[8] Typically, foreign aid

---

8. Andrew M. Scott, *The Revolution in Statecraft: Informal Penetration* (New York: Random House, 1965), makes this distinction.

programs are supportive not only of a regime but of the particular government of the day. The organization of revolutionary opposition is subversive.

There are some cases in which foreign personnel participate in the authoritative decision-making system of a state, their roles being accepted as having the same authoritativeness as indigenous personnel. This seems to have been the case in Egypt with respect to some of the Soviet personnel present after the 1967 war with Israel. It is often the case with foreign technical assistants who sometimes occupy authoritative positions in the bureaucratic structure of a country. When this phenomenon occurs, the polity may be referred to as a penetrated political system.[9] If foreign personnel participate authoritatively in the politics of an opposition group rather than as recognized foreign advisers, we would also use the term penetrated political system.

Diplomatic Means

Diplomatic means may be sharply differentiated analytically from political means in that diplomacy occurs through formal channels and there is no blurring of the distinction between political systems. Diplomats clearly represent their respective countries and act on behalf of them. Moreover, diplomats generally do business with other diplomats. It would not be possible for diplomatic personnel to be recognized as authoritative within a foreign political system. In addition to communicating, negotiating, and persuading, diplomatic functions generally involve the coordination of other specialized representatives of a country on foreign soil.

Although analytically distinct, there can be practical problems of confusion of diplomatic and political means. Political personnel are often attached to embassies, and problems of coordination have arisen on occasion, sometimes with substantial consequences.

Diplomatic means are the personnel and skills of communication and coordination on behalf of one country conducting official and recognized intercourse with another country. Although the means may be employed secretly or openly, they rely on official channels and operate under a legal structure governed by international law and custom. Sometimes, diplomatic functions may be performed by persons who do not have official diplomatic places in a government, such as Harry Hopkins who was simply an adviser to President Franklin D. Roosevelt. Even in such a

---

9. For an extended discussion of the meaning of "penetrated" system, see James N. Rosenau, "Theories and Pre-Theories of Foreign Policy," in his *The Scientific Study of Foreign Policy* (New York: The Free Press, 1971).

case, however, the person acts as an agent of an official and his status relies entirely on his capacity as a representative of an official. Moreover, in this sort of case as well as in more orthodox cases, communication relies on an official channel at the other side of the relationship.

Informational Means

The difference in the receiving side of the communications relationship partly distinguishes informational means from diplomatic means. Informational means are those communications that occur between the official sender of one state to the population or a segment of a population in another state. Control of the origins of information lies in the hands of the authorities of State A, and the authorities of State B are, at best, marginally influential in channeling or disrupting the flow of information. Discretion over receptivity is in the hands of individuals in State B, although, as will be noted in a later chapter, the determination of which individuals are more likely to be receptive to foreign messages can be made by identifying group affiliations.

Informational means include the use of mass media—newspapers, radio, and television. Radio and television are most prominent because they may cross state borders without the permission of the government of the receiving country. As electronic technology has diffused in this century and more people have acquired receiving equipment, informational means have increased in importance.

There are other techniques, too, of disseminating information. Some of these are libraries, conferences, and exhibitions. Any technique that purveys information from the government of one country to the people of another would be included. Although informational means are directed toward selected or mass audiences, the officials of the recipient country may also receive at least part of the information directly. Although informational means, like other types, are primarily employed by larger countries, certain smaller countries have the capacity for massive employment of such means and utilize them extensively. For example, Egypt and Cuba have powerful radio transmitters and broadcast voluminously in the Middle East and Latin America, respectively.

Economic Means

Economic means are those resources—goods and services, capital and technological skills—normally associated with economic activity, production, and distribution. Anything that is exchanged in an economy or the media of exchange may be employed. However, we need to distinguish between economic activity which is divorced from political activity in a market economy and governmentally controlled economic activity, whether in a market or a planned economy. Unless a private enterprise becomes an international actor within the meaning explained in chapter 2, our concern is exclusively with the use of economic means by countries or other international actors for foreign policy purposes.

Economic means may be utilized either through the transfer of resources or through their deprivation. Some examples will illustrate some of the ways in which economic means may be employed to achieve foreign policy goals.

In the aftermath of World War II, the Marshall Plan, aimed at bringing about the recovery of Europe from the war's devastation, was launched. The United States transferred $17 billion to western Europe on the condition that the recipient countries cooperated to plan the use of the capital. On the grounds that the Second World War had been caused fundamentally by an excess of nationalism, the objective was to overcome nationalism through cooperation and integration. This transfer of economic resources was a successful venture of bringing about not only economic recovery but also the reconciliation of former enemies, political stability, and the inauguration of a far-reaching process of economic and possibly political integration. The presence and success of the political aims does not deny the Churchillian characterization of the program as the "least sordid act in history."

Just as resources may be transferred, they can also be deprived. Economic sanctions have been tried in numerous cases, an example being those against Rhodesia in the wake of its unilateral declaration of independence in 1967. Economic deprivation requires cooperation among all of a country's trading partners for effectiveness, but sometimes a single country can deny economic resources to an adversary. Economic sanctions alone are not decisive in most cases, but they can have a substantial impact on a country.[10]

In addition to transfers and deprivations, the manipulation of nonpolitical economics can affect foreign policy, and nonpolitical economic factors may become foreign policy instruments under some conditions. Cooperative regulation of trade and money is a form of friendly intercourse among countries. However, the development of nationalistic policies on these matters can become an issue of conflict. United States' manipulation of trade in the Far East before World War II probably was a factor in Japan's decision to attack the United States at Pearl Harbor in 1941. The imposition of harsh reparations upon Germany following World War I undoubtedly contributed to the rise of Hitler and his expansionist foreign policies.

---

10. See E. H. Carr, *The Twenty Years Crisis, 1919–1939*, 2d ed. (New York and Evanston: Harper & Row, 1964).

Foreign Determinants

The distinction between private and governmental economic matters is impossible to make in the case of countries with planned economies, and it is sometimes difficult to make in the case of market economy countries. A criterion to employ in making the distinction, however, is whether the government of one country is using economic instruments to gain control over an international situation for political ends. When governments transfer, deprive, or manipulate economic means for reasons other than making profits, we can regard the economic means to be instruments of foreign policy.

Military Means

We do not have such problems of drawing distinctions with respect to military means. Although there are several uses to which military means may be put, they are clearly identifiable by a single criterion: the application of force. Military means are applications of force by one actor upon another. A wide variety of instruments occur—from the garrote and the knife to tanks, machine guns, and airplanes to rockets and thermonuclear weapons. Personnel and skills for applying the instruments of force and supporting personnel and *matèriel* are also included.

The most obvious use of military means is the direct application of force. The very existence of military capabilities, however, may be used to convey threats and to conduct diplomacy. Capabilities need not be invoked explicitly to be effective. Military forces may be used also as symbols of national unity and as instruments of nation building through the socialization of young men. These uses are particularly apparent in pre-mobilized systems.

A useful distinction to apply in thinking about the use of instruments of force for foreign policy purposes is that developed by Thomas C. Schelling.[11] He draws a distinction between deterrence and compellence. Deterrence is the use of force to prevent an adversary from doing something. Compellence is the use of force to induce the adversary to stop doing what he is already about or to get him to do something he is not prone to do. Schelling's discussion of the limits of the use of force is worthwhile reading for the student of foreign policy. We shall return to his distinction in the chapter on the application of instruments and techniques.

Consequences

All of these means have both direct and indirect consequences. The direct consequences are fairly predictable, but the indirect are far less

---

11. See his *Arms and Influence* (New Haven and London: Yale University Press, 1966).

easy to project. For example, one can reasonably predict that a bomb will explode, and even that a given number of people will be killed or that a certain amount of property damage will occur as a result, but it is far more difficult to predict what the psychological reaction of the survivors will be. It may be an improved will to fight back or it may be a diminution of spirit and undermining of morale. There may be a greater propensity of certain nations to respond in a certain way than other nations, but we know too little about such national characteristics to allow us to predict indirect consequences with anywhere near the degree of accuracy which we can in predicting direct consequences.[12] It is important to recognize the distinction, however, and we can see this more clearly as we discuss the concept of targets.

Because the application of means is directed toward having an impact on the foreign policy of other countries or actors, the targets are the three components of foreign policy action which are elaborated at much greater length in subsequent chapters. The targets then are decisions, resources, and instruments of other states or actors. Decisions are on the whole indirect targets, the direct targets being the domestic determinants which help to shape decisions.

Means applied to resources and instruments may be direct, but means must usually be applied indirectly to decisions. The exception to the latter is the use of a political instrument in a penetrated system in which the agent of State A can actually make an authoritative decision for State B. As we shall see later, however, means may be employed directly upon aspects of the decision-making process. To give just one obvious example, personnel from State A may assassinate a central decision maker in State B, thus transforming the decision-making system radically. The example, which is extraordinary although not without precedent, indicates the unusual occurrence of such direct action on the decision-making process.

On the whole, the application of instruments to decision targets is indirect. Thus, as we saw above, the predictability of such applications is less reliable than applications to other targets.

Patterns of Foreign Determinants

Having outlined the categories to be used in the analysis of foreign determinants, one can now chart foreign determinants and portray several

---

12. Klaus Knorr, in *Military Power and Potential* (Lexington, Massachusetts: D. C. Heath and Company, 1970), has developed the idea of "national propensity to use military power" as a concept for distinguishing among nations.

Foreign Determinants

gross patterns. A focus on the pattern of foreign determinants as seen from the point of view of a given initiating state is needed. Figure 6 shows schematically the pattern of expectations on the part of the given initiating state about the responses of other parties interested in a situation. In this table, the policy makers in a given country chart their

FIGURE 6
Pattern for Schematizing Expectations about
Respondent States in Decisional Phase

	Inaction	Supportive	Oppositional	Neutral	Inducive
Allies Rank 1 Rank 2 Rank 3		promised diplomatic economic			
Adversaries Rank 1 Rank 2 Rank 3			threatened diplomatic economic		
Neutrals Rank 1 Rank 2 Rank 3				expected diplomatic	

expectations in a very simplified form which ideally fits a situation in which all allies have promised to support the intended action, all adversaries have threatened to oppose it, and all neutrals are expected to take neutral action. This hypothetical pattern is extremely rare and is much too simple to reflect most real situations. Nevertheless, the chart enables us to schematize a pattern of expectations in an ideal situation. As we will see, it is also possible to sort out the pattern of actual responses in the execution phase and compare it with the pattern of expectations. That exercise will give us a criterion for determining the effectiveness of planning in the decisional phase of a foreign policy undertaking.

When analyzing either phase, two types of information need to be included in this sort of chart. The first type of information is with respect to the grounds for the expectations. That is, whether the action is promised (or threatened), whether it is expected by the given state's decision makers, and actual activities. The second type of information is what instruments are used or expected (or promised or threatened) to be used. The simple table above presents a capsule of this sort of information in the decisional phase.

The sort of analysis represented by figure 6 does not address itself to the variety of targets toward which respondent actors might direct their instruments. The most obvious targets will be those of the initiating state, but other targets are the allies and other actors of the respective respondent states themselves and the targets of the initiating actor's allies. We do not need to address the complexity of these patterns of interaction, for our view is still focused upon the behavior of the single state whose foreign policy we wish to analyze. We do, however, need to address the question of what targets the instruments of the initiating actor are directed to. A second chart will be useful for this purpose.

Figure 7 plots the instruments in the hands of the initiating state against the targets presented to it in the situation. Depending upon the kind and intensity of a foreign policy undertaking, very complex activity may occur which involves applying instruments across a wide spectrum of targets. Major foreign policy initiatives involve wide-ranging activity not only with respect to the primary targets but also with respect to other states interested in a situation. Depending upon the situation, more or fewer boxes may be filled. The more boxes that are filled in actuality—that is, in the execution phase of a successful undertaking—the wider the scope, the more widespread the control, and the more engagement in the situation. Conversely, the fewer the boxes filled under the same conditions, the narrower the scope of the situation, the more limited the control, and the more the situation is insulated.

On the other hand, if fewer boxes are filled in the decisional phase than in the execution phase, there would be revealed a miscalculation of what instruments and activities were required by the situation. If the differences were gross, it would probably indicate an unsuccessful undertaking.

The x's in the boxes in figure 7 represent the sort of pattern that one might expect in a set of disarmament negotiations among not only the great powers but also smaller, neutral countries, such as we have had at the Geneva Disarmament Conference where NATO, the Warsaw Pact, and non-aligned countries have been represented.

The aim of the country upon which we are focusing is to achieve a disarmament treaty. This sort of undertaking includes using the diplomatic instruments which are directed to the diplomatic instruments of other countries represented at the conference. The indirect targets are the decisional structures of other countries, and informational activities are employed in order to influence the decisions. Of course, the

FIGURE 7
Instruments and Targets of Given State in a Negotiating Situation

INSTRUMENTS	TARGETS								
	Allied States			Adversary States			Neutral States		
	decisions	resources	instruments	decisions	resources	instruments	decisions	resources	instruments
Political									
Diplomatic	x		x	x		x	x		x
Informational	x			x			x		
Economic									
Military									

given country is also using the informational instrument in order to protect its own prestige should the negotiations fail. This example is a simpler one than might occur in more complex situations.

What is suggested by even the very simple undertaking plotted in figure 7 is that a foreign policy undertaking as straightforward as ordinary negotiations represents more complexity than is normally associated with such activity. How much more complex are crises and wars! We shall see, when we analyze a specific case of a more complicated undertaking, how the boxes can fill up. We shall also see that the charts developed so far provide us with a useful tool of analysis in trying to understand the complexity of a foreign policy undertaking.

Although the charts introduced thus far are greatly simplified aids to analysis, the components in the charts can be reduced even further to illustrate extreme hypothetical patterns of foreign determinants. The following two examples represent this greatly simplified form of analysis which helps us to see, in essential form, patterns of foreign determinants with respect to a given country's foreign policy. The pattern illustrated in figure 8 is one of complete conflict in which there are no neutrals and in which all types of means are used. Figure 9 represents another simplified and extreme pattern in which a given state is isolated but is not at war or under the imposition of economic sanctions.

FIGURE 8
Model Pattern of Complete Conflict

	ACTIONS	
	Supportive	Oppositional
Allies	Actual All Means	
Adversaries		Actual All Means

These charts are suggestive of the range and variety of patterns that might exist. They also provide the beginning for charting configurations for development over time. As shifts occur in the pattern of foreign determinants, a feedback process to a given state will require adjustments in the domestic determinants and possibly in the choices that can be

FIGURE 9
Model Pattern of Isolation without War or Economic Sanctions

	ACTIONS		
	Inaction	Supportive	Oppositional
Allies			Actual Diplomatic Informational
Adversaries			Actual Diplomatic Informational
Neutrals	Actual		

made. By means of a graph, the development of the pattern of foreign determinants can be plotted. Depending upon the case and the questions posed by the analyst, time graphs may be put on an hourly, monthly, yearly, or any time span that is useful to understanding the patterns. An example of the dynamic analysis which is referred to here will be given later in this chapter as a case study.

Foreign determinants, thus, can be usefully analyzed statically and dynamically. Static analysis enables us to chart patterns which give us insight into the kind of environment foreign policy makers face and assists us in evaluating foresight and effectiveness in foreign policy conception and execution. Dynamic analysis enables us to see the way in which foreign determinants operate over time and how they induce changes in foreign policy by a given state.

It needs to be noted, however, that all of the charts employed in this chapter—including those following which try to abstract real events—are only suggestive and should not be construed as hard data.

Case Study: Britain in the Middle East in 1956

The considerations that have been developed in this chapter can now be applied to an actual set of historical events. Although the mode of analysis can be applied to any case, the one used here to illustrate this analytical scheme is the case of the Israeli-British-French invasion of

Egypt in October-November 1956. Since our focus is on one country, we will follow the British in their activities in the case.[13]

There are several reasons for using this case for illustrative purposes. One is that it occurred sufficiently far in the past that there is a substantial record of the events and interpretations in the form of memoirs and secondary analyses upon which we can draw. Another reason is that it is a case of failure in a foreign policy undertaking, and one can determine through this mode of analysis at least some of the reasons for failure. The situation in the Middle East was also linked with other important situations which allows us to explore the way in which linkages between situations operate. An additional reason is that the aftermath of the events seems more clear than if we were placed in time closer to the events themselves. It is important for the foreign policy analyst to understand not only the sequence leading up to a set of events but also the repercussions and ramifications of the events.

In the treatment of this case, real countries will be filled in on the charts rather than the hypothetical illustrations used above. Nevertheless, the categories will be employed, and the same structure in the charts as developed in the general discussion above will be used. The case study will not be so comprehensive as the traditional case study, for the intention here is to sort out only the foreign determinants of Britain's foreign policy and to trace their impact upon that policy. The simplification will lead, however, to better understanding and one which can be compared with other cases which use the same mode of analysis. Let us now turn to the case itself.

The background to the events of October 30 to November 7, 1956, with which this case study is concerned, is complex. The Middle East had long been a region of great power conflict, but the countries of the area were struggling in 1956 to gain a larger measure of control over their own affairs. Great Britain had withdrawn its forces from the Suez Canal, under pressure from Egypt, earlier in the year. France, in 1954, had agreed to supply Israel with aircraft and agreed to revise the agreement in April 1956 in response to the influx of Soviet bloc arms to Egypt as a result of a 1955 accord. France had faced an armed insurrection in Algeria since 1954 and, convinced that Egypt was giving crucial support

---

13. The following sources have been consulted in preparing this case study: Peter Calvocoressi, ed. Anthony Moncrieff, *Suez: Ten Years After* (New York: Pantheon Books, 1966); Anthony Eden, *Full Circle* (London: Cassell, 1960); Herman Finer, *Dulles Over Suez: The Theory and Practice of His Diplomacy* (Chicago: Quadrangle Books, 1964); Richard E. Neustadt, *Alliance Politics* (New York and London: Columbia University Press, 1970); Charles L. Robertson, *International Politics since World War II: A Short History* (New York, London, Sydney: John Wiley and Sons, Inc., 1966); Hugh Thomas, *The Suez Affair* (London: Weidenfeld and Nicholson, 1967).

to the Algerian rebellion, shifted from a traditional pro-Arab policy to this support of Israel.

Egypt had been the subject of a military takeover in 1952 and Colonel Gamal Abdel Nasser had emerged as the prominent leader of the Egyptian revolution in 1954. He moved clearly to a position of non-alignment following the Bandung Conference in 1955 and perhaps in response to the pressures of the Western powers who wanted him to join an anti-Soviet alliance. The alliance was established under the concept of the "northern tier" (of Middle Eastern states) as the Baghdad Pact (CENTO since Iraq's withdrawal in 1958). Although Colonel Nasser's ambitions extended to exerting leadership over the Arab world, his main concern was the development of the Egyptian economy and political system. The key to Egyptian hopes for economic development was the projected Aswan High Dam. When a loan promised for this enterprise was abruptly cancelled by the United States in July, Nasser announced that he would nationalize the Suez Canal. The Suez Canal had previously been operated by the Suez Canal Company under a treaty of 1888 which guaranteed that it would remain available for the shipping of all countries in peace and war. British and French shareholders were the main owners of the stock in the company. By taking revenues from the Canal, Nasser hoped to finance the projected dam himself.

The British government determined that Egypt could not run the Canal and were intent upon retrieving it from Nasser. The British prime minister, Anthony Eden, looked upon Nasser as a dictator equivalent to Hitler. American policy during the summer and fall of 1956 was to improvise arrangements such as the Suez Canal Users' Association in an attempt to stave off the use of force by the British and to find an alternative solution to an invasion. The American government (particularly President Dwight Eisenhower) felt that an invasion would undermine Western influence in the Arab World and cause substantial resentment.

Diplomacy seemed to be working when, in October, Secretary-General of the United Nations Dag Hammarskjöld was able to obtain agreement upon six "principles" by the users of the Canal and Egypt. Eden, however, fearing for the dependence of Western Europe upon the Middle East for oil and hoping to bring about a comprehensive solution to the problems of instability in the Middle East by toppling Nasser whom he considered to be at the root of the problem, continued to plan with the French to use force to gain control of the Canal.

On October 18, the British and French governments agreed at Sèvres to a plan for joint action. The French government was also collaborating with the Israelis, but the United Kingdom refused to engage intimately in planning with Israel because its plan was to be justified in terms of separating the combatants after Israel had attacked Egypt.

In treating the pattern of foreign determinants of British foreign policy in this situation, charts will be developed, in the first instance, for three times: October 30, when Israel invaded Egypt; November 5, when substantial pressures from other countries worked their impact upon British; and November 7, when the ceasefire had been established and the United Nations Emergency Force began to be mobilized for deployment a few days later.

In figure 10, we view the pattern of expectations of the United Kingdom on October 30. It is not necessary to include every country interested in the situation, for several responded in essentially the same way. Syria is used to represent the Arab states other than Egypt, and Brazil and Yugoslavia to represent the neutral countries that responded to the United Nations General Assembly's request for contingents to make up the Emergency Force. The major actors are all included.

At the time that this chart represents, Britain was preparing to deliver jointly with the French an ultimatum to Egypt and to engage in military action against Egypt. Israel had already invaded Egypt, as indicated on the chart. The collaboration of Britain and France is indicated by France's promise of military assistance. Britain expected that only Egypt would fight back militarily. It was also expected that Nasser would be overthrown in the wake of military defeat. The Soviet Union, bogged down in Hungary at the time, was expected to be effectively neutralized by the United States. The Soviets would engage in propaganda efforts to condemn Britain and its allies and perhaps use diplomatic efforts to isolate the invaders. The British also had to expect condemnation by what they regarded as an ineffective Secretary-General. With respect to North American allies, Britain expected diplomatic support from the United States in neutralizing the Soviet Union and economic support by way of supplying oil. Canada was expected to be inactive.

This pattern of expectations pointed to probable success in the goals of securing the Suez Canal. As the Israeli army rolled through the Sinai Desert, the British and French launched an air attack against Egyptian military targets on October 31 and sent ground troops from Cyprus that landed in Egypt five days later. We can see how this pattern of expectations was grossly in error by charting in figure 11 the actual pattern of foreign determinants on November 5.

The shift in the pattern between the expectations of October 30 and the reality of November 5 was remarkable. Comparison of figures 10 and 11 illustrates that Britain made a severe miscalculation with respect to its major ally, the United States. Whereas Eden expected Eisenhower

FIGURE 10
United Kingdom—October 30, 1956
Expectation of Pattern of Foreign Determinants

COUNTRY (rank)	ACTIONS				
	Inaction	Supportive	Oppositional	Neutral	Inducive
Allies United States (1)		Expected–DE			
France (2)		Promised–DIM			
Israel (5)		Actual–DIM			
Canada (3)	Expected				
Adversaries U.S.S.R. (1)			Expected–DI		
Egypt (5)		Expected–P	Expected–DIM		
Neutrals Syria (5)	Expected				
Brazil (3)	Expected				
Yugoslavia (5)	Expected				
Secretary-General			Expected–I		

D = diplomatic means   M = military means

I = informational means   E = economic means

P = political means

to "lie doggo"[14] until after the American presidential election, the American administration turned on its ally, condemning it for the use of force and refusing to allow Britain to withdraw capital from the Inter-

---

14. This is the phrase used by Neustadt in *Alliance Politics*.

FIGURE 11
United Kingdom—November 5, 1956
Pattern of Foreign Determinants

COUNTRY (rank)	ACTIONS				
	Inaction	Supportive	Oppositional	Neutral	Inducive
Allies United States (1)			Actual–DIE		Urged withdrawal
France (2)		Actual–DIM			
Israel (5)		Actual–DIM			
Canada (3)			Actual–DI		Proposed UNEF–Burns
Adversaries U.S.S.R. (1)			Actual–DI Threatened–M		Urged joint U.S. action & withdrawal
Egypt (5)			Actual–DIMP		
Neutrals Syria (5)	Actual				
Brazil (3)			Actual–DI		Promised UNEF troops
Yugoslavia (5)			Actual–DI		Promised UNEF troops
Secretary-General			Actual–DI	Actual–DIE	Set up UNEF Urged withdrawal

D = diplomatic means M = military means
I = informational means E = economic means
P = political means

national Monetary Fund. Britain needed the capital to protect the position of the pound sterling which came under severe pressure in the wake of the invasion. The comparison also shows a much stronger reaction by the Soviet Union than Britain had envisaged, and it shows that, instead of retaining oligopolistic control of the situation, Britain and its allies

Foreign Determinants

were not only the subject of other countries' influence: they were actually losing all control over the situation as forceful and rapid inducive action began shaping up. Within Egypt itself, the political action which Britain had been counting on to topple Nasser actually supported him or remained neutral.

The next step in the process is shown in figure 12 as the neutral and inducive actions take effect and the three allies who invaded Egypt were isolated. The initiative had passed to the neutral activists, and the allies

FIGURE 12
United Kingdom—November 7, 1956
Pattern of Foreign Determinants

COUNTRY (rank)	ACTIONS				
	Inaction	Supportive	Oppositional	Neutral	Inducive
Allies United States (1)					Actual–DIE
France (2)		Actual–D			
Israel (5)		Actual–D			
Canada (3)					Actual–DM
Adversaries U.S.S.R. (1)					Actual–DI
Egypt (5)					Actual–DI
Neutrals Syria (5)	Actual				
Brazil (3)					Actual–DM
Yugoslavia (5)					Actual–DM
Secretary-General					Actual–DM

D = diplomatic means   M = military means
I = informational means   E = economic means
P = political means

became the object of concerted efforts to seek their withdrawal from Egypt. The reversal of the situation became complete at the end of December when Britain and France removed the last of their troops and in March when Israel removed the last of its troops from Egypt.

By the end of this sequence of events, Britain had lost most of its ability to influence events in the major countries of the Middle East. It had certainly lost all influence in Egypt. Moreover, Nasser became more solidly entrenched than he had been before.

For Britain, the Suez adventure was an important experience in shaping future policy, as it was for France. Both countries, distrusting the reliability of their major ally, the United States, became intent upon developing independent nuclear deterrents. Thus, the situation we have analyzed had important repercussions for the linked situation of the North Atlantic alliance. It also had the important consequence for the United States of reinforcing the view that, where a power vacuum exists by virtue of British withdrawal, it needed to be filled by American commitment. This view led to the Congressional support for the Eisenhower Doctrine in 1957 and to the landing of American marines in Lebanon in 1958 and the continued diminution of American prestige in the Arab world. Although there were these far-flung consequences, analysis of them is beyond the scope of this case study. Let us now return to the limited time which we have been analyzing.

The events which have been discussed can now be charted across time. This is done in figure 13 which plots foreign determinants actions against the times which were represented in the three preceding charts. The shift in the pattern of foreign determinants from the October 30 expectations of Britain through the actual events of November 7 is shown. This shift demonstrates clearly the miscalculations made by the Eden government. Now we can simplify this pattern by impressionistically aggregating the response of the international community interested in the situation and show the contrast between British expectations and actual events.

In this plot, by aggregating the response of the international community, we can show the gap between British expectations and the actual course of events. British expectations were that there would be a mixture of support and opposition in the first instance, with the opposition either being neutralized or withering away to inaction within a relatively brief period. Instead, the United States opposed the invasion, the Soviet Union took a stronger posture than the British expected, and the middle and small powers and the Secretary-General took inducive action. The interested international community, then, was able to work its will upon Britain which, with its immediate allies alone, was isolated.

Foreign Determinants 131

FIGURE 13
United Kingdom—October 30 to November 7, 1956
Changing Patterns of Foreign Determinants

ACTIONS	October 30	November 5	November 7
Inducive		Neutrals–DI	Neutrals–DE U.S. (1)–DIE U.S.S.R. (1)–DI Egypt (5)–DI Canada (3)–DE U.N.–D
Neutral			
Oppositional	U.S.S.R. (1)–DI Egypt (5)–DIM	U.S.S.R. (1)–DIMt Egypt (5)–DIMP U.S. (1)–DIE	
Supportive	U.S. (1)–DI France (2)–DIM Israel (5)–DIM Egypt–P	France (2)–DIM Israel (5)–DIM	France (2)–D Israel (5)–D
Inaction	Neutrals		

DATES

D = diplomatic means   M = military means
I = informational means   E = economic means
E = economic means   t = threatened

This case illustrates how powerful foreign determinants can be in influencing the outcome of a foreign policy undertaking. There was a fundamental miscalculation about the way in which the foreign determinants would work, thus a mistake of conception. In addition, there were difficulties in the execution of the undertaking which need not be analyzed here. But there was another aspect of the undertaking that was faulty and which will be revealed as an instruments and targets table for the British undertaking is developed. The paucity of the British undertaking in this respect as contrasted with what would have been appropriate to the operation becomes clear when we examine figure 15.

Britain thought of the problem essentially as an Egyptian one. Except for diplomatic collaboration with France and diplomacy in Syria aimed

FIGURE 14
United Kingdom—October 30 to November 7, 1956
Expected and Actual Developments of Patterns of
Foreign Determinants

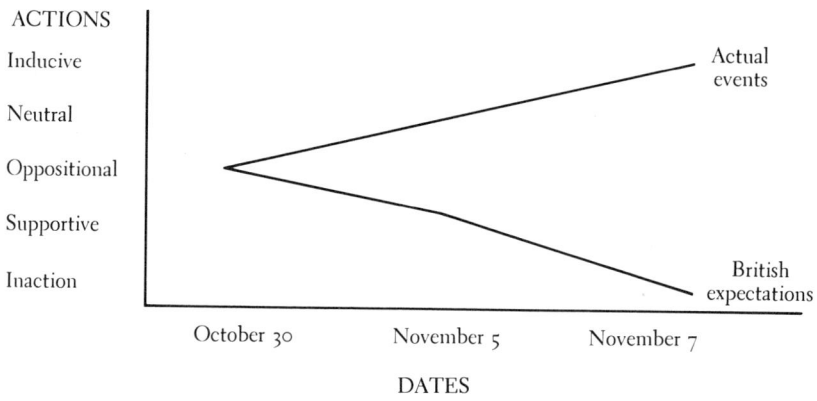

at neutralizing that country (similar action also took place with regard to Jordan and Iraq), all of British policy was aimed at Egypt. The italicized targets which Britain did not take action on are those which, as we have seen, were most influential in resisting British policy. Had their response to the British action been foreseen, the British would either have attempted to neutralize that action or developed a very different conception of what its objectives were in the Middle East. The paucity of the undertaking is shown in figure 15, and the gross assumption that the United States could be taken for granted to be at least neutral is illustrated. Since the United States at the time was seeking a negotiated settlement of the Middle Eastern situation, the British problem was either to recognize its dependence upon the United States or to induce Eisenhower and Dulles to support its undertaking against Egypt. It did neither. The other gaps in the table could perhaps have not been foreseen by the most astute foreign policy maker. Only in retrospect can one see the importance of neutral decisions and the effectiveness of the United Nations' reactions.

FIGURE 15
United Kingdom—Suez Undertaking
October–November 1956
Instruments and Targets

INSTRUMENTS USED	TARGETS									
	Allies			Adversaries			Neutrals		
	decisions	resources	instruments	decisions	resources	instruments	decisions	resources	instruments
Political				Egypt					
Diplomatic	France Israel U.S. Canada			Egypt			Syria SecGen		
Informational				Egypt					
Economic					Egypt				
Military						Egypt			

Conclusion

In this chapter, it has been attempted, through the development of analytical tools and an illustrative case study, to show how foreign determinants influence both the planning and execution of foreign policy undertakings. The case study of the British undertaking against Egypt in October-November 1956 illustrates how greatly dependent upon foreign determinants a country's foreign policy may be. In other cases, foreign determinants may not be so nearly controlling because the foreign policy makers may not misperceive the pattern so grossly and may choose more appropriate instruments for a given situation. Nevertheless, foreign determinants always have a great deal to do with the success of foreign policy undertakings, for it is in the nature of international politics that success depends not only on an initiating country but also upon responding countries in the environment.

The classification system of actions that was developed also indicates something about the probability of success. With the exception of inaction, each of the classes of action is intended to gain some measure of control over a situation. Support and opposition are very likely to achieve the intended consequences of giving support or opposition to a given state's policy. Successful achievement of the objectives of the policy being opposed or supported, however, depends upon the overall pattern of the situation and the realism of the conception involved and the skill of execution. Neutral action is intended to bring a set of events to a stop or otherwise prevent actors from what they are at a given time doing. This consequence is more difficult to achieve. Finally, inducive actions are intended to get an actor or actors to do something that it or they would not otherwise do. It is the hardest class of action to implement successfully.

Considering the 1956 Middle East crisis in this light makes the successful United Nations action seem all the more remarkable. This classification should also make clearer why the United Nations is not more effective, for its tasks are largely defined as belonging to neutral and inducive actions, the most difficult to achieve.

6

Domestic Determinants

The capacities and predispositions of countries are, as noted in chapter 2, affected by many factors. Although the concepts could not be altogether operationally defined, several crude measures were introduced which helped to get at the concepts, and it was possible to treat variations among countries by the use of the measures. This chapter carries forward that discussion by further analysis of the many factors which make up capacity and predisposition. In addition, the political process in which these factors operate to produce policies will be discussed.

Domestic determinants are those attributes, characteristics, conditions, and processes which—together with foreign determinants—help to shape foreign policy acts. They are, in turn, also targets for the influence of other countries because, in altering the determinants, other countries would alter acts. Domestic determinants are subject to development and change, so it will be useful to explore what sorts of changes are likely to occur, how they are likely to occur, and the conditions under which they are likely to occur.

Although all of the domestic determinants are susceptible to change, some are more stable than others. The discussion is organized, then, by grouping the determinants into three broad categories according to their pace of change.

First, there are *highly stable determinants*. These are geographical size and location, terrain and climate, population, and resources. Change in these determinants proceeds slowly, and there is little likelihood of abrupt change in them. Another country can alter these factors in a given country usually only through the use of force.

Second, there are *moderately stable determinants:* political culture and political style, and political leadership and political process. Change in these proceeds somewhat less slowly than in the highly stable determinants. Political leadership, in particular, is somewhat more likely to be susceptible to abrupt change.

Finally, there are *unstable determinants*. These are short-term attitudes and perceptions as well as accidental and fortuitous factors. They are susceptible to abrupt change in a situation. In particular, mass attitudes may change very rapidly and can be influenced by all of the different kinds of means used in foreign policy.

Just as situations and foreign determinants provide the *external* environment with which a given country's foreign policy makers must cope, so domestic determinants provide the *internal* environment with which the foreign policy makers must cope. Domestic determinants also provide the elements which can be drawn on for coping with the external environment. The more stable the determinants, the more foreign policy makers can take them for granted either as elements which can be drawn on for coping with the external environment or as elements which impose settled restrictions on what they may do. The more unstable they are, the more foreign policy makers must attend to them as elements of their environment which have to be coped with. On the whole, the stable determinants provide continuity in foreign policy, whereas the unstable determinants provide change.

Highly Stable Determinants

The highly stable determinants are least susceptible to abrupt change. They are geographical size and location, terrain and climate, population, and material resources. Some crude indicators of size, location, and population have already been dealt with in the size and location indexes. Nevertheless, the ensuing discussion will treat all of these factors.

Size and Location

A large geographical area provides security because it is difficult to occupy and hold. Climate and terrain contribute similarly to the security of a country. The history of western and central European invasions of Russia testify eloquently to the importance of the vast space and the harsh climate in protecting Russia from conquest. All of these factors are modified with technology, but Hitler's mechanized divisions were no more successful than Napoleon's foot soldiers, and even very sophisticated technology does not completely overcome the geographical and climatalogical environment. The application of highly sophisticated chemical technology substantially altered the terrain in South Vietnam, but the hills and jungles continued to be major influences on the course of the war there.

Size and location contribute not only to security and capacity but also to predisposition. The size of the country is an independent variable contributing to the identity of a country. Very small countries are most unlikely to think of themselves as having major world responsibilities. The leaders of the largest countries, on the other hand, are likely to have attitudes of confidence and pride, based on their relative security, and to define for themselves more ambitious roles to play upon the international scene.

By comparing the sizes of countries in a region, one can determine which are more likely to play leading roles. If it is found that a smaller country is playing a particularly ambitious role in a region and a larger country is also active, one can predict that the smaller country will probably be displaced in its leadership role in the long run. This appears to have been the case in West Africa. For a period Ghana was the most ambitious country, but Nigeria had the potential to play a leading role. Nigeria began to assume this role in the early 1970s and can be expected to continue to play it in the future.

At some times and under certain conditions, size changes. When this happens, the change itself becomes an important variable, and adjustments need to be made to the new size. Settlements at the end of wars are one of the circumstances under which states change their size. On the whole, victors tend to expand and losers tend to contract. Sometimes small states disappear, being annexed by neighboring countries.

Under conditions of federating leadership, unions change the size of states, as the union between Germany and Austria did in 1938, and as the formation of modern Germany and modern Italy did in the last half of the nineteenth century. During wars there may also be transfers of territory as the belligerents trade territory to neutrals for other advantages. Examples of this are the Louisiana Purchase of 1803 and the destroyers-for-bases deal in 1940. States also change size under conditions of internal disintegration. In the Nigerian civil war, for example, Biafra came into existence as an international actor and Nigeria was diminished in size. Upon winning, Nigeria was restored to its former size. Large migrations under conditions of turmoil also change the size of states in substantial ways, as happened in the Bangladesh situation.

There are varied repercussions on foreign policy when the size of states changes. Settlements at the end of war create occasions for elements of conflict among allies, and the adjustment in the condition of interaction requires adjustments in the foreign policies of the allies. When new states are formed through federating processes, the basis of foreign policy formation in terms of domestic determinants is changed, and other countries must make adjustments to the new actor. When size is enlarged by conquest, this poses a new threat to other actors interested in a situation. When countries change size through disintegration—as happened to Pakistan in 1971—the new actors seek to adjust their relationships, and other countries find new opportunities in the situation.

In chapter 2, the importance of location in terms of relationships with immediate neighbors was discussed. In addition, let us note that capacity is influenced by whether a state is riparian or landlocked. Moreover, the location of a particular country in a continental or broadly cultural context shapes its development and identity. Several countries on the periphery of China, for example, not only have the problem of accommodating to great power relationships but also have been heavily influenced by Chinese culture through overseas Chinese ethnic communities. The location of countries with black populations in Africa gives them a different identity and assigns a different meaning to blackness than the location of such countries as Haiti or Trinidad and Tobago in the Caribbean.

Terrain has the sort of security influence which was discussed above, but it also has an influence on the development of penetration by a national government and the participation by a population in national life. People living in remote hills or jungles are much less likely to be mobilized into a modern national system than people who are more accessible in cities or in more easily reached rural terrain.

In like manner, climate has an impact beyond the security ramifications discussed above. For the most part, high levels of economic development have occurred in the temperate climates.[1] Modern technology

---

1. See Gunnar Myrdal, *The Challenge of World Poverty* (New York: Pantheon Books, 1970) for a discussion of the meaning of this largely ignored phenomenon.

Domestic Determinants

makes it more likely that development can occur in arctic climates like those of Soviet Siberia and in tropical climates like those of Nigeria and Brazil, but special problems are presented. Although we do not have much knowledge about it, we can expect that there might not only be differences in economic factors such as working conditions but also differences of morale and attitudes that might possibly affect foreign policy.

Population

Various aspects of population are related to foreign policy analysis. The absolute size of the population gives us the basic data for constructing the size index which we are using. We need also to be concerned with the age distribution and geographical distribution of population. In addition, the integration of the population and its skills are important factors in the calculation of capacity. Finally, it is necessary to comment on the developmental nature of these various population characteristics.

The productive age groups—approximately 15 to 65 years—provide the manpower pool for economically supporting the entire population and the manpower pool for armies and other instruments of foreign policy. The nonproductive age groups represent an important domestic demand on resources. Under most conditions, resources will be consumed by this portion of the population. But under some conditions—the Biafra secession was an example of one—resources will not be allocated to the unproductive portion of the population. Children may be deprived of housing, clothing, the skills of teachers, and—as in the case of Biafra—food.

A different aspect of age distribution to be considered is the percentage of the population in the fifteen to thirty-year-old range. Particularly important in democratic societies, a younger generation will have different experiences and different memories than older generations and may wish to make different adaptations to world as well as domestic politics. There are also very important continuities and processes of passing down values, but generational change is important. The larger the proportion of the population in the age group 15–30, the greater will be the pressure for changes, particularly under conditions of frustration in foreign policy and a lesser level of skills of inspirational leadership by the political elite. There will often tend to be general instability when this age group is larger, and this condition would have an impact on foreign policy.

Geographical distribution of population affects the mobilizability of the population for national political purposes. The more dispersed it is, the more it is susceptible to political influences not under the control of the national elite. These alternative influences may be local politicians or revolutionary elites attempting to gain a base of power for national government overthrow.

Concentration of population also makes a country vulnerable to certain kinds of external influences. The more concentrated the population, the more likely that there will be groups susceptible to certain kinds of informational activities from abroad. This is because concentration of population leads to the aggregating of groups which reinforce individuals' attitudes. These attitudes, in turn, become the condition for receptivity to certain kinds of messages. For example, peace groups in the United States tend to reinforce individuals' fears of major war. Threatening messages from abroad tend to enhance the fears of these groups and they become more active in response.

Concentration of populations also makes a country more vulnerable to aerial attack in the case of war. General dispersal of population makes aerial attack less promising as an instrument to an adversary.

In addition to the above aspects of population, we also need to be concerned with two other questions. The first is integration of the population in a cohesive society. If there are large segments of a population that belong to a minority linguistic, cultural, religious, or racial group, they may not support the foreign policy of the country. This is particularly true where there are ethnic kin in contiguous states. Where an ethnic group rules in a state contiguous to one in which there is an identical ethnic minority, the situation can be a dominant factor in both states' foreign policies.

The pools of skills available in a given country make a difference in the possibilities of utilizing certain instruments of foreign policy. For example, ethnic identification in a contiguous state is not an important operative factor without skilled cadres of political and military leaders if a given country wishes to fight a guerrilla war in the neighboring country. Countries cannot have widespread diplomatic relations without skilled diplomatic personnel, and countries cannot build nuclear weapons without the skilled manpower to solve the engineering and production problems involved in such an undertaking. Countries cannot have developed missile systems without skilled electronics engineers and computer specialists. Technical assistance experts are necessary for foreign aid programs, and trained officers are necessary for leading armies.

These particular skills will be dealt with in the chapter on the mobilization of resources. Two crude indices of skills are the literacy rate (which is related to the level of technology of the country and its ability to absorb sophisticated equipment) and the number of scientists as a percentage of the population. In comparing countries, such data give

Domestic Determinants

us an idea of the skills that foreign policy makers can draw on. To assess the weight to give to these factors, however, we need to put them in the context of particular situations and apply them in specific cases.

Although population is subject to abrupt change only under the most exceptional circumstances, we need to note the developmental nature of population characteristics. First, there is the question of growth of numbers which will affect not only the total population but also the age distribution. The application of medical technology to reduce death rates induced very substantial rates of population growth in this century, and the further application of medical technology to bring down birth rates may reduce rates of growth through effective conception control programs.

Second, skills change with the introduction of educational programs and with industrialization. Industrialization also brings about shifts in geographical distribution and changes in culture, ranging from attitudes to fundamental social units including the family.

Third, modernization includes the mobilization of populations into national life with increased participation. With the resulting enhanced capacity, there is likely to be a shift in predispositions.

Finally, although each country is responsible for its own development and necessarily must rely on its own resources, other countries are marginally functional in bringing about development, particularly by transferring technology. The foreign policies of many underdeveloped countries are primarily aimed at gaining assistance to develop their human and material resources.

Material Resources

There is a vast amount of data that might be explored in analyzing material resources. In some cases, concentration upon relative minutia can have tremendously significant consequences. For example, if British and American bombers had concentrated on destroying ball-bearing plants in Germany during World War II, all of the production of German mechanized military machinery would have come to a standstill.[2] To take another example, comprehensive knowledge of Egyptian radar in 1967 enabled the Israelis to gain complete air supremacy in the war of that year. It would be impossible, however, to undertake in this book comprehensive analyses of all of the resources that bear upon foreign policy. In studying a particular case, the analyst would want to under-

---

2. See Albert Speer, *Inside the Third Reich*, trans. Richard and Clara Winston (New York: The Macmillan Company, 1970), p. 285.

stand completely the myriads of resource factors that are relevant in the given situation.

This analysis is necessarily limited to a few crude data which can be used for gross comparison of countries and for the illustration of a few hypotheses. Gross national product, despite its difficulties, is the best single datum for measuring the overall power of a country and its resources. The GNP per capita gives us an indication of the relative wealth of a country.

Wealth is a precondition for undertaking certain kinds of foreign policies; it conditions attitudes and behavior; and it carries its own peculiar problems. Wealth determines that a country will be more interested in stability than revolution, and wealth is necessary for large-scale economic assistance programs. Wealth is necessary for bribes, and it is necessary to sustain beleaguered allies. Wealth enables countries to sustain large armed forces, and it is probably also true that the wealthier the country, the more money it will waste on preparing for contingencies that will never eventuate. Poorer countries do not have this luxury.

Wealth leads to foreign investment which brings its own complications to foreign policy, and it leads to dependency on others for raw materials which are consumed in the wealthier state. It also leads sometimes to balance of payments problems and to participation with considerable power in international organizations like the World Bank and the International Monetary Fund. Wealth is also an index of status in the world, and it marks the difference between aid-giving and aid-receiving states. Wealth assures independence which is more difficult to secure in a state of poverty.

Wealth allows countries to engage in prestige projects like international exhibitions with some luxury, and it enables countries to engage in scientific enterprises like space exploration. Wealth enables a country to spend money on the training of people and on the support of large bureaucracies and on keeping a population well-fed and healthy.

Poorer countries tend to be less stable in a generally modernizing world. Consequently, they are more vulnerable to "frontal assault" revolutions and to foreign intervention.[3] They are also less able to mobilize their resources, particularly the population, for the pursuit of national goals. The foreign policies of poorer countries are very often shaped largely toward the object of securing the resources which will help them to grow richer, a condition which makes them vulnerable to

---

3. See Hugh Seton-Watson, *Neither War Nor Peace*, rev. ed (New York: Frederick A. Praeger, 1962), for a useful classification of revolutions and from which the notion of the "frontal assault" revolution is taken.

penetration. Poor countries are also likely to be primary product-producing countries and therefore at less of an advantage in trading than richer countries.

Two other useful indicators of material resources are manufacturing as a percentage of GNP and foreign investment as a percentage of total investment. Manufacturing is an indicator of how modern a country is and the extent to which resources (particularly military instruments) which are dependent upon manufacturing enterprises are likely to be resources useful to the foreign policy elite. Such data also tell us something about the vulnerability of a country to certain kinds of attack. The percentage of foreign investment tells us something of the extent to which a country is dependent upon others and, consequently, must defer to others in their policies.

All the questions with respect to the use of resources are dependent not so much on their existence as on the political will to use them. That will is dependent upon other factors, to some of which we now turn.

Moderately Stable Determinants

The moderately stable variables are political culture and national style, and political leadership and political process. Neither of these variables has obvious quantitative measures associated with it.

Political Culture and National Style

The classic definition of culture is Tylor's:

> Culture . . . is that complex whole which includes knowledge, belief, art, morals, law, custom, and any other capabilities and habits required by man as a member of society.[4]

An aspect of this is political culture, defined by Almond and Powell as "the pattern of individual attitudes and orientations toward politics among the members of a political system," and includes cognitive, affective, and evaluative orientations.[5]

---

4. Quoted in Anthony F. C. Wallace, *Culture and Personality* (New York: Random House, 1961), p. 6.

5. Gabriel A. Almond and G. Bingham Powell, Jr., *Comparative Politics: A Developmental Approach* (Boston and Toronto: Little, Brown and Company, 1966), p. 50. They note that the three components are derived from Talcott Parsons and Edward A. Shils, eds., *Toward a General Theory of Action* (Cambridge: Harvard University Press, 1951), pp. 58 ff.

These patterns of attitudes and orientations are more coherent and consistent in some countries than in others, but, whatever the coherence, they affect the political life of each country, including the foreign policy aspects of political life. As discussed in chapter 2, the identity of people and their experiences produce predispositions. Identity is an important component of political culture.[6] Other components of political culture which affect foreign policy are patterns of memory, values, perceptions, and fears. We shall also be interested in patterns of affective orientations toward the regime and will discuss in the next section the concepts of loyalty, legitimacy, and alienation.

In this analysis, a distinction is drawn between the components of political culture which are regarded as moderately stable and thus long-term determinants of foreign policy, on the one hand, and short-term attitudes, perceptions, fears, and so forth, which are unstable, on the other hand. This is a difficult distinction to draw empirically, but it is useful conceptually, and it suggests that political culture helps to shape predispositions and produces long-term political styles.

Two aspects of the American style of conducting foreign policy may serve as illustrations of political style. The first is the pursuit of policy by doctrine. From the Monroe doctrine issued in 1823 through the Stimson doctrine of 1931, the Truman doctrine of 1948, and the Nixon doctrine of 1969, we can see a similar style despite the immense changes in all of the other variables, including parties, power of the country, alliance patterns, executive power, public opinion, and so forth. The other aspect is the tendency to define security interests in very broad terms. From the war with the Barbary Coast pirates to the Truman doctrine, the United States has defined its security interests in broader rather than narrower terms. One can trace this back to something in American political culture which gives rise to bold conceptions, soaring rhetoric, and a belief in the importance of the United States in the world arena.

To use another example, an understanding of the concept of the "mandate of heaven" in China provides insight into the question of the legitimacy of the Chinese government. Without that concept, which is unique to China, a John Foster Dulles as United States Secretary of State could claim that the Communist government in China was not

---

6. See Sidney Verba, "Comparative Political Culture," in *Political Culture and Political Development* ed. Lucian W. Pye and Sidney Verba (Princeton, N.J.: Princeton University Press, 1965), pp. 555–56, where he discusses "national identity and political history" and refers to the importance of revolution and war in creating "identification with the nation."

legitimate. The concept provides insight that helps to analyze foreign policy more rationally.

Another example of political style illustrates contrasting responses to similar experiences. These responses then had the effect of influencing subsequent policies. It is the contrast in the German and Japanese response to defeat in World War II. The Germans were willing to displace all the guilt onto a few war criminals and were thus much less reluctant than the Japanese to enter into foreign policy coalitions. In contrast, the Japanese people all accepted responsibility for the militaristic policies of Japan in the 1930s and 1940s, and this helps to explain Japan's reluctance as late as the early 1970s to exercise the leadership that its power would suggest it could.[7]

In addition to these peculiar kinds of characteristics, one may note that there are more common characteristics of nations that may provide some basis for affinity with other states. There are, first of all, political characteristics that help to bring people together. For example, the Christian democratic movement in Western Europe provided a basis for the communities of the Six. Language, culture, and political institutions were to a large extent responsible for the United States' assistance to Britain before 1942. Religious affinity sometimes provides the basis for cooperation among countries, as does race in the case of many black African countries. Wealth, too, induces cooperation, the most notable example being the rich-poor division in the world. Ideological affinity operates too, as in Soviet aid to North Vietnam, a beleaguered Communist fellow.

All other things being equal, affinity characteristics tend to produce cooperation. As we have seen in the case of the Sino-Soviet dispute, on the other hand, affinity characteristics can also provide the issues on which allies divide, at least in the case of ideological affinity.

Despite the unique character of political culture and style, there are certain values and fears which are common to all countries. There may, nevertheless, be peculiar ways of seeking the achievement of the values and of coping with the fears.

Common Values

The people and the elites of every country in the world value their own protection, safety, and well-being, and strive for self-respect and some measure of deference. These universal values are embodied in the goals

---

7. See Edwin O. Reischauer, *The United States and Japan*, 3d ed. (Cambridge: Harvard University Press, 1965) where the contrast in political cultures is drawn.

of sovereignty, independence, and security. The means for achieving these goals vary as situations and the relevant determinants vary, but the values are widely shared.

In the northern hemisphere, at least, there is a universal fear of complete nuclear destruction. In all countries, there is a large segment of the population that fears civil disorder, natural disasters and other threats—immediate or remote—to well-being, order, and security.

The elites of countries that exist next to or are otherwise subject to heavy influence by more powerful countries fear the repercussions of the extension of influence into their national life by the dominant country. Other countries fear invasion by neighbors, particularly in situations of irredenta where neighbors make historic claims to territory that is presently part of one's own country.

Some elites have specific fears. For example, based on their memory of the invasions of 1812, 1914, and 1941, the Soviet elite has a predominant fear of invasions from central or western Europe, and one can explain part of Russia's foreign policy in Europe on the basis of that fear. In this case, the Soviet leadership sees a specific threat to its values, and fearing the worst from a reunited Germany, opposes reunification unless it can be brought under Soviet control through a Communist Party. Control of Eastern Europe and the long-term goal of eroding American influence in Western Europe are other Soviet policies that can be explained in this way.[8]

Political leaders of countries that have been colonial subjects have fears of redomination and, consequently, seek alternative sources of assistance to allow them to retain their highly valued independence. There is some difference between most of the former French colonies and others, for the payoffs for the French colonies is greater than their fears of continued French domination. When these countries become stronger, however, we can expect fissures to open up between their policies and French policies. The outcome of these conflicts will depend upon the skill of French policy and the development of demands of the particular countries involved.

Security is a core value of all countries. Governments wish, at a minimum, to preserve themselves as independent entities and to retain con-

---

8. Although there is a tradition in the literature of conflicting interpretations of Soviet motivations in respect to European policy, based on the question of national interest vs. ideology, the most convincing interpretation is Richard Lowenthal's which is accepted here. See his "The Logic of One-Party Rule," in *Russia Under Khrushchev: An Anthology from "Problems of Communism,"* ed. Abraham Brumberg (New York: Frederick A. Praeger, 1962).

trol over their national life and decisions within their own territory. Each country is, in some senses, in a unique situation, but there are—as we saw above—particular types of situations that are more general and comparable, and there are also some typical ways of coping with security situations. A fear for one's security implies that there is a threat to it. Therefore, elites identify threats. There is, then, a relationship between threats and fears, although they are not the same thing, and fears may be more or less well-grounded in relationship to threats. On the whole, we will find it more useful to employ the assumption of rationality in analyzing threats and fears.

In identifying threats to its security, the foreign policy makers of a given country will determine that the predominant threat to its security emanates from a specific or a diffuse source at any given time. For example, the Nationalist Chinese government identified a very specific threat to its security: the Communist Chinese government. On the other hand, India in the years from 1947 to 1962 saw the major threat to its security as coming from the general world situation of bipolarity, hostility between blocs, and the threat of nuclear war. American leaders have seen both specific and more diffuse threats emanating from the Soviet Union and from instability in the world at large. Changes in these perceptions of threats occur over time, and sometimes the shift in perceptions may be cyclical, being diffuse at one time and specific at another.

Western European governments generally shifted perceptions of threat as specifically emanating from the Soviet Union in the 1950s to a relaxation of fears of the specific threat in the 1960s. In 1968, with the Czechoslovak invasion, however, there were some slight shifts toward the 1950s perceptions.

Canada's decision in 1969 to withdraw some of its forces from NATO is a reflection of the diminished fears of a direct Soviet threat and a shift to a perception of a more diffused threat coming from the nuclear arms race. Elements of this perception were apparent in Canadian foreign policy much earlier, however, as for instance, in Canadian perceptions of the Middle East in 1956 which supported the Hammarskjöld doctrine of insulating smaller conflicts from the cold war to avoid the spreading of the major conflict to new situations.

The response to fears for one's security will vary with the perception of threat. In terms of a direct-diffuse dichotomy, one hypothesizes that the more the threat is perceived as direct, the more the tendency for a given country to seek engagement. Conversely, the more the threat is perceived as diffuse, the more likely it will be that the country will seek insulation.

The Cambodian situation can illustrate this hypothesis. Under Sihanouk, the Cambodian government perceived the threat to its security as diffuse and feared the consequences of becoming embroiled in the conflict situation that was moving forward in Southeast Asia. When Sihanouk was overthrown—and the difference in perception was one of the reasons for overthrowing him—the Lon Nol government saw the major threat to its security as emanating specifically from the Viet Cong and North Vietnamese forces which were operating on Cambodian territory. In the former case, Sihanouk sought to keep Cambodia insulated from the Vietnam war. In the latter case, Lon Nol sought engagement in that war.

Political culture assists us in understanding the basis of alignments and the reasons for particular approaches to situations. It also suggests that new experiences are a very significant influence on the political culture of a country and one of the major sources of significant change in the general directions of the country's foreign policy.

When one is analyzing a country's foreign policy, he would have to examine deeply the self-identity and the major experiences of the country. What is apparent at a glance, however, is the fact that different countries' elites would bring quite different perspectives to bear on their foreign policy problems. As we shall see later in this chapter, the memories of people have important and hypothetically predictive impacts on their behavior. The major experiences of countries provide at least some clues to future policy.

To take one example, following the Cuban missile crisis, the Soviet Union dealt cautiously with the United States and pursued a detente policy wherever possible. At the same time, it built up its navy and in the early 1970s was projecting its power into the Mediterranean and Indian Ocean. Although difficult to document, it is likely that the 1962 experience revealed to the Soviets the importance of a navy in a crisis. At the same time, it revealed the foolhardiness of embarking on adventures like the implantation of missiles in Cuba without the instruments to protect them against American pressures. Since the memory of that crisis in the United States has been very different, the contrast underlines the importance of analyzing the particular memories and identities of specific elites.

Without systematically examining every political system, one can discuss a number of components of political culture and hypothesize how variations in each component might affect foreign policy. Although some illustrations will be used, it needs to be noted that these are not tested hypotheses. They are, rather, statements of how the author impressionistically thinks the components affect policies. Suggestions are made as to how one might go about examining them and what data might be used. We also need to maintain awareness of the difficulty of separating long-term from short-term components. With these caveats in mind, let us discuss fears, goals, memories, attitudes, and perceptions.

Fears

The two fears that are most critical in foreign policy are fear of attack and fear of disintegration. Fear of attack or conquest is usually fear of a neighbor or other country in the range of insecurity on the location index developed above. Fear of disintegration can apply to three realms: internal disintegration, spheral disintegration, or balance of power disintegration. Other predominant fears that may occur are fear of loss of regime and fear of loss of prestige. These two are particularly susceptible to change in the short run.

In addition to the kinds of fears that may be predominant, we must also be concerned with the immediacy or remoteness of the object of fear and of the strength or weakness of the feelings of fear themselves. We can identify at any given time the predominant fears existing in all of the countries we are analyzing, but it must be remembered that these change as the other factors affecting foreign policy change. Therefore, a few examples of shifts in predominant fears will be cited, and the circumstances in which these shifts occurred will be indicated through the statement of hypotheses.

The first hypothesis is that strong, immediate fears of internal disintegration make it more likely that regimes will pursue policies of insulation. These fears occur under several different conditions. When a regime comes to power by illegal means, there is a period of time in which it needs to consolidate its position, sometimes in order to overcome opposition, sometimes merely to gain legitimacy. In either case, it is not in a position to follow policies of engagement in foreign policy because of a fear of internal disintegration.[9] Russia in 1917 is an ex-

---

9. This interpretation of the relationship between internal stability of a regime and external policy, which is also carried through in the next chapter, is contrary to the major conclusion of Richard N. Rosecrance in *Action and Reaction in World Politics: International Systems in Perspective* (Boston and Toronto: Little, Brown and Company, 1963), chapter 12. He argues, on p. 304, "that there tends to be a correlation between international instability and the domestic insecurity of elites." I argue in this book that any external thrusts by a country rely on command by the political elite of the resources of their country. One of the cases which Rosecrance cites as supporting evidence is the expansionist policies of Nazi Germany. My argument would be that the outward thrusts of Germany in the late 1930s were in conformity with Hitler's ideology and had to be delayed until his regime was consoli-

ample when, in order to consolidate the regime in a situation of disintegration, Lenin decided to leave the war. Fears of disintegration in the United States in the late 1960s led to withdrawal from the war in Vietnam.

Fears of spheral disintegration also have an impact. Strong, immediate fears of spheral disintegration lead a hegemonial power to intervene, as the Soviet Union did in Czechoslovakia in 1968 and as the United States did in the Dominican Republic in 1965. In both of these cases, there was a reinforcing fear of internal disintegration in the absence of action.[10]

Fears of disintegration in a balance of power also have consequences. American fears of balance of power disintegration in the Cuban missile crisis were part of the motivations for oppositional action, and similar fears partly motivated the intervention in Vietnam. This fear is also partly at the basis of foreign aid programs.

Strong, immediate fears of attack lead to a search for allies and the mobilization of resources within the country. When such fears become extremely intense, there is a possibility that a given country may make a "preventive" attack against its neighbor, the fear leading directly to war. This was the case with Israel in 1967.

Fear for the loss of regime is more likely to be a predominant consideration in states in which there is not a fixed term of office, but it will be a lesser consideration in all countries. In the 1958-62 crisis over Berlin, though, it became a major consideration for Premier Khrushchev. In the politics of the Middle East, one could observe that President Nasser was motivated by fears for loss of his regime, and when these fears diminished, he was free to pursue national or foreign policies that were otherwise constrained by this fear.

Fear of loss of prestige accounted for President Nixon's decision to launch the attack against the Communist sanctuaries in Cambodia in April 1970. It also accounted for the American feeling of need to uphold its commitment to South Vietnam lest its adversaries would not believe its commitments elsewhere, and its allies would lose confidence. Similarly, the Soviet Union assisted North Vietnam.

---

dated and Germany had improved its capacity. It was Nazi ideology, not insecurity of tenure, which was the crucial variable which led to World War II. I am persuaded by this argument which is made convincingly by Gerhard L. Weinberg in his *The Foreign Policy of Hitler's Germany* (Chicago and London: The University of Chicago Press, 1970), chapter 1. On the other hand, this is obviously a controversial point, and the reader may wish to read further and think it through.

10. There was no fear in either case of a collapse of the regime but rather simply of marginal disintegration.

Domestic Determinants 151

Sometimes fears are expressed in public, but often one has to infer them. Public expressions can be measured by examining speeches and documents. However, other fears can be gotten at only by examining memoirs or by interviewing the participants in the foreign policy process.

Goals

Goals of elites in foreign policy are both complex and simple, both broad-ranging and narrow, both direct and indirect, and both specific and diffuse. For our purposes, however, four continua will be constructed and distinction between long-term and short-term goals will be made in each. The four continua are: independence-integration; hegemony-submission; preservation-extension; and stability-revolution. These continua along which goals may be classified are states of affairs that goals are expected to achieve. Goals are always defined with respect to given situations and represent states of affairs that given leaders wish to bring about in the future. What we are interested in here is what statesmen are attempting to achieve. Each of the extremes of our continua tend to lead to certain kinds of foreign policies, as the following hypotheses indicate.

A predominant goal of independence leads to policies of insulation, and a predominant goal of integration leads to policies of cooperative engagement. One can contrast French policy under DeGaulle with the policies of West Germany. French goals of independence led to policies which served to insulate France from NATO, and German objectives led to policies which served to tie Germany to the United States and other allies as closely as possible.

The hypotheses with respect to the hegemony-submission continua are that a predominant goal of hegemony leads to policies of integration engagement and that a predominant goal of submission leads to policies of cooperative engagement. Czechoslovakia and Poland after World War II, fearing a resurgent Germany, sought cooperative arrangements with the Soviet Union. Poland, already under the control of the Soviet Union, submitted completely. Czechoslovakia, on the other hand, hoped to act as a bridge between East and West, and sought cooperation only. In 1948, the German fear led to its willingness to submit completely to Soviet domination. The Soviet Union sought to integrate both of these countries under its hegemony.

To turn to the next continua, there are hypotheses with respect to preservation and extension goals. A predominant goal of preservation leads to policies of cooperative engagement in order to form support against a specific threat. In the absence of a specific threat, a predominant goal of preservation leads to policies of insulation. Preservation goals are most likely to be predominant in weaker states, for the states which feel relatively secure are likely to develop other predominant goals once they feel that their preservation is assured.

A predominant goal of extension leads to unilateral warlike policies and policies of engagement aimed at inducing inaction in other countries; under such conditions, it may be necessary to form a two-actor coalition as the price of not having the second actor interfere with specific actions of the given country. This is the situation of the Molotov-Ribbentrop agreement, and failure to pursue this line of policy is one way of accounting for the failure of the 1956 expedition against Egypt by Britain and France.

The final set of goal hypotheses is as follows. A predominant goal of stability leads to cooperative engagement with governments, and a predominant goal of revolution leads to cooperative engagement with alternative elites. The policies of the Soviet Union and China in the late 1960s may illustrate this set of hypotheses.

Goals may be instrumental as well as final expectations, and they may change over time. One may infer goals from public documents and from statements of ideology.

Maximum and Minimum Goals—Countries seek as many values as human beings do. Thus, countries seek prestige, deference, respect, dignity, wealth, power, and so forth. There is an immense variety of ways of doing this, but all of the methods and policies are included in policies of insulation, policies of engagement, and policies of expansion.

We have already seen that policies result from a complex of motivations, fears, and values. Moreover, we have seen that policies may aim at broad or narrow goals and that goals may change. At this point, it will be useful to introduce the notion of maximum and minimum goals.

To cite an example, one can analyze Soviet objectives vis-à-vis Western Europe. A minimum goal is to prevent a major threat to Soviet security from developing in Western Europe. The Soviet Union's concern with German rearmament and its policy of preventing German reunification under any circumstances short of Communist control and client status represent reflections of this minimum goal. On the other hand, it would be desirable from the Soviet Union's point of view to eliminate American influence in Western Europe, to keep it divided, and to assert Soviet influence as the predominant influence there, to "Finlandize" Western Europe. Although it is conceivable that a new maximum could be established in a flow of events that would entail Soviet conquest of Western Europe, that is most unlikely in view of the threat that such action would pose to the United States. Moreover, it has not been the Soviet Union's maximum goal up to the early 1970s.

On the basis of this notion, one can say that it is much more likely that a country will employ more resources to achieve minimum goals than maximum goals and that maximum goals are unlikely to be pursued vigorously in the absence of some progress in achieving minimum goals. One can also say that minimum goals are more likely to have a closer geographical reference than maximum goals. In any close analysis of a given country's policies, it is useful to concentrate on the minimum goals, but it is also useful to keep the maximum goals in mind in order to explain features of a policy which do not seem to make sense in terms of minimum goals.

French foreign policy under DeGaulle, for example, aimed, at a minimum, to secure freedom of action for France vis-à-vis NATO and the bipolar structure of international politics. It also had more far-ranging goals, however, and a maximum goal of achieving true great power status with an extension of French influence to many parts of the world and a France acting as an alternative center in a world of several blocs. At a maximum, France would lead a restructured and confederal Europe encompassing both East and West up to the Ural boundary and, of course, including the European part of a truncated Russia. While many observers think of DeGaulle's maximum goals as visionary, utopian, or absurd, it is easier to understand the French posture under DeGaulle if we keep the maximum goals in mind.

Maximum goals, while often utopian, provide insight into the perceptions of leaders and a clue to their operating conceptions of what forces are at work in the world. DeGaulle's concept of his maximum goals rested on a deep belief that the nation-state was the most important entity for the future but also that nationalism as a force was at least somewhat likely to lead to a breakup of current states. His conception of a "Europe from the Atlantic to the Urals," of a "Quebec Libre," and his sympathy with the Biafran secession are all consistent with this conception. It was also a useful conception in opposing the alternative conception of the United States of integration of states into larger aggregates.

Memories

Every country's members—elites and masses—have memories of the past. These memories provide continuity in policies under some conditions, and disjunction in policies under others. At any given time, policies are made with reference to memories. Memories are the context into which countries' leaders put new events, and they are the stuff of analogies. Memories are of the means of foreign policy, of conditions, of the relations a country has had with others, of the responses of others to initiatives, and of policy outcomes. Different memories help to account for generational change in foreign policy as well as in other areas of national life.

The sets of memory categories that will be dealt with here are peace-war, success-failure, support-betrayal, insulation-engagement, freedom-dependence, and adulation-humiliation. The hypotheses which relate these memory categories to policies follow.

Memories of success in peace or war will tend to influence policies in the repetition of behaviors, and memories of failure will tend to influence policies in the opposite direction. Like other hypotheses, this one is subject to the *ceteris paribus* condition. Perhaps the memory of Munich as an attempt at the peaceful settlement of a dispute is as good an example as any that the memory of failure has led to avoidance of such behavior.

Memories of support will tend to solidify alliances, and memories of betrayal will tend to produce either policies of insulation or policies of realignment. Alliances are necessarily based upon identical or coincident interests of the members, but alliances are not random, and realignments are influenced by the past behavior of allies.

Memories of success in insulation or engagement will tend to perpetuate those respective policies, and memories of failure will tend to influence policies in the opposite direction. Sweden's neutrality has been successful and is perpetuated, while the other European neutrals whose neutrality was unsuccessful have joined alliances.

Memories of adulation will lead to attitudes of confidence, and memories of humiliation will lead to attitudes of caution. The Soviet Union was humiliated in the Cuban missile crisis and became more cautious in ensuing policies. In contrast, the United States was adulated and became much more confident in, for example, its MLF policies and in its intervention in Vietnam.

Memories of dependence lead to fears of integration and make policies of integration engagement less likely. Such memories led most of the newly independent countries to assume postures of nonalignment.

Memories are invoked in public speeches and in the deliberations of policy makers. They also appear in memoirs. Although one needs to be very cautious in making interpretations, memories are based on real

Domestic Determinants

historical experiences, and a reading of the history of a nation may give at least clues to kinds of memories that might prevail.

Attitudes

Attitudes also help to shape foreign policy determinations. They are variable by individual, and one may find contradictory attitudes among the members of a decision-making group and among different constituencies. Attitudes affect styles of conducting foreign policy and of leadership of supporters. Attitudes do not determine policies, but they do make given policies which are determined by other factors more or less likely by their reinforcing or their repellent effect. Attitudes are, then, conditions under which policies are more or less likely to occur when determined by other factors. In treating attitudes, a set of continua will once again be constructed.

The first is the confidence-caution continuum. Under attitudes of confidence, countries will be more willing to undertake initiatives without making careful calculations of ends and means. Attitudes of caution induce leaders to make these calculations and make bold initiatives less likely.

The second attitude continuum is trusting-suspicious. Trusting attitudes are more likely to occur in democracies. Attitudes of trust show more willingness to enter into new engagements, while attitudes of suspicion make countries less willing to enter into new engagements. Severe attitudes of suspicion will deter policies of integrative engagement except on conditions under which the suspicious country can penetrate its ally and under which it cannot be penetrated itself.

Open-secretive is the next attitude continuum. Attitudes of openness will lead rulers to engage in justification, while attitudes of secrecy will not. Attitudes of secrecy lead to more criticism of adversaries and reinforce distrust of allies, while attitudes of openness reinforce trust.

The next continuum is hopeful-despairing. Hopeful attitudes will reinforce tendencies to action, and despairing attitudes will reinforce tendencies to inaction. These are important attitudes for the governors of a country considering an initiative to take into account. If an elite wishes inaction on the part of others, attitudes toward the despairing end of this continuum are helpful, from its point of view.

Attitudes ranging from sanguine to urgent fall along our next continuum. Attitudes of urgency tend to produce decisional activities, whereas attitudes of sanguinity reinforce tendencies to avoid decisions.

Attitudes toward risk fall on the next continuum. It runs from willingness to take high risks to willingness to take low risks. High risk attitudes reinforce tendencies to take military action, while attitudes of low risk work against these tendencies.

Finally, we have the attitude continuum gratified-frustrated. Attitudes of gratification reinforce tendencies to repeat behaviors. Attitudes of frustration reinforce attitudes of change, either in the direction of other action, perhaps more radical than before, or in the direction of apathy and withdrawal.

Attitudes may be inferred from speeches, but also from the tone and atmosphere of a series of events. Although very intuitive, intersubjective judgments might be used to operationalize attitudes.

Perceptions

The way in which elites see events helps to determine how they will define problems and this will lead to policy making. Perceptions may be inferred from speeches and documents as well as from actions. Interviews also will elicit responses with respect to perceptions. It will be most useful to divide the analysis of perceptions into five parts. There are perceptions of threat, of process, of situations, of expectations of other countries, and of the self. Each of these is treated in a separate section, with hypotheses about how each set of perceptions affects foreign policy process and outcomes.

Perceptions of Threat can be treated on three dimensions. Threats may be *specific* or *diffuse*. That is, a country's elite may perceive a threat emanating from a specific country or alliance, or it may see a threat in more diffused terms. One can contrast the United States' and the Soviet Union's perceptions of the nuclear proliferation problem. The United States saw a threat in the general problem of nuclear proliferation (diffused threat), whereas the Soviet Union saw the particular problem of West Germany's acquisition of nuclear weapons (specific threat). Until the United States dropped its advocacy of the MLF, which the Soviets viewed as giving nuclear weapons to Germany, the nuclear nonproliferation treaty could not be initialled.

Threats may also be perceived as *immediate* or *remote*. The more immediate the threat, the more likely that specific decisions will be made to respond to it. The more remote the perceived threat, the more influence on the situation policies has the bureaucracy; the more immediate the perceived threat, the more the political elite will have influence. Perceived threats are one of the three major elements of crisis.

The third dimension of threat perception is the *probability* of the threat's materializing. For this dimension, we construct a continuum

Domestic Determinants

of probable-improbable. The more probable the threat, the more likely it is that action will be taken to counter it. The more improbable, the more the likelihood of policies of drift. When probability reaches imminence, there is a greater likelihood of unilateral action. When probability lies toward the center of the scale, there is more likelihood of a search for allies.

The fourth dimension is the *severity* of threat. Severity means the amount of damage that might be caused if the threat were carried out. The continuum of this dimension is very severe (great damage)-not severe (little damage). The more severe the threat, the more likely that action will be taken to counter it.

Perceptions of Process—There are many ways to view the process of international politics in general or of specific situations in particular. Several important differing ways are given here by constructing continua and developing hypotheses about the way in which perceptions of process affect other determinants and outcomes.

One set of differing ways of perceiving process is along the continuum ranging from controllable through manageable to uncontrollable. Perceptions that view process as controllable lead to greater internal feelings of frustration when policies fail. Perceptions that situations are manageable lead to attitudes of confidence, while perceptions that process is uncontrollable lead to attitudes of despair. Perceptions that process is more controllable than not lead to action, and perceptions that it is uncontrollable lead to inaction.

Another set of perceptions ranges from the view that the process is scientific—that is, it occurs according to explainable and predictable patterns—to the view that it is pragmatic—that is, each problem is a discrete one which must be managed on an *ad hoc* basis. The hypothesis is that perceptions that the process is pragmatic lead to greater inconsistencies in actions than perceptions which see the process as scientific. In other words, there is a self-fulfilling prophecy at work in terms of perceptions of the process.

One may also analyze the time period in which perceptions of the process are put. Perceptions may vary from the view that the process at work is a long-term one to the view that it is a short-term one. The hypothesis is that perceptions that the process is long-term lead to concerns about support of other states, whereas perceptions that process is short-term lead to attempts to keep control in as few hands as possible.

The process may also be viewed as radical or incremental, and perceptions of the process as radical lead to policies of disruption whereas perceptions that the process is incremental lead to policies of regulation.

This dimension of perceptions, too, has a quality of the self-fulfilling prophecy.

Perceptions of the rate at which change occurs vary from abrupt to slow. Perceptions that process is abrupt increase the influence of the political executive, whereas perceptions that it is slow increase the influence of the bureaucracy and the legislature.

The final way in which perceptions of process will be analyzed is in terms of a view of conflict or harmony. Perceptions that process is dialectic lead to greater willingness to use military force, whereas perceptions that process is harmonious lead to less willingness to use military force.

Perceptions of Situation Structure and Dynamics—Here categories will be used which are identical to those used in analyzing situations. There are three dimensions along which to plot the perceptions of given countries at given times. The first is the perception of the number of actors involved. Is the situation viewed as a two-actor or multiple actor situation? This perception will affect how many other actors a given country deals with. If the perception is erroneous and does not square with the objective situation, we can expect miscalculations of policy.

The second dimension of perceptions of situation structure is with respect to scope. Is the situation of wide or narrow scope, and is it linked with other situations? The policies that are pursued will be affected by this dimension of situation perception. Perceptions of narrow scope will lead to simpler policies, and perceptions of wider scope will lead to more complex policies. Perceptions of wider scope are more likely to lead to alliance behavior than to unilateral policies, and perceptions of narrower scope are more likely to lead to unilateral policies.

The final dimension of perception of situation structure is with respect to the mix of conflict, competition, cooperation, and integration. Perceptions of conflict will lead to hostile actions, whereas perceptions of competition will lead to actions intended to achieve an advantage without provoking hostility, and perceptions of cooperation will lead to attempts to link policy with other actors, and perceptions of integration will lead—on the part of the dominant partner—to attempts to gain support of clients and—on the part of clients—to take independent actions.

Perceptions of Other Countries—In addition to perceptions of a situation, elites will also have expectations about other countries and about the international community in general. In the chapter on foreign determinants, we saw how the actions of other states affect the foreign policy of the given state. Here, we are concerned with the way in which the given state expects others to act.

Domestic Determinants

On the whole, there will be general expectations of friendliness or hostility to the contemplated actions of the given state. In addition, calculations will be made with respect to inaction and supportive-oppositional-neutral-inducive actions of other states and the international community.

States are unlikely to take actions which they do not expect to be able to achieve, but, because success often rests on the cooperation or weakness of others, this kind of calculation is important. If the perceptions are accurate predictions, and the appropriate capacity is available, then success may be achieved.

Perceptions of Self—Not only are perceptions of the rest of the world important determinants of the actions of a given country, but the self-image of that country also influences the kinds of actions it takes in the world. There are three dimensions along which self-images will be placed.

The first of these is self-effacing-messianic. Countries which view themselves more modestly are more likely to defer to others and not to initiate policies. Those which are more messianic are more apt to exert roles of leadership, acting as federators in coalitions and less apt to be swayed by the opinions of other countries. These are the countries which are willing to exercise vetoes in appropriate situations.

The second dimension of self-image is powerful-not powerful. Countries which view themselves as powerful are more apt to take on responsibilities outside their own countries. They will also feel secure from smaller neighbors and they are more likely to be willing to intervene.

Stabilizer-revolutionary is the third continuum of self-image. Countries which view themselves as revolutionary are more likely to take destabilizing actions and to support counter-elites in other countries. Revolutionary self-images also lead to more initiative than stabilizing self-images. Stabilizing self-images lead more to policies of response and to less acceptance of instability in the world.

Summary

The components of political culture are the complex psychological orientations to the political system and to the external environment.[11] The patterns of these components are seldom coherent and simple,

---

11. For useful analyses of mass psychological correlates of foreign policy, see the chapters by Herbert McClosky and Johan Galtung in *Domestic Sources of Foreign Policy*, ed. James N. Rosenau (New York: The Free Press, 1967). The best study of the psychological variables of elites with reference to foreign policy is Joseph de Rivera, *The Psychological Dimension of Foreign Policy* (Columbus, Ohio: Charles E. Merrill Publishing Company, 1968).

but more often show cleavages both between elites and masses and among different members of elites. We may think of these phenomena as well as the other domestic determinants as providing constraining and facilitating factors upon political leaders. Political leadership, then, is the link between political culture and a country's foreign policy. We will examine that phenomenon in the next section.

Political Leadership and Political Process

Every country is headed by a political executive. The executive not only links political culture with foreign policy, as was suggested above, but also provides the link between domestic and foreign affairs. The notion of leadership suggests relationships between leaders and led, and this section deals with those relationships.

In chapter 2, a four-fold scheme of political executive systems was devised: presidential, parliamentary, dictatorship, and junta. Although the scheme was based on the criteria of number in the top political leadership of the state and whether the political system is democratic or authoritarian, the different types also have different relationships with their constituencies. Before proceeding to discuss those relationships and the process by which they are acted out, let us first elaborate on the types of political executive systems and define what we mean by constituencies.

It is sometimes difficult, in the changing contemporary world, to classify every political executive system easily, for there are shifts from one to the other, particularly in the premobilized modern systems.[12] It is also not always clear to the outside observer whether one man fulfills the functions of the chief executive or whether a group of persons share chief executive prerogatives. Indeed, even in mobilized parliamentary systems, the prime minister has often emerged as a leader who shares some of the characteristics of a president.[13] These difficulties of classification, however, need not deter us. In the first place, we recognize that there can be changes from one system to another, and this implies that there might be "mixed systems" and periods of uncertainty. These are empirical, not conceptual questions.

---

12. It is also difficult to classify systems as democratic or authoritarian. One can operationally define these, however, by using series of measures from the Yale *World Handbook* data. See footnote 9 in chapter 2.

13. See the interesting debate on this topic in Thomas A. Hockin, ed., *Apex of Power: The Prime Minister and Political Leadership in Canada* (Scarborough, Ontario: Prentice-Hall of Canada, 1971), particularly the selections by Denis Smith and Joseph Wearing.

Domestic Determinants 161

Second, what interests us is functional equivalency rather than formal arrangements. Thus, a weak presidential system may require the president to defer to the advice of politically important colleagues, and a strong prime minister may be able to downplay his cabinet, thus making the two contrasting formal systems functionally equivalent. As we shall see, the political process does vary as between these types of political executive systems.

The differences between one-man and collective political executive systems and between democratic and authoritarian systems are substantial at the extremes, but the differences are relative rather than absolute. The categories, therefore, should not be considered as airtight compartments but rather as points on continua and as guides to understanding concrete examples. The functions of governance are performed by all of the types.

In both democratic and authoritarian systems headed by one person, there is more reliance on that one person than in systems headed by a collectivity. On the other hand, a president operating in a democratic system is bounded by constitutional and legal restraints and tends to be more responsive to the demands of the mass public and interest groups than a dictator because he is subject to reelection, among other reasons. The dictator is freer to define the needs of his system and is free to respond or not to demands from groups in his system. At the extreme, he can—as Stalin did—repress and eliminate rivals.

Collective leaderships in both democratic and authoritarian systems tend to rely on groups of individuals with independent political bases. Thus, even the top leader of the political executive in a collective system has political constraints placed upon him that are different from presidents and dictators. The latter tend to have more direct contact with mass supporters, whereas the former's contact with mass supporters is more mediated by political colleagues. One-man systems rely on political advice, too, but executive advisers draw their legitimacy from the ruler, whereas the political advisers in collective systems draw their legitimacy to a large extent from other sources that are somewhat independent of the ruler. These and other differences will be explored further in the discussion of political process. First, it is necessary to define and explain the notion of constituencies.

Constituencies

Constituencies are those persons who are led by the chief executive. They exist in every political system, providing demands on and supports for the political executive. The components vary by political system, and the relationships of the chief executive to each of the major categories of constituency vary according to the type of political executive.

In this analysis, three categories of constituencies which exist in every political system are used. They are (1) political elites, (2) bureaucracies, and (3) mass publics and other nongovernmental actors. For some purposes, one can treat interest groups as a distinct subcategory of (3). Each of these categories of constituencies has different characteristics from the others, but all may be thought to provide tools for and constraints upon the chief executive. Each may be thought to have at its disposal opportunities for relating to the political executive along a continuum that ranges from complete support to complete opposition. Each operates differently in concrete terms because of different characteristics and differential access to the political system. Their actions nevertheless fall along the support-opposition continuum, regardless of differing characteristics and modes of operating. As an illustration, let us suggest very briefly how a military bureaucracy and mass public opinion in a democratic system might be handled within this framework.

Military bureaucracy is hierarchically organized, disciplined, often politically skillful, and armed. In addition, the military comprises a set of instruments that may be employed by the political authority. A mass public, in contrast, is undisciplined and has scattered political skills dispersed throughout it. These political skills are not organized into a coherent force, and a mass public is unarmed or at least not armed with sophisticated weapons. Although a mass public may be mobilized on behalf of a country's politics, it does not represent a cohesive instrument of policy.

Both military bureaucracy and mass public may be loyal and concede legitimacy to the political executive in general or specific terms. On the other hand, both may resist the authority of the political executive by a variety of means. Military officers may refuse to obey orders, threaten to resign and enter the political arena, or they may conduct civil war or engage in a coup d'état—in the extreme. A mass public may demonstrate or vote to remove political leaders from office or—in the extreme—engage in terrorism and conduct a revolution.

The chief executive relates to the various constituencies across the whole spectrum of politics and policy, not simply with regard to foreign policy. Keeping this in mind, our subsequent definitions of constituencies and discussion of relationships between political executives and constituencies will nevertheless stress a foreign policy orientation.

Political elites comprise the first category of constituency to be defined. Political elites are those persons who occupy authoritative positions and governing roles and whose source of authority rests partly on a legitimizing constituency. In functional terms, political elites are those persons who perform rule-making functions. Their decisions are taken on behalf of the society they represent as a whole. Recruitment into political elites varies by the type of political system, although stable systems—whether democratic or authoritarian—tend to recruit through political parties. One party monopolizes the recruitment process in authoritarian states, while competing parties share the recruitment function in democratic states. In unstable political systems, political elites may emerge through less specialized channels, the military being only the most prominent. Political elites include cabinet ministers and other members of parliament in parliamentary systems, legislators in presidential systems, and functional equivalents in authoritarian systems.

The second category of constituency which interests us as foreign policy analysts is *bureaucracy*. Bureaucracies are composed of persons recruited on the basis of their specialized skills to perform rule-application functions. Their positions do not rest on a legitimizing constituency but rather on power derived from the regime as a whole and on their qualifications. In less developed political systems, members of the bureaucracy may serve at the pleasure of the incumbent political elite, while in more developed systems, the bureaucracy is more secure and continuous. The development of large and specialized bureaucracies has the effect of creating independent modes of thought and different standards from political elites. The result is that, despite the theoretical subordination of the bureaucracy to political control, bureaucracies develop their own interests.

This has led in highly developed systems to the creation of bureaucracies in the direct service of the chief executive to assist its control of the large general bureaucracy. An example is the National Security Council staff in the United States.

The third category of constituency is *mass public and other nongovernmental actors*. This constituency performs legitimizing and interest-articulation functions, but it also provides the instruments for mobilization on behalf of political system goals. For some purposes, it will be useful to distinguish between interest groups and the mass public. This would be particularly true in doing case studies of certain issues and in the detailed examination of particular countries. In this general analysis, however, we can treat the mass public and interest groups as a single category of constituency of the chief executive.

The chief executive faces the problem of relating to each of the three categories of constituencies, building and retaining legitimacy, inspiring them to follow him, and conceptualizing obtainable goals which gain the support of constituencies. Each category of constituency in any type of political system has—assuming differential risk factors and levels of probability of success—some choice in conceding legitimacy to or resisting the authority of the chief executive. These relationships between the chief executive and the three categories of constituencies co-vary by the characteristics and actions of the chief executive, on the one hand, and by the characteristics and actions of the constituencies, on the other. One can hypothesize that significant differences may be found among the four types of political executive systems in terms of each of the three categories of constituencies.

In each of the twelve sets of relationships, one can further hypothesize, there is a political process which characterizes it under normal conditions. These characteristics are shown in figure 16.

FIGURE 16
Political Process Characteristics of Relationships between
Chief Executives and Constituencies under
Normal Conditions

POLITICAL EXECUTIVE SYSTEM TYPE	CONSTITUENCIES		
	political elites	bureaucracies	mass public and other nongovernmental
presidential	public bargaining	competitive	egalitarian
parliamentary	private bargaining	supportive	deferential
dictatorship	submission/repression	submissive	acquiescent
junta	elite struggle	factionalized	apathetic

Treating Britain and the United States, Richard Neustadt has suggested that the decision-making process in the two countries is essentially similar even though it appears to be different.[14] What does remain different is the style of bargaining—public versus private—that makes the process appear to be quite dissimilar in the two countries. This difference in the bargaining style of the United States and Britain is

---

14. In ibid. under the title, "White House and Whitehall," abridged from *The Public Interest* 2 (1966).

reflected in figure 16 and applied to the relationships between the chief executive and the political elites in all presidential and parliamentary systems.

In the relationships between the chief executive and the political elite, the chief executive shares the rule-making function with others regardless of the type of system. Thus, the differences are not absolute but rather represent different ways of conducting the relationships. Moreover, the differences described are not watertight compartments; they simply suggest the different tendencies in dissimilar political structures.

Democratic systems are characterized by bargaining among political elites, but the institutional differences between presidential and parliamentary systems lead to contrasting ways of conducting the bargaining. The bargaining must be conducted because the political elite members represent their own constituencies which have a claim to a voice in policy making. The separation of powers in the presidential system tends to bring this bargaining into the public arena, whereas the cabinet system tends to conceal the bargaining that occurs. There is some private bargaining in the presidential system, and there is some public bargaining in the parliamentary system—particularly between the government and the opposition—but the different methods of conducting relations between the chief executive and the political elite in the two systems are characteristic.

Authoritarian systems include bargaining too, but they have the additional feature of a lack of stable succession. Therefore, bargaining over policies includes an element of struggle over positions of leadership. Although such considerations are not unknown to democratic systems, they are characteristic of authoritarian systems. Dictators are in a better position to enforce their will upon the political elite, and in the extreme case such as Stalin's regime the political elites either submit to the dictator's will or are repressed. In any dictatorship, it is characteristic for the political elite to defer and submit rather than challenge as the political elite in a democratic system does. The struggle for position in a collective authoritarian system is more pronounced than in a dictatorship. Although one person is generally more powerful than the other members of the junta, his position is not so secure as that of the dictator, and he will attempt to make his position increasingly secure until he is a dictator while his colleagues will attempt to replace him. There are many different ways of resolving such a struggle, but it is a feature of juntas and makes the formation of coherent policy difficult.

The relationships of the political executive and bureaucracies also vary by type of political system. As the rule-application agencies, bureaucracies are important tools for the political executive. In mobilized modern systems, they are also involved in at least the preparation for the rule-making function, despite the fact that they are not in a political sense responsible or accountable for this latter function. Their impact on both functions varies with both size and specialization. For example, there will be variation in the role that a bureaucracy with a large military composition plays and the role that a bureaucracy with a small military component plays.

In a presidential system, the bureaucracy tends to be more competitive with the chief executive while the bureaucracy in a parliamentary system is more deferential. There is more of a tendency for a presidential system bureaucracy to develop independent goals and to use competitive techniques such as leaks to the press. In part, this stems from the institutional arrangements through which the political elites operate. In the United States, for example, members of Congress may gain information and allies in parts of the bureaucracy to be used in bargaining with the president. Bureaucrats similarly may find spokesmen in Congress for their interests. The bureaucracy in a parliamentary system may sometimes compete with the chief executive, but the relations are more characteristically deferential. Again in part, the institutional arrangement whereby the bureau has an official spokesman in the cabinet usually obviates the necessity of seeking other spokesmen among the political elite.

Authoritarian bureaucracies also reflect the political elite structures. Without an electoral base of support, political elites in authoritarian systems often have their constituencies in segments of the bureaucracy. In the Soviet Union, for example, political elites represent and have their bases of political support in the party, the army, and the managerial elite. Consequently, to the extent that political elites in a dictatorship are submissive, so is the bureaucracy. And, to the extent that there is a lack of coherence and struggle for power in a junta, so these same characteristics are features of the bureaucracy in a collective authoritarian system.

Finally, the chief executive has relationships with the mass public and intermediary interest groups. The most important variables affecting these relationships are the political and economic development of society and the mass political culture, but they also vary by type of regime. Lack of education and skills, income, participation and penetration, and other features of development affect the relationships of leaders and masses, but they also tend to produce more authoritarian regimes, as the recent history of the underdeveloped countries testifies.

In mobilized democratic systems, the mass public and the chief executive have more egalitarian relationships in presidential systems whereas the mass public is more deferential in parliamentary systems. These characteristics reflect the more direct electoral linkage between a president and the electorate as contrasted with the more indirect relationship between a prime minister and his country's electorate. Insofar as a party in a parliamentary system is electorally dependent upon the party leader (a growing tendency), the relationship with the mass public may come more to resemble that of a presidential system.

Authoritarian systems, in which mass publics do not have the political rights and opportunities of democratic systems, are characterized by acquiescent and apathetic mass publics in dictatorships and juntas, respectively. Mass publics in a dictatorship give support and legitimacy to the regime but do not have the means to articulate demands upon it. Their relationship to the chief executive is one of acquiescence. In junta regimes, the factional struggles lead mass publics to apathy rather than acquiescent support. There are not generally opportunities for articulation of demands, but neither is there the security which allows positive support for coherent elites. During times when collective elites are stable and coherent, of course, the mass public may give acquiescent support.

As indicated, these relationships vary by different characteristics of constituencies and by the actions of both leaders and led. There are substantial variations within categories, and there are transformations from one type of political system to another or from one kind of chief executive system type to another. What this analysis of relationships does is not to specify exact relationships but rather to suggest normal characteristics of the political process under different types of systems.

These chief executive-constituency relationships can now be related to the three kinds of acts comprising the conduct of foreign policy.[15] The three kinds of acts, which will be examined more fully in the next three chapters, are (1) the making of decisions, (2) the execution and implementation of policy, and (3) the mobilization of resources. These three kinds of acts tend to fall largely into the three pairs of relationships between the chief executive and his three categories of constituencies. Acts do not fall exclusively into these patterns, but the patterns appear to predominate.

Decisions generally involve chief executive-political elite relationships. Execution and implementation generally involve chief executive-bureaucratic relationships. Mobilization of resources largely involves chief ex-

---

15. Although the ensuing analysis does not draw directly on his work, it has been inspired by the mode of thought of Theodore J. Lowi. See his *The End of Liberalism* (New York: W. W. Norton & Company, 1969), particularly chapter 6.

ecutive-mass public and other nongovernmental actor relationships. There are some exceptions to these patterns. For example, when a president or a prime minister attends a summit conference, he is executing policy. Bureaucracies, to cite another type of exception, are involved in the formulation of policy and help to shape decisions even though they are not responsible. However, this analysis is consistent with functional analysis and with theories of governmental accountability particularly in democracies. Political elites perform the rule-making function, and bureaucracies perform the rule-application function. In democratic countries, it is the political elite which is held accountable for decisions.[16]

Moreover, when a type of act falls outside the relationship associated with it, we often think of it as improper. Perhaps the most obvious example of this is the criticism of the military-industrial complex in the United States based on the fear that part of the bureaucratic and part of the nongovernmental actor constituencies combine to exert undue influence in decision making. It also seems true that when an appropriate relationship is not fulfilled we often think of that as improper. The obvious example of this phenomenon is the Johnson "credibility gap" in which critics held that the president did not appropriately perform his functions in his relationships with the mass public.

These relationships and the three kinds of foreign policy acts with which they are associated will be elaborated in the next three chapters. One chapter is devoted to each kind of act.

Unstable Determinants

The discussion of political culture earlier in this chapter pointed out that there are substantial difficulties in separating stable and longer term attitudes, fears, perceptions, and similar psychological factors from more unstable and shorter term factors. The difficulty is exacerbated by the dynamic nature of attitudes and by our inability to discriminate between permanent and ephemeral changes in attitudes.

From the unification of Germany and the Franco-Prussian War in 1870 until well after the end of World War II, the French feared Germany and were very concerned to protect their security against their eastern neighbor. With the development of western European integration and the division of Germany, this French fear seems to have

---

16. See the excellent discussion of this issue by Stephen D. Krasner, in "Are Bureaucracies Important? (Or Allison Wonderland)," *Foreign Policy*, number 7 (Summer 1972).

diminished. Should the integration movement be reversed and should Germany be reunited, however, the French fear might be revived. In retrospect, one could view cyclical shifts such as this as relatively stable phenomena, but they are difficult to predict and appear from the present to be fairly unstable attitudes.

There are psychological phenomena, however, which seem more assuredly to be unstable. These are the unpredictable emotional factors which may affect elites, bureaucracies, and masses and their relationships. The emotional outbursts of a dictator or the anger of a president can have a substantial impact on foreign policy decisions, yet such phenomena are very short term and unstable. In August 1972, General Idi Amin, the President of Uganda, announced that God had revealed to him in a dream his duty to expel most Asians who held British passports from his country. The presence of large numbers of Asians in a country whose regime was intent on Africanization of all aspects of its political and economic life as well as the fact that many of them held British passports would lead one to predict a certain problem that would one day have to be resolved. The suddenness and the form of this particular decision was fired not by these more stable factors but by the unstable factor of General Amin's dreams, or—if one should not wish to take him literally—his arbitrary personality.

The incidence of such phenomena among chief executives whose decisions affect many people is more apparent than their occurrence among others. Short-term attitudes and emotional responses, however, affect everyone. Just as President DeGaulle could stake his tenure in office on the outcome of a referendum that was seemingly irrelevant to that question, so major segments of the French electorate could respond by voting against him or by abstaining.

Great shifts in mass attitudes can occur in a relatively short period of time. It appears that some three million voters in the United States shifted to President Eisenhower in the course of the week following the Israeli-British-French invasion of Egypt in 1956. A massive shift in attitudes occurred among elites, the bureaucracy, and the mass public in the United States in the wake of the North Vietnamese Tet offensive in early 1968.

In addition to these short-term attitudes, there are other unstable determinants. Political assassinations occur which can have remarkable consequences as did the infamous Sarajevo assassination in 1914. Sudden illnesses of elites as well as fortuitous phenomena such as the physical location of a leader at a critical time can also have broad consequences. The possibilities of an accident or the unauthorized use of nuclear weapons is another easily conceivable unstable determinant.

It is not possible to catalog the entire range of psychological, accidental, and fortuitous phenomena which have the potential for significantly affecting foreign policy. Any analysis of foreign policy which did not include the category of unstable determinants would, nevertheless, be incomplete.

Although the accidental and the fortuitous are included in the category of unstable determinants, the psychological factors are not necessarily accidental or fortuitous. They are to some extent manipulable. It is not uncommon for political elites to manipulate mass short-term attitudes. During periods when regimes lack legitimacy and the capability of solving internal problems, the political elite may call attention to a real problem or may manufacture a problem in the external environment to draw mass attention away from domestic problems.

Conclusion

The political life of a country is shaped by many forces. Although the complexity of factors has not been underestimated, neither has it been possible to simplify this political life as it shapes the way in which countries cope with their external environments. What has been suggested is that the capacities and predispositions as well as the specific foreign policies of countries are shaped by many domestic determinants.

The characteristics and resources of a country shape both capacity and predisposition. Different countries respond to their environments differently because of their background, experiences, ideas, and affections which the notion of political culture tries to capture. Although the features of political culture seem to be relatively permanent, there are also related expressions of a psychological nature that are more unstable and ephemeral. These plus the other unstable factors of accident and fortune help us to understand foreign policy but not to predict it.

It has also been suggested that the nature of political systems and regimes varies among countries and that the political process associated with the differences has an impact on foreign policy. The next three chapters are an elaboration on the three kinds of foreign policy acts and an expanded discussion of the relationships among the political components and constituencies which are involved in the political process.

III

Acts

7

Decisions

Policy decisions involve the selection of objectives from among alternatives and the selection of means to be used in the pursuit of those objectives. Although means are always limited, countries with more complex means available have more opportunities for choice. In a sense, then, the means determine the ends which may be sought.

Any time that an appropriate authority feels a need to make a choice is an occasion for making a decision. If the choice involves making a determination that certain means are worth using to achieve the selected objective, there is an occasion for a policy decision. Some decisions involve making a conscious choice that the objectives desired are not worth making sacrifices for. That too is a policy decision, albeit a negative one.

Classification of Decisions

Decisions may be classified along two dimensions: stage and dynamics. The dimension of stage refers to two types of decisions: basic and sequential. A *basic decision* is one which involves the choice of new objectives. These are fundamental decisions which may inaugurate a new policy, reverse a previously established policy, or respond to a new situation in the environment. Basic decisions are normally made by political elites exclusively. They set into motion new processes. They are the equivalent, in the foreign policy field, to major pieces of legislation in the domestic policy field. Examples of basic decisions are decisions to go to war, to begin new programs such as the Marshall Plan, to enter disarmament negotiations, to reconstruct a war-torn country, or to respond in a certain way to an international crisis.

Basic decisions provide the context for *sequential decisions*. Sequential decisions are those that follow from basic decisions. A basic decision to go to war, for example, involves making decisions about diplomatic maneuvers to gain support or to neutralize critics. It involves logistical decisions, and it involves battlefield decisions. As the war progresses, there is an immense number of tactical decisions that must be made. Invasion routes must be chosen, and experiences often recommend changes in methods.

Although it is sometimes difficult to know exactly where to distinguish between a basic and sequential decision, the general concept is still a useful one. It is difficult to distinguish because some sequential decisions, in turn, become basic ones. For example, in World War II, the decision of the United States to go to war against Germany was clearly a basic decision. The decision to invade through northern France, in the context of the previous basic decision to fight Germany, was sequential. But the decision to invade northern France was basic to a series of sequential decisions that had to be made to implement the invasion.

One can say, however, that basic decisions are always made at very high levels of the political elite and involve the chief executive. Lower levels of both political and bureaucratic elites only make sequential decisions, never basic ones. The higher levels, however, make both basic and sequential decisions. Depending upon the sort of problem which we wish to analyze, basic decisions can sometimes be treated as sequential ones. However, the distinction is worthwhile because basic decisions set the boundaries for sequential decision making. The most important decisions are basic.

Basic decisions not only provide a set of boundaries for sequential decisions, they also set into motion processes that provide momentum. Sequential decisions must somehow be perceived as consistent with basic decisions. Many people become psychologically and materially committed to the course of action implied by the basic decision. The burden for change or reversal is on those who want it and who must demonstrate that the costs of innovation are less than the investment in the given policy. This phenomenon of momentum also inhibits abrupt changes by policy makers who wish to capitalize on opportunities by actions that appear to be inconsistent with the basic decision. Because more people are involved in the active support of policies in democracies than in authoritarian political systems, the momentum is more difficult to reverse by the action of the political elite alone.[1] Moreover, highly mobilized systems tend to be more ponderous than less mobilized systems for the same reason.[2]

In classifying decisions along the dynamics dimension, three categories will be used: initiative, response, and drift. *Initiative decisions* are those which inaugurate actions in the international system. Initiative decisions originate through internally determined processes. We can say that initiatives cause movement in the international system. Although the policy makers of a given country perceive their environment and identify opportunities, nothing in the international environment causes them to make the policy selection to begin or inaugurate a new process. Hitler's decision to invade Poland and Khrushchev's diplomatic notes on Berlin in November 1958 were initiative decisions. They can be explained exclusively in terms of domestic determinants and internal processes.

Response decisions are taken in reaction to events outside a given country. When events occur in the external environment that, when apprehended by the decisional elites of a given country, induce feelings of need for decision, the decision makers respond by taking decisions with respect to the situation in question. Whereas initiative decisions affect actions and tend to be basic, response decisions may be either basic or sequential. When, in August 1971, the United States government announced a set of new policies including a surcharge on imported goods and a change in the price of gold to improve its balance of trade and to stabilize the American economy, trading partners were faced with the necessity to respond. For Japan, the United States' economic initiative plus the visit of President Nixon to China induced feelings of a need to review the most fundamental premises of Japanese foreign policy.

Drift decisions are those which, upon reconsideration of alternatives, reiterate previously made decisions. These also may be either basic or

---

1. This point has been made, among others, by George F. Kennan in his *American Diplomacy*, 1900–1950 (New York: The New American Library, 1952).

2. See Karl W. Deutsch and Richard L. Merritt, "Effects of Events on National and International Images," in *International Behavior: A Social-Psychological Analysis* ed. Herbert C. Kelman (New York: Holt, Rinehart and Winston, 1965).

sequential, but differ from initiative and response in that no new processes are set in motion. Drift decisions, on the other hand, may give impetus to processes within a state representing the efforts of those who wish to change the direction of policy. For example, continuing efforts were made over a period of years in the late 1960s and early 1970s in the United States Senate to reduce the size of American troop deployment in western Europe. The failure to get a decision to reduce the size, however, did not stop those promoting change. Instead, those advocating change continued to pick up votes and were thus encouraged to continue their efforts.

Internal Pressures for Decisions

Although occasions for decision are defined as any time that appropriate authorities feel a need to make a decision, there are many factors at work in the foreign policy process which may press that felt need upon the decision makers. Decisional occasions always represent an opportunity for change, and every kind of decision except drift decisions is a choice on behalf of change. Therefore, one can relate the various factors that press for decisions to the channels of change that were outlined in chapter 1.

There are four such channels or means of change: personnel change, perceptual and goal changes in authorities, a shift in the political coalition which dominates a given policy-making process, and new governmental structures. In discussing the factors which work for change within these channels, a differentiation will be made between those that are internally determined and those that are externally determined, remembering also that initiative decisions can only come from internal factors and that response decisions are prompted by external factors. Drift decisions, being reiterations rather than changes, may result from either or both sets of factors.

Felt needs for decisions may be generated by the individual personality of an elite member, but this is unlikely in a complex organization like the modern state. The role of an elite member in decision-making is more like that of the judge who hears arguments and chooses from among them rather than the kind of process one associates with the autonomous individual.[3] The more complex the state and its foreign affairs business, the less one is likely to find self-generated felt needs for foreign policy decisions. Still, the personality component is apparent in

---

3. See Dean Acheson, "Thoughts About Thought in High Places," in Andrew M. Scott and Raymond H. Dawson, *Readings in the Making of American Foreign Policy* (New York: The Macmillan Company, 1965).

electoral campaigns in a democracy and in the accession of new leaders in authoritarian systems. The individual personality interacts with other variables, and it is difficult to separate this factor from others. On the whole, however, the individual personality appears to shape the way in which decisions are made and the style of interaction with other persons who share in the process, rather than generating felt needs to make a decision.[4]

We cannot expect that reverses of basic decisions will occur through autonomous processes. It is even unlikely that, having committed a country to a basic course of action, top level decision makers will autonomously change. Reversals come only in response to drastic changes in either the domestic or the international environment. Even in pursuing a policy that is failing, it is unlikely that the perceptions and goals of given decision makers will change sufficiently to abandon the policy. Much more likely is a change of personnel or of the dominant coalition governing that particular aspect of policy. Perceptions and goals do change over time, but abrupt changes are most unlikely.

To be discussed is a large number of factors that operate internally and which cause pressures to be exerted on behalf of decisions. These will be treated in random order of importance. It is impossible to specify that a particular factor works only through one of the channels, for often factors will affect all channels, although perhaps one more than another and one more directly or more immediately than another.

In modern states, technological innovation and improvement are constant factors at work. Innovation does not occur at a fixed rate, but there are continuous pressures for development of new machines, new techniques, new organizational arrangements, and new applications. When innovation does occur, it is very often communicated to elites and a pressure is created for incorporating the innovation into the country's foreign policy. In the highly technological society, research is sponsored by bureaucratic agencies whose purpose is to search and find technical innovations that may be used in foreign policy. This is particularly true of military bureaucracies, who sponsor both pure and applied research where they contract for a technical innovation which will meet certain specifications. These specifications have been developed because they are needed to achieve a particular military mission.

---

4. For a good analysis of the role that individual personality plays in decision-making, see Joseph de Rivera, *The Psychological Dimension of Foreign Policy* (Columbus, Ohio: Charles E. Merrill Publishing Company, 1968), chapters 4 and 5. An intriguing case study of the impact of the individual personality on decision making is Alexander L. and Juliette L. George, *Woodrow Wilson and Colonel House: A Personality Study* (New York: Dover Publications, Inc., 1956).

Except under extreme conditions of wartime secrecy, in a democratic country, technological innovations are processed through a bureaucracy and come before the legislature in the form of budget requests. They then pass through a legislative process and may be adopted by the legislature's authorizing appropriations. In nondemocratic countries, a similar process occurs except that it is handled with secrecy and cannot be researched so easily. Nevertheless, in both types of countries, technological innovations and improvements are a constant factor which creates pressures for decisions.

Technology is one form of ideas. There are other forms, and these too are factors which create pressures for decisions. New ideas may be generated by bureaucracies as they process information and think about problems. They may also be generated by legislators, journalists, academics, interest group elites, and other members of societies who take an interest in foreign policy. There are specialized agencies in some countries whose mission is described as the generation of analyses and ideas with respect to foreign affairs. The agencies may be within or without bureaucracies. The Department of State in the United States, for example, has its Bureau of Intelligence and Research and the Policy Planning Council. The staff of the National Security Council is also charged with the task of generating new ideas. Outside the bureaucracy are such agencies as the Rand Corporation, the Hudson Institute, and the Institute for Defense Analysis. The concept of deterrence and related ideas which became official policy in the United States, for example, originated in the Rand Corporation.

Another factor that presses for foreign policy decisions that is related to ideas is revolutionary ideology. When a revolutionary regime comes to power—as in Russia in 1917, in China in 1949, in Cuba in 1959—there is a logic to its ideology, a momentum in revolutionary accomplishment, and a high value of rectitude that presses for the implementation of the revolution beyond the domain where it has gained its initial success. The revolutionary fervor itself does not automatically bring about expansion, but it does create a pressure for decisions. The political elite may process the pressures for decision and choose to expand. It can do so under two conditions.

The first condition is when it believes that spreading of the revolution is necessary to gain the support of elements of its constituency. The second condition is when the political elite has gained sufficient legitimacy in its own country to feel that it can engage in foreign adventures with some chance of success. The point at which the elite feels confident enough to expand is difficult to pin down. The elite may even decide to expand in order to gain further support of its people. That is, it may engage in foreign activities in order to solve internal problems. It cannot do this, however, without a certain measure of legitimacy and without command of the country's resources.

A more general phenomenon that leads to pressure for decisions is that decisional systems—whether individuals or large organizations—are information-processing entities. As information flows, it is incorporated into the conceptual constructs that the system maintains. Several consequences flow from the processing of information, all related to the question of how well new information fits into the conceptual framework.

New information can lead to dissatisfaction with present policy in two directions: failure and success. Perceptions of failure lead to searches for modifications and revisions of policy. If it is very adaptable, a given elite may alter policy along new lines. Depending upon how the problem is perceived, the elite may make major changes in the policy, thus making basic decisions. Alternatively, it may make minor modifications, or sequential decisions. The elite's perceptions and fears determine whether basic or sequential decisions are made. If the elite is less adaptable, a struggle to gain dominance over it or to replace it will be inaugurated by alternative leaders. By either of these means, policy changes of this nature will always be defined in terms of the previous policy. Thus, policies of engagement which are perceived to be failing will lead to reactions in favor of policies of insulation and vice versa, if the struggle is over basic decisions. If the struggle is over sequential decisions, there will be an attempt to deemphasize that aspect of the policy which is perceived to be failing.

Dissatisfaction with policy can proceed from success as well as failure. Dissatisfaction may arise because new information leads some segment of the elite to apprehend that more can be achieved than was previously thought possible. When new higher goals are perceived as capable of being accomplished, there tends to be dissatisfaction with given goals, and there is a pressure created for decisions to adopt the new goals as policy.

Related to this are newly perceived opportunities in situations where a policy is successful. Having achieved lesser goals, an elite may perceive that there is more to be gained in a given situation than was originally thought possible, or the experience of successfully accomplishing certain goals may bring to light opportunities that were not previously seen. In either case, success—particularly easy success—creates pressures for new decisions to take advantage of the opportunities provided by that success.[5] Once again, this does not mean that there is any kind of automaticity to this phenomenon, but a pressure for choice is generated.

Information processing also sometimes leads to the identification of new problems. When these new problems are apprehended, there is another pressure for decision.

Changes in regime usually bring pressures for decision. There is usually some change, although on the whole continuities of policy are more impressive and more common, particularly in stable democratic countries. Where there is no constitutional provision for succession, there is a greater possibility for change after a time has elapsed in which the new regime gains legitimacy. The very act of conducting an election or of otherwise seeking power creates pressures for justification. Justifications then create pressures for implementing programs. Most often, these are related to domestic rather than foreign policy questions, but often enough foreign policy is part of the program of an alternative elite's attempt to gain power.[6]

In the long run, even domestic programs may create pressures for foreign policy decisions. In an underdeveloped country, for example, an alternative elite may come to power on the justification of providing better leadership in the country's modernization program. This, in turn, leads to a search for means of modernizing which entails finding donors of aid, a foreign policy undertaking. The solution of the Nazis to Germany's unemployment problem led to the building of an armaments industry which, to be used, required the creation of a large army. This in turn required an ethic which was embodied in the master race and pan-German conceptions. All of this process led to pressures for decisions on behalf of German expansion.

In addition to these various factors which create pressures for decision, there are relatively routine factors which similarly create pressures. One of these is standard reviews that are conducted by bureaucracies and highly organized political elites. A special case of a standard review is the budgetary process which, in addition to being an instrument of control for a political elite, creates its own pressures for decisions. Although not quite routine, speeches create pressures for decision. State holidays, political campaigns, and other "speechifying" occasions create pressures for decision because high-level elites either reiterate old policies or announce new ones on such occasions.

---

5. This appears to have been the case in the Korean war when, in the summer of 1950, the United Nations' successes led to the decision to invade North Korea.

6. See the discussion of the impact of elections on foreign policy by Kenneth N. Waltz, "Electoral Punishment and Foreign Policy Crises," in *Domestic Sources of Foreign Policy*, ed. James Rosenau (New York: The Free Press, 1967).

Decisions 181

Finally, processes of internal disintegration create pressures for decisions, particularly if they are related to foreign policy questions. When some major constituencies become alienated, they create pressures for decision to deal with them and with the problems that appear to be causing the alienation.

Conditions for Decision Making in Response to Internal Pressures

It has now been suggested that there is a variety of factors at work internally in a country that create pressures leading to occasions for decision making. The problem now is to specify the conditions under which internally generated pressures for decision are more and less likely to culminate in actual decisions. To put the problem somewhat differently, the present task is to distinguish between those conditions under which a country will have an active initiative foreign policy; that is, when internal pressures result in the making of basic initiative decisions. One will also wish to specify the conditions under which a country's foreign policy will be dormant.

One hypothesizes that a country will have an active foreign policy, defined as a period in which a relatively large number of basic initiative decisions are made, under conditions of internal integration and of political elite legitimacy and cohesion. Countries will have an inactive foreign policy, defined as a period in which few if any basic initiative decisions are made, under conditions of internal disintegration and of political elite division and weak legitimacy.[7]

When the Chinese entered the period of the Cultural Revolution, for example, they withdrew their ambassadors from around the world and did not take any new initiatives in foreign policy, concentrating rather on internal problems. The Cultural Revolution was characterized by a lack of elite cohesion, and the political life of the country was in a state of disintegration. By 1970, when segments of the elite had been thrown off and the country gained a measure of integration, the Chinese once again dispatched ambassadors around the world and otherwise launched policies of engagement.

The French Fourth Republic provides another example of fragmented political elites, with foreign policy largely conducted by the bureaucracy —which does not make basic decisions—and of disintegration processes at work. Not until the Fifth Republic under General DeGaulle did the political elite secure cohesion and legitimacy; and as the army and other threats to the integration of the society were brought under control, France once again pursued an active foreign policy.

---

7. See footnote 9 in chapter 6.

Before World War II, the United States was unable to have an active foreign policy. The social cohesion necessary to enter and conduct the war were finally induced by the Japanese attack at Pearl Harbor and the German declaration of war against the United States. Subsequently, with major attempts at producing political elite cohesion through the activities associated with bipartisanship, the United States was in a position to be active in the foreign affairs field. Korea and Vietnam produced fragmentations both within political elites and within constituencies which led to less activity. Only after President Nixon reduced the amount of discord in the United States over the Vietnam war by withdrawing American ground combat forces was he able to take a variety of initiatives in foreign policy including his famous trips to Peking and Moscow.

The analysis of these conditions suggests that periods of active foreign policy—the making of basic initiative decisions—are short-lived if not cyclical. This phenomenon points up the importance of the domestic political process and of the relationships of the chief executive to his various constituencies. In order to make basic decisions, he needs to have a minimum level of support by both elite and mass constituencies.

External Pressures for Decisions

This political process is also affected by the actions of other states. Here the external pressures for decision making which result in response decisions, both basic and sequential, will be dealt with. Certain external events create not only pressures but also occasions for decisions. As with the internally determined pressures, there are both more random and more routine types of determinants.

One external factor is the change or collapse of a government. Any change of government in a country with which a given country has relations or which could pose a threat to the given country is an occasion for either reviewing policy or searching for alternatives. If the change comes about through a constitutional succession, the period in which the new political elite seeks power may alert a given country to the kinds of policy questions that it might expect the new elite to open. On the other hand, a change of government in a country in which there is no succession law may be a surprise to other countries, and they must grapple with the policy implications of the new government in a briefer time and without the benefit of advance planning.

In most cases, changes of government do not present new threats or new opportunities to other countries. However, a new regime may occasionally pose a threat, for example, by incarcerating foreign nationals resident in its country. Major powers would respond to such a threat by acting to protect their nationals, sometimes through military intervention. On other occasions, a new regime may appear to be the target of an adversary. In such a case, a major power would act to deprive its adversary of access to the new government or otherwise attempt to prevent its influence from gaining ascendancy. What might be noted here is the fact that new regimes, regardless of their means of obtaining power, do not cause immediate foreign threats because they need some time to consolidate their power. That is not to say that their internal problems may not be foreign policy problems for other countries, but it is to say that they will not immediately project their country's power externally.

The reverse may be true, however. That is, a country which is following a policy of engagement may, under a new regime, almost immediately begin to turn its policies around toward insulation. For allies, as well as direct adversaries, this can have consequences for decision making in order to adapt their policies to the changed situation.

Not only do given countries have to be alert to possible threats from a new government, but they may also be confronted with new opportunities provided by that government. If the new government seeks to change alignments or otherwise alter its relations with other countries, then previously excluded or disadvantaged countries may find opportunities that did not previously exist. Such circumstances provide occasions for decisions where opportunities for new engagements are present. Following the 1965 coup in Indonesia, for example, opportunities were presented to the United States which had not existed before.

There are related circumstances where opportunities and threats create pressures for decisions. These are when political vacuums are created through the collapse of a government's regime over all or part of its domain. In an area where larger powers are interested, this kind of situation creates fears in those larger powers that their adversaries will gain an advantage. Consequently, they are subject to pressure to make decisions, sometimes to intervene, as when the United States intervened in Lebanon in 1958.

Another set of factors which create pressures for decisions are the initiatives of other governments. Such initiatives may be unilateral acts, such as the invasion of a country or diplomatic initiatives which call for the alteration of some status quo. Interested governments in these cases are pressured to make decisions which will give them responses to the initiatives.

When such actions represent a perceived threat, induce a sense of urgency, and involve risks in responding for a given country, that is a foreign policy crisis. Crises involve somewhat different sets of behavior than non-crises.[8] Decision-making routines are bypassed and high level policy makers develop responses. There is a set of possible responses to crises which may be categorized as immobilism, acceptance, management, restoration, and transformation.

The first category is that of *immobilism*. The initiating act or event may be of such short duration that there is too little time for respondent action. In such a case, the new situation created by the action creates a different crisis with different characteristics from the situation created by the initiating action and immediate response. The seizure of the *Pueblo* in 1968 by North Korea was such a situation in which the respondent state, the United States, was precluded from any response other than immobilism. Having secured the ship and crew, North Korea was in a different relationship with the United States than it had been during the hours in which the seizure was occurring. Immobilism can occur only when the natural time of events is very brief. The natural time of an event is the time in which it will be completed if unopposed. This may be contrasted with critical time, which is a calculation of a point in time preceding the end of the natural time by which a respondent in a crisis must act in order to gain some measure of control over the course of events or to stop the initiating event from being completed.

A closely-related category of response is *acceptance*. Acceptance is allowing events to continue without action by the respondent state. The difference between immobilism and acceptance is twofold. Immobilism is a systemically imposed condition, whereas acceptance is the result of conscious decision. Second, there is a time differential: immobilism occurs only when the natural time of events is very short, but acceptance must occur in a longer duration. The United States' response to the August 1968 Warsaw Pact invasion of Czechoslovakia was an example of acceptance.

The third category—*management*—is the most common type of response. Management means that the respondent state acts to engage in events in such a way as to minimize their deleterious impact upon itself or other states with which it is identified. The essential intent of crisis management is to gain some measure of control over events which, if uncontrolled, would cause some harm to the valuables of the respondent state.

The fourth category is *restoration*. Restoration is to act to restore the status quo existing before the initiating act. When the initiating act

---

8. A good description and analysis of this point is contained in Ole R. Holsti, "Political Processes and Foreign Policy: Decision Making in Crisis and Noncrisis Situations," in *Systems and Actors in International Politics* ed. LeRoy Cramer (Scranton, London, Toronto: Chandler Publishing Company, 1971).

Decisions

is a verbal one, this is a possible response. When the initiating act is of an irrevocable character, restoration is not an alternative.

In all of the preceding four categories, the respondent state remains in the respondent posture and plays what might be called a defensive role in the two-actor situation established by the crisis. The final category represents a departure from this role.

The fifth category is *transformation*. A transformation response is one in which the respondent state acts in such a way as to create a new situation in which it becomes the initiating state and its adversary becomes the respondent state in a new crisis. Such a transformation involves increasing the risks to both actors, but when it can be effected, the original crisis may lead to advantages for the original respondent state that it may not have been able to achieve in the absence of the crisis.

Although the categories listed above are mutually exclusive, it is possible for two types of response to occur simultaneously. In the Cuban missile crisis, the United States responded with restoration insofar as the initial act—the emplacement of Soviet missile launching sites in Cuba—was concerned. Simultaneously, the deployment of ships to enforce a selective blockade was a transformation response because that development was an initiating act directed at Soviet shipping and placed the Soviet Union in the role of respondent state.

Wars and peace settlements also create pressures for decision. However much a given country, by its internal determinants, opts for inaction, crises, wars, peace settlements, and diplomatic initiatives force it to make decisions of the response type. It is the domestic determinants, however, which will shape the type of response that a country will make.

Apart from these more forceful pressures for decision making, there are also many routine pressures. There are meetings of the organizations and alliances that a given country belongs to which need to be prepared for, and the preparation creates pressures for decision. There are also routine reports and diplomatic correspondence that need to be handled, each calling for some kinds of decisions. Many of the routine matters which deal only with sequential decisions may be handled by bureaucracies. It is, of course, one of the tasks of the bureaucracy to alert the political elite of the need for basic or very important sequential decisions.

Another factor which creates pressures for decision is disintegration in the external realm. If a country perceives a threatening process of disintegration occurring in a sphere of control or a more general disintegrating process such as a threat to a balance of power, it will be subject to pressures for decision.

Conditions for Decision Making in Response to External Pressures

We have now to pose the same problem as we did with respect to internally generated pressures for decision. That is, what are the conditions under which externally generated pressures are more or less likely to culminate in actual decisions? Since sequential decisions are, on the whole, handled routinely, our problem is to specify the conditions under which basic response decisions are most likely to be taken.

The hypothesis is that decisions are most likely to result under external conditions of high threat or major opportunity. Diplomatic initiatives, crises, wars, and peace settlements are the most important external determinants. However, the equation has been defined in such a way that these external factors must be joined with internal factors. That is, not only must an opportunity exist in the external environment but it must also be seen as an opportunity by the political elite. The political elite is most likely to perceive an opportunity under conditions in which it has an active foreign policy with the characteristics which were outlined above, that is, elite cohesion and legitimacy.

No external event, by itself, can axiomatically cause a decision to be taken. The external event must be apprehended and perceived in a certain way. The external events themselves create pressures for decision, and on the whole perceptions will be largely influenced by those events (there is an assumption of rational behavior), but the intervening variable of perceptions is crucial.

For example, it is highly unlikely, given attitudes of despair, that a country would perceive opportunities as readily as the same country, given attitudes of confidence. Attitudes of suspicion and fears of an adversary are more likely to make an elite feel threatened by a hostile action of that adversary, and so on. Thus, external events must be joined with unstable domestic determinants to produce decisions in response to those events.

Process of Decision Making

The final problem of this chapter is to analyze the process of decision making in foreign policy.[9] The general characteristics of the process were outlined in the chapter on domestic determinants by noting that

---

9. The literature on decision making is vast, but the seminal work of Richard C. Snyder, Burton Sapin, and H. W. Bruck, *Foreign Policy Decision Making* (New York: The Free Press of Glencoe, 1962) remains as a useful statement of the complexity of the process at work and of the myriad considerations in analyzing decisions.

Decisions

the process of policy formation involved the relationships of the chief executive with other members of the political elite, each of which had the support of some constituency. The task here is to extend and to detail that framework of analysis.

Underlying the discussion of the process of decision-making is the assumption that, like war in the international politics field, revolution is always a possibility in domestic politics. Just as there may be limited wars and hostilities that do not quite deserve the label of wars, there may be limited revolutions, hostilities short of revolution, and demands made upon political leaders which (if they are to remain in power) they must recognize and meet. Political leaders must have followers who believe that the leaders ought to govern, and the major problem of the political leader is to convince those followers—who may have different ideas from his—that he ought to do so. In short, the assumption underlying the following discussion is that of Machiavelli: the prince (political elite and especially the chief executive) must work to retain his power.

The problem is complicated for the political elite because it may have different constituencies, making contradictory demands. The Vietnam war illustrates this problem very well insofar as the United States is concerned. A basic decision was made to commit American troops to the defense of South Vietnam against indigenous guerrillas and North Vietnamese invaders. The decision entailed, for the American political elite, a commitment to the military and large segments of the public constituency to support the military in its mission. Otherwise, the military and large segments of the public would have felt betrayed, with significant problems arising in the direction of revolution. On the other hand, large segments of the public and of the political elite (particularly the Senate), desired American withdrawal from Vietnam, and some segments demanded a major change in American policy from the primacy of foreign policy to the primacy of domestic policy. Added to this most difficult problem were the United States' commitments to its allies and the problem of its very important role in the international system. This case provides, in sharp relief, the outlines of the political elite problem of staying in power and fulfilling the functions of elite leadership and governance.

Most political struggle is not so sharply apprehensible, for the processes at work are not so near to the revolutionary threat. There is more often an acceptance of the authority of the political elite. Nevertheless, the process of struggle over the making of decisions always involves the kinds of ingredients that we find in the more extreme case. That is, the political elite always has to be concerned with keeping power and authority. The elite does this by attempting to keep control of the bureaucracy, particularly of the military or segments of it (like a secret police) which have the tools for directly challenging the power of the elite, satisfying its various constituencies, and maintaining a ruling coalition of elite members and warding off the challenges of alternative elites.

Although the problem for the chief executive and the political elite is constantly one of control and depends upon the skills, the personalities, and the fortunes of those involved in the process, some identifiable general problems and some circumstances affect the relationships in a predictable way. For example, in a crisis, a small group at the top political elite level tends to retain close control over decision making. Bureaucratic routines are bypassed, and the rational model of decision making is adhered to.[10] In contrast, the bureaucracy is more influential in noncrisis, routine decision making. In addition, certain segments of the bureaucracy tend to be more influential when the problems faced by a country are within the competence of that segment. The obvious illustration of this is the increase in the influence of the military during times of war when the political elite is more dependent upon the military.

This illustration raises another problem. Every time a political elite gives an assignment to a segment of a bureaucracy, it loses some measure of control over the issue within its own political system. This is because in performing the rule application function, the bureaucracy elaborates and expands on the rules that have been made. Although this is a concomitant of using the tools of bureaucracy, it does present some control problems for the political elite. Occasionally, this leads to a major problem of control such as that which developed in the challenge by General McArthur to President Truman in the Korean war.

Moreover, the political elite needs to be concerned with assigning achievable tasks to the bureaucracy, particularly the military. Over time, the frustration of the military can have dire consequences for the regime. The French army is a case in point. Defeated in 1940 at home, in 1954 in Indochina, and losing political support for its role in Algeria in 1958, the frustration of the French army was a major factor in bringing France to the brink of civil war in 1958 and in the demise of the Fourth Republic.

There are other problems and circumstances affecting the control of the political elite over decision making. As countries are more de-

---

10. The assumptions and utilities of this model and other models of decision making are examined in Graham T. Allison, "Conceptual Models and The Cuban Missile Crisis," *The American Political Science Review* 63 (September 1969). The thesis is elaborated by Allison in his, *Essence of Decision: Explaining the Cuban Missile Crisis* (Boston: Little, Brown and Company, 1971).

veloped, they staff bureaucracies with professional personnel. Professionals are more likely to set independent goals—including styles of operation, codes of behavior, self-protection, and certain beliefs or frameworks—from the political elite. Professional foreign services, professional armies, professional intelligence agencies, professional secret police, and so forth are all examples of these.

If there are tendencies in any of the segments of bureaucracy toward independence, this poses a political problem of control for the political elite and can lead to severe complications in the conduct of foreign policy. These complications may occur in two directions. The first is that the independent agency can precipitate situations which will force the political elite to take actions that it otherwise would not have taken: one can call this indirect political power of the bureaucracy over the political elite. The second direction is that the independent position may be used directly to persuade the political elite to make decisions that it otherwise would not in order to retain overall control over the segment of the bureaucracy which is pressuring it. This, one can call direct political power. It needs to be noted here that political elites may also initiate actions to satisfy bureaucratic elites in order to gain control over them, as President DeGaulle did with the French army: in this case the action was in conformity with DeGaulle's purposes. He assigned the military a role in national defense, apart from NATO, thus reintegrating the army into French national life.[11]

The military is a special case of bureaucracy because, controlling the arms and the skills of combat and being organizationally disciplined, it is in a much more powerful position than other segments of the bureaucracy which do not have arms and whose skills and organization are never capable of the same kind of threat that the military can make. Secret police and intelligence agencies pose some of the same problems, but they are neither so common nor so well-armed as to have the same amount of potential power. An additional factor that makes the military so powerful is that the political elite is so dependent upon it for certain actions. Thus, the more the political elite gives tasks to the military which rely exclusively on the military for execution, the more dependent it is upon the military. A final source of military power is that it always contains a high level of organization and may contain a high incidence of political skills which, under certain circumstances, can make it an alternative political elite, with the instruments of coercion that can bring it to power.[12]

---

11. See Edgar S. Furniss, Jr., *DeGaulle and the French Army: An Appraisal of a Civil Military Crisis* (New York: Twentieth Century Fund, 1964).

12. See Morris Janowitz, *The Military in the Political Development of New Nations* (Chicago and London: The University of Chicago Press, 1964).

All the segments of bureaucracy have their own constituencies and can both lead, respond to, and otherwise maintain contact with them. For some bureaucracies, this constituency may be largely the organization itself. For others, there may be a broader constituency. In a modern democratic state, the military may have a very large constituency. In the United States, for example, the military has not only its very large organization but also supporters in Congress, military contractors and workers in military-related industries, veterans' organizations, nationalistic associations, many citizens who have served in the armed forces, and other voters who may be influenced to support the military elite against the political elite on given issues.

Democracies have somewhat different problems with military bureaucracies than do authoritarian states because the military in authoritarian countries has less opportunity to develop outside constituencies. Developed and underdeveloped countries vary in the complexity of constituencies involved in this political process.

Each constituency has different patterns of values, and one may say that the larger and more complex the constituency, the greater mix of values that may be found within the constituency. Since cohesion on values gives strength to a constituency and, by support, to its related elite, smaller numbers can often be a weightier factor than larger numbers, when these are characterized by cleavages within the constituency.

The relations of authority, obligations between elites and supporters, and styles of constituencies vary. Bureaucratic structures are hierarchical, for example, while public opinion is not. Bureaucracies have direct access for aggregated opinion while public opinion's direct access is unaggregated. The timing of participation in debate is different.[13] Public opinion is less reliable and less predictable than other constituencies.[14]

Where the press is free, it intervenes between the political elite and the public and thus is an important factor in the policy process. The press also serves to inform entire bureaucracies about policy questions that are outside the jurisdictions of most segments.[15] The existence of a free press complicates the policy process by giving information to publics that would not otherwise have it, by providing information to everyone

---

13. See Bernard C. Cohen, *The Political Process and Foreign Policy: The Making of the Japanese Peace Settlement* (Princeton: Princeton University Press, 1957).

14. See Gabriel A. Almond, *The American People and Foreign Policy* (New York: Frederick A. Praeger, Publisher, 1960).

15. Bernard C. Cohen, in *The Press and Foreign Policy* (Princeton: Princeton University Press, 1963) makes this point about the "elite" press in Washington.

interested enough to absorb it, and by offering alternative interpretations to those of political elites.

What kinds of actions do constituencies have at their disposal for influencing elites and on what elites can they exert influence? All constituencies have a range of actions for supporting and opposing elites. They can all confer legitimacy on the leadership by obeying laws and orders, as the case may be. Other kinds of support include financial contributions and votes for politicians; press leakages to support bureaucratic elites; withholding information on the part of the press; and log-rolling between, for example, military contractors and military procurement officers. All of the actions of support that can occur in a domestic political system can be taken in the foreign policy process.

On the opposition side, constituencies can question, persuade, publicly debate, refuse to obey or carry out instructions, resist through more positive actions, and violently overthrow their elites. At the milder end of this continuum of actions, we can expect frequent recurrence of such activities. The problem is to specify the conditions under which more positive resistance to elites will occur.

On the whole, one can say that when there is a gap between the expectations which an elite has led a constituency to develop and the fulfillment of those expectations, there will be activities of positive resistance. There will also be positive resistance when the values of segments of constituencies come into great conflict with the values of the elites or when the fears of the actions of the elites become greater than the fears of the objects against which the elites are taking action.

At some point, when the opposing actions of constituencies become sufficiently severe, the political struggle between elites and constituencies becomes a more salient conflict than relations with other countries. This occurred, for example, in Russia in 1917 and led to the withdrawal from the war, and it was one of the phenomena of the Chinese Cultural Revolution.

In order to retain control, then, the political elite must satisfy the constituencies that have power over them. The expression of satisfaction takes place in democracies through elections and in authoritarian systems through the continued approval of the political elite.

This general problem and the processes associated with it cover both domestic and foreign policy. An attempt is made here only to discuss the processes associated with foreign policy, but it will be useful to keep in mind the more general problem of the maintenance of elite power as the essential phenomenon at work.

The many factors—internal and external—which create pressures for decision and the factors which inhibit decision have been discussed. It has also been stated that there are four channels through which the processes of decision making operate, and the assumptions and the general character of the processes have been stated. Let us now discuss the processes of each of the channels.

Change in Personnel

One of the channels is a change in personnel. Personnel changes occur under several conditions. Succession processes—whether elections or political elite struggles where there are no constitutional succession procedures—bring new leaders into office. These are fairly predictable in countries where there is a stable constitutional order. Predictions of change can be made with exact accuracy as to timing in presidential systems and with rough accuracy in parliamentary systems. In systems without legal succession laws, it is much more difficult to predict the timing of change of personnel. The death, whether through natural causes or assassination, of a leader is another mechanism that sets into motion processes that bring new leaders into office. *Coups d'etat* are another.

Changes in the elite may also be made through cabinet shuffles or otherwise bringing new influences into a political elite. On occasion, resignations of segments of a political elite will create the need for new appointments. The more high-level and the more extensive the change, the more pressure for changes in policy.

New personnel bring different expectations about themselves, and their constituencies have different expectations of them than of their predecessors. Therefore, new goals, new perceptions, etc., accompany new personnel into office. The amount of time needed varies with the elite's command of information, the legitimacy conferred by its constituencies, and its own sense of confidence and ability to make decisions. This time period of adjustment of elites provides a unique opportunity for others to attempt to influence them. A discussion of several cases will illustrate this problem.

President Eisenhower was elected largely on the expectation that he would bring peace in Korea. His own and his constituencies' expectations were immediate. A brief time was required, however, for him to grasp the office, but his earlier command responsibilities made this time shorter than a less experienced leader. Within six months after assuming office a truce was negotiated and signed.

When President Kennedy was elected, a segment of the bureaucuracy— the Central Intelligence Agency—was able to influence him to approve the Bay of Pigs invasion which occurred within three months after his inauguration. Despite the advice of political scientist Richard Neustadt, who pointed out the problem of the president's keeping power,[16] President Kennedy decided to give control of this operation to his bureaucracy. He was acutely embarrassed when he decided to keep power by not assigning the U.S. Air Force the mission of giving air support to the Cuban invaders. While this case can be used to demonstrate how a bureaucracy is provided with an opportunity to increase its influence, it should also be noted that the constitutional succession system conferred sufficient security of office on the president that he could make a basic decision without question.

Another example follows which demonstrates that a political leader who is not secure in office is immobilized in his decision making. The example is King Hussein of Jordan whose entire preoccupation in much of the 1960s had to be with maintaining himself in office. His constituencies were his army, his citizens, Palestine refugees, and guerrilla organizations. He also relied upon Egyptian nonintervention in his country and he satisfied his army by obtaining arms from the United States and Great Britain. In such a situation, he could make no basic foreign policy decisions except those which were absolutely necessary to preserve himself from threats to his regime. These were largely those intended to appease Egypt or the guerrillas whose policy demands were directed externally.

In systems which determine succession by a struggle among the political elite, there is an interaction between gaining power and foreign policy decision making. By manipulating the demands of other members of the elite, a single man may rise to the top of the leadership. Such manipulation requires the balancing of the demands of the different members of the elite and their constituencies. For example, Premier Khrushchev of the Soviet Union rose to the top of the Soviet hierarchy by, among other things, gaining international respect by going to summit conferences in 1955 and 1959. He also conceded many of the demands of those who wanted more domestic consumption. In 1957, he gained the support of Marshall Zhukhov, later dismissing him when he was able to gain the support of other members of the elite. Only when he became secure after 1957 could he take basic foreign policy initiatives like the proposals for revision of the status quo in Germany and Berlin. The ability to gain control in such a system depends upon the skill of the leader and his ability to capitalize on the mistakes of others. Although we know little of the actual workings of such systems, the evidence that we do have suggests that the hypothesis that security in office is required

---

16. Neustadt's argument is contained in *Presidential Power: The Politics of Leadership* (New York: John Wiley & Sons, 1960).

to make basic initiatives in foreign policy is confirmed. However, in the struggle for leadership, basic initiatives in foreign policy may be related to gaining power. Although these may be either policies of engagement or of insulation, they are more often the latter.

Change in Policy By Incumbent Elite

The second channel for change is that in which an elite reverses or substantially modifies its previous policies. Once new personnel gain office and the security of office necessary to make basic decisions, they will attempt to implement them. Beyond that, perceptions and goal changes are required to make new decisions. The factors which bring pressures for decision will be at work in any system, although at different rates and in different magnitudes. Changes in perceptions and goals will occur under conditions of new experiences. The extent to which these changes will lead to new decisions depends upon the problem-solving and learning capacities of the political elite. If these are effective, then decisions will be made through this channel. Otherwise one of the other three channels will be used to bring the decisions.

The new experiences which lead to decisions may come from either the environment or from the political system itself. Perceptual and goal changes leading to foreign policy decisions are more likely to be induced by the experiences provided by the external environment than by internal processes. Internal processes are likely to lead to decisions through the other three channels.

Examples of externally induced experiences are threats, attacks, crises, and so forth. The North Korean attack on South Korea, for example, induced such new perceptions and goals in the United States that a large number of decisions that were before thought impossible could be made. Then the experience of success led to changes of goal to include the forceful reunification of Korea.

Some new experiences provided by the domestic political system can sometimes lead to the changes referred to here. For example, internal disintegration and civil war may lead to changes in perceptions that induce new foreign policy decisions. As the example of both the Czarist regime and the liberal democratic regimes in Russia show, however, even extreme internal division including massive desertions of army units in wartime do not necessarily lead to changes in foreign policy decisions. In the case of Russia in 1917, it required structural change in the government and personnel change to bring about basic decisions in foreign policy.

Less profound internal events can lead to change in foreign policy. For example, technological innovation may seem to provide new op-

Decisions 195

portunities. The development of the atomic bomb is one example of this, and the development of an anti-missile system is another. In both these cases, however, it may be argued that these innovations led not to basic decisions but only to sequential ones. In Canada, the Liberal government's apprehension of American business domination of Canada may be cited as a change in perception that could lead to shifts in foreign policy, although the issue is largely a domestic one.

This channel is the one through which constituency influence works. It is highly unlikely, however, that constituency influence can bring about basic changes. The more important facet of constituency influence is in demanding the continuance of policy in the face of contrary demands by alternative constituencies and their elites. Thus, the American Joint Chiefs of Staff influenced policy in the Johnson administration by threatening resignation with its consequent political implications as they would then be in a position to join or lead an alternative elite and appeal to the President's public constituency against him.

The problem for the political elite is one of maintaining a winning coalition. As Riker has explained, this problem is governed by the size principle.[17] The size principle is derived from the theory of n-person, zero-sum games. Riker holds that, in such games, a process of coalition formation occurs which leads to a winning coalition of minimal size. That is, there is a tendency to include only enough members in the coalition to win. Additionally, a winning coalition which exists at any given time will tend to reduce itself to the minimal size necessary for winning. Thus, constituencies other than those which back members of the winning coalition have little influence. Members of the winning coalition have the power to influence the central elite only insofar as they are necessary to the maintenance of the winning coalition. Thus, a political elite would rather slough off a segment of its coalition than accede to its demands unless it is large enough to diminish the coalition to a size smaller than that necessary to winning. Because of this phenomenon, change in basic decisions in foreign policy are more likely to work through one of the other channels.

Dominant Coalition Change

The third channel is that of dominant coalition change. This channel is restricted to political systems which give access to oppositions and it works only under conditions of failure. If there is no access for political oppositions, then there will be an alternative elite struggle. Depending

---

17. See William H. Riker, *The Theory of Political Coalitions* (New Haven and London: Yale University Press, 1962).

upon the type of political system, this struggle may be conducted through elections, through a civil war, or it may be eliminated by a very powerful dictator.

In discussing this channel, one assumes that there are opponents to a given policy who are members of a regime. For present purposes, it does not matter whether these opponents oppose the policy out of conviction or because it offers them an issue which they may use to become dominant. Given the latter motivation, they are more likely to form an alternative elite if that is feasible within the political system.

As a policy is perceived by constituencies to be failing, the opponents have an opportunity to press their own particular leadership. Thus the members of a collective leadership may attempt to gain dominance by persuading the dominant leader to listen to their advice rather than to that of others who are associated with the given policy. One can trace this kind of struggle in Indonesia between the Communists and the army in their attempts to influence Sukarno. Another example is the United States' Senate's struggle with the President for control of foreign affairs in the 1970s. According to some versions, this was the process at work leading to the decision of March 1968 to greatly restrict the bombing of North Vietnam by the United States.

Change in Government Structures

The final channel for decision making is a change in government structures. All governments are subject to changes which influence the making of different decisions in the long run, and it is difficult to separate out the shifts in structure from the shifts in personnel, for personnel changes usually, though not always, accompany structural changes. In treating structural changes within the frame of time reference which this book is largely concerned with, the slow and long-term changes will be taken as constants and concentration will be on more abrupt structural change.

The coming to power of revolutionary movements is the most obvious and dramatic impetus to major structural changes in governments which lead to changes in foreign policy. However, there are lesser changes that occur. A few examples will illustrate.

The structural change that occurred in Egypt from the time when there was a collective leadership of colonels to the emergence of President Nasser as a dictator is one example. Premier Khrushchev's ascendance and downfall marked structural changes in the Soviet government to and from a single dictatorship. The reorganization on two or three occasions of Nigeria's federal system marks another example of structural changes that made a difference in foreign policy decision making. There are lesser changes: for example, when the United States instituted

Decisions 197

the National Security Council, coordination of political and military affairs became more manageable.

Structural changes that are important for foreign policy decision making are those which alter the relationships of segments of elites and those which give direct access to central decision makers to new elites which head new constituencies. These shifts alter the mix of domestic determinants which leads, in turn, to new decisions.

Conclusion

A decision has been defined as the choice to pursue certain goals with certain means. An occasion for decision is when a foreign policy elite feels the need to decide. There is a number of pressures, coming from both the internal and external environments of the policy makers, for decisions. On the other hand, there are factors of inertia which provide pressures for avoiding decisions. The discussion has tried to show that under certain conditions, the pressures for decision will overcome the forces of inertia and decisions will be made.

When referring to these decisions, it has been found useful to make a distinction between basic and sequential decisions, for sequential decisions can be made in the context of dominant inertial pressures, whereas basic decisions are only made under the conditions specified and under the pressures for decisions which have been described. Distinctions have also been made among decisions in terms of initiation, response, and drift.

Decision making, however, is not the only kind of act that foreign policy makers engage in. Unless the means are available or can be generated, it is not possible to implement the decisions. Thus, there is a need to be concerned with a different sort of foreign policy act, the mobilization of resources, a subject to which we now turn.

8

Mobilization of Resources

Means determine the ends that may be sought. The political elite of a country is constrained and facilitated in choosing goals by the resources that are available to them. The resources are not composed of a steady-state fund, however, for the political elite acts to generate and to mobilize the resources which it needs to accomplish its objectives. These resources include human and material capabilities, tangible and intangible components, and quantitative and qualitative factors. Countries vary immensely in the resources at their disposal and in their political will to use them for varying purposes.

As noted in chapter 6, the mobilization of resources involves particularly the relationship between the chief executive and the political elite, on the one hand, and the mass public and nongovernmental groups, on the other. Depending upon the stage of political and economic development and the democratic or authoritarian nature of the political system, there are different patterns of consumption and governmental control over resources. In any society, regardless of the character of regime, there are competing demands upon resources for domestic and foreign policy needs. One of the tasks of the chief executive is to shape and balance these demands.

The resources to be mobilized are developed primarily in the society as a whole and out of the domain which the regime rules. In addition, however, the political elite may gain resources from other countries. Such resources may include foreign troops and *matériel* for foreign policy purposes, capital and technical assistance for economic development purposes, and trade for consumption and development. This category of foreign policy acts, then, does not lend itself to a simple dichotomy of domestic and foreign policy.

Neither does it lend itself to easy distinctions among academic disciplines. The major focus of this discussion will be on the political side, on the leadership associated with developing and mobilizing the resources to conduct foreign policy. The analysis of such resources, however, involves economics; geography; science, technology, and engineering; education; sociology; and psychology. There have been many checklists of the capabilities of countries, and it is not proposed to reproduce them.[1] What will be emphasized are the many ramifications and complications of the type of foreign policy act which is called the mobilization of resources.

The most important resource of a country is its people. The analysis will begin by an examination of the concepts of and the problems associated with loyalty and legitimacy, and a discussion of the variations among countries according to their political development. Then there will be an examination of the distinction between what are here called mobilized instruments and mobilizable resources. Then, under the rubrics of conditions of mobilization and limits on mobilization, the discussion will include attention to the political relationships between the political elite and the mass public and nongovernmental groups.

Legitimacy and Loyalty

In preceding chapters, it has been held that the political elite of a country must enjoy legitimacy and must be able to command the resources of their country in order to conduct an active foreign policy.

---

1. Among the leading analysts of capabilities are Harold and Margaret Sprout, whose works have been cited. See also the work of Klaus Knorr, in particular his *The War Potential of Nations* (Princeton: Princeton University Press, 1963) and *Military Power and Potential* (Lexington, Mass.: D. C. Heath and Company, 1970).

Legitimacy is the right of a regime to exist and of a government to rule. In mobilized modern systems, legitimacy rests on the confidence of elites and on the loyalty of masses. There are other claims to legitimacy in traditional systems, particularly claims based on divine right.

Loyalty is the positive affect of citizens for regimes and governments which leads to a willingness to support the regime and to obey the government. Although individuals have loyalties to primary groups and intervening groups, the loyalty with which we are most concerned is that toward the nation. Conflicts in loyalties are particularly prevalent in premobilized modern systems where modernizing elites are engaged in the process of generating participation in national life in the context of family, village, and tribal loyalties. In mobilized modern systems, loyalty to the nation is the normal state of affairs, and primary and intermediary groups tend to be instrumental in building and reinforcing national loyalties. There is some evidence that in highly mobilized societies there is an increase in the development of loyalties beyond the nation, but the lack of strong objects of loyalty in the international sphere makes this development problematical. Even in western Europe, where the Common Market has developed functioning institutions, the loyalty of the masses is not showing signs of shifting away from the nation to supranational institutions, myths, and symbols.

Analyzing the phenomena of nationalistic loyalty, Kelman argues that loyalty is derived from two sources: instrumental and sentimental sources.[2] That is, people give their loyalty to the nation because it embodies for them the values with which they identify or because it is a means of achieving their values. To put the matter more crudely, people are loyal if the nation conforms to what they cherish or if it gives them what they want. On both grounds, there is an important distinction between premobilized and mobilized political systems.

Highly developed political systems have certain advantages by virtue of the fact that their populations have largely grown up in the context of nationalistic loyalties. They have well-established symbols, myths, and identities. Moreover, most of the institutions of the society exist in the context of the nation and thus reinforce nationalistic loyalties. Certain countries such as Britain, Germany, and Japan are more homogeneous than others such as the Soviet Union, Canada, and Switzerland. In the latter countries, there are particular—as opposed to national—loyalties

---

2. Herbert C. Kelman, "Patterns of Personal Involvement in the National System: A Social-Psychological Analysis of Political Legitimacy," in *Foreign Policy and International Politics*, ed. James N. Rosenau, rev. ed. (New York: The Free Press, 1969).

that do not completely reinforce nationalism. Nevertheless, these countries accommodate in various ways to the particular loyalties, and, through both domestic and foreign policies, usually retain the national loyalties of their citizens.

Particularistic loyalties in premobilized systems, on the other hand, tend to be characteristic. In India, for example, there are very strong loyalties to language, a condition which has made it impossible so far to implement a single language policy as a tool of national integration and as a means for conducting national business. The strength of particularistic loyalties was demonstrated in Nigeria when the Ibo Tribe (which could as well be called a nation) seceded under the name of Biafra. Fear of similar secessions in other countries led the political elites of most other African countries to support Nigeria rather than Biafra. Pye has explained the difficulties of this problem even for political elites in his study of Burma.[3]

There arise in some premobilized systems personalities who command the loyalty of the masses. This may be a substitute for national loyalty, but because individuals are more ephemeral than national institutions and symbols, such loyalties are necessarily unstable. Thus, Indira Gandhi in India was able to mobilize the support of the Indian people on behalf of her policies with respect to Bangladesh, but it is not certain that another Indian leader could have done the same. The disappearance from the scene of such leaders as Nkrumah, Sukarno, and Sihanouk illustrate the point. The imminent passing of Tito raises the same problem. The successors to these charismatic leaders do not have the established base of sentimental loyalty to the nation to draw on that successive leaders in mobilized systems have.

Mobilized and premobilized systems may similarly be differentiated on the basis of instrumental sources of loyalty. In mobilized systems there are many more roles in which citizens participate which are a function of the nation. From more extensive bureaucracies and mass armies to interest groups and political parties to ordinary citizen roles, the mobilized system provides livelihood for many citizens and important segments of their lives for others. Moreover, the mobilized system provides more services and supports to its citizens than does the premobilized system. Thus, the mobilized political system is important to the achievement of the goals of its citizens. Moreover, as systems develop, the citizens make more demands upon it, thus reinforcing the process of building loyalty on an instrumental base. The corollary of

---

3. Lucian W. Pye, *Politics, Personality, and Nation-Building: Burma's Search for Identity* (New Haven and London: Yale University Press, 1962).

this process, of course, is that if the system is unable to satisfy the expectations of its citizens, the result may be political instability and possibly revolution.[4]

In premobilized systems, not only are there fewer roles to provide the instrumental source of loyalty, but also the expectations of those citizens who do participate in the political system tend to outrun the capacity of the system to fulfill them. Moreover, there is a lack of institutionalized means of succession and policy making, of a tradition of a loyal opposition which can criticize the government of the day in the context of loyalty to the regime, and of sufficient roles for alternative elites. This leads to a great deal of political instability and a lack of instrumental loyalty. Regardless of their own confidence in themselves, the leaders of premobilized systems cannot normally rely on the loyalty of their masses to concede legitimacy to them. In addition, they cannot normally rely on the basic loyalty of their masses as a foundation for the mobilization of resources to achieve political system goals.

Foreign policy for premobilized modern systems, then, very often consists largely of mobilizing resources within and without to solve the more basic problems of nation building. For example, all of the new countries which have become independent in the post–1945 period have sought membership in the United Nations. Such membership confers status on the new state which helps to build nationalism at home. The new states also seek economic and technical assistance from abroad to modernize the economic and other aspects of their societies. Such modernization builds the foundations for both sentimental and instrumental loyalties. It also provides increasing capacity to determine internal affairs, reducing the influence of other countries. This is not the exclusive thrust of policy of these countries, but it is an important one.

What is suggested by this discussion—most starkly in the case of premobilized systems but also apparent in mobilized systems—is that loyalty and legitimacy are the foundation for mobilizing the resources of a country. In addition, these concepts are the basis for understanding the relationships of the chief executive and the political elite with the mass public and nongovernmental groups. The masses place demands on the system which must be met by the elite, and the elite not only tries to meet those demands but also helps to shape them and attempts to build support through both the sentimental and the instrumental sources of loyalty. More scope is given for demands in democratic sys-

---

4. For an excellent analysis of political violence and an explanation based on a theory of relative deprivation, see Ted Robert Gurr, *Why Men Rebel* (Princeton: Princeton University Press, 1970).

tems, and more resources are generated by mobilized systems. Loyalty is more characteristic of mobilized systems, but elites in any system need to work to secure support for policies.

However legitimate the political elite and however loyal the masses, there are many ramifications to the mobilization of resources. In discussing these a distinction is drawn between mobilized instruments of foreign policy and mobilizable resources.

Mobilized Instruments

There is such a multitude of factors to be taken into account in describing the capabilities of countries that exhaustive descriptions are extraordinarily difficult to make. In addition to complexity, one needs to be concerned with the relative capabilities of different countries and the developmental nature of capabilities. Many factors, moreover, are intangible and immeasurable. Leadership, imagination, and skills are factors that can make a difference in the conduct of foreign policy, yet there are no means of measuring them or even conceptualizing them adequately. Finally, capabilities take on meaning only in the context of objectives and situations. Capabilities are illuminated by the intersecting searchlights, to use Stephen B. Jones' metaphor, of power inventories and strategic theory.[5]

Countries vary, nevertheless, in obvious ways in the instruments which are mobilized for foreign policy purposes. We can draw clear distinctions between nuclear and non-nuclear powers, for example, and between countries with large military forces who are highly trained and who are equipped with sophisticated weapons and those with the opposite characteristics. As stated at the outset of this chapter, the countries with more mobilized instruments have more opportunities, and those with less are unlikely to develop goals which are unachievable without the instruments.

Keeping in mind the need to assess mobilized instruments in terms of goals, one can discuss some of the factors that could be measured on a comparative basis. Comparison is particularly difficult because of what Jones calls "modifiers of power inventories."[6] For example, two countries might each possess 100 identical tanks. The personnel of both countries might have each received the same number of hours of training. These

---

5. See Stephen B. Jones, "The Power Inventory and National Strategy," in *Foreign Policy and International Politics* ed. James Rosenau (New York: The Free Press, 1961). Reprinted from *World Politics* (1954).

6. Ibid.

Mobilization of Resources

power factors need to be modified, however, by such intangibles as the tactical skills of commanding officers, the risk-taking propensities of political leaders, and the willingness of the population to support the use of the tanks in given circumstances. If these modifiers are substantially different in the two countries, it would be misleading to think of the military capabilities as equal even though the power inventory would make them seem so. If we recognize the limitations of the exercise, we can, however, usefully compare countries along the dimension of mobilized instruments.

One measure would be the number of men who are mobilized in association with the various categories of foreign policy instruments. For example, the number of persons in the military and its various branches, and their training or other characteristics could be compared. Numbers in diplomatic service and in informational and economic assistance contingents of the bureaucracy could also be counted and their characteristics noted. We might add the numbers of all personnel in these categories to arrive at total mobilized manpower and to calculate this as a percentage of the whole population. If equivalent manpower from other countries is at any given time were mobilized and at the disposal of a government, it would provide an increment to these figures. These figures would need to be modified, among other ways, by indicating whether the personnel so counted were mobilized under a strategy that looked to the international environment or were largely conceived to be domestic instruments or both.

Capabilities analysis to a large extent focuses on military instruments. Thus, we could compare numbers of weapons within various types.[7] We would also wish to know the transportation capabilities of different countries to deploy forces long distances.[8] If the weapons have been bought or otherwise transferred from foreign sources—as most countries' weapons are—it would be useful to know the sources and their reliability for continued transfers or sales.

Other hardware can also be inventoried. For example, the number and range of radio transmitters would help us to know the capabilities of countries in the international area. The extent of library and other informational outlets and the capabilities of countries for conducting trade relations would be other things to compare. Budgets allocated to cultural exhibits and diplomatic representation are other indices.

---

7. A good source is *The Military Balance*, prepared and issued each year by The International Institute For Strategic Studies in London.

8. Attention was focused on this problem by Albert Wohlstetter in "Illusions of Distance," *Foreign Affairs* 46 (January 1968).

Closely related to the actual instruments of foreign policy are scientific and technical personnel working for the government or on governmentally-sponsored research and enterprises. We could also compare the amount of investment in or the products of industrial plants that are run by or contracted to governments.

These and many more things could be measured in order to assess the comparative capabilities of countries to do certain things. Additionally such assessments would have to include projections into the future, particularly when dealing with factors subject to technological innovation. Moreover, given the lack of knowledge about the precise developments in any country by others, the capabilities analyst would want to guess what likely lines of development would be pursued by adversaries. Certainly, policy makers behave in this way. For example, during World War II, it was a fear that Germany would develop an atomic bomb that gave an impetus to American research and development.

Underlying all of the specific factors that need to be considered in capabilities analysis is general economic growth and development. The greater the overall economic level which includes developments in the basic factors of land, labor, and capital with all their ramifications, the greater are the possibilities for mobilizing specific instruments. There is not a straight-line relationship between economic development and mobilized instruments, for different governments mobilize and allocate their resources differently.

When the Soviet Union's gross national product was only 45 per cent of the United States', the Soviet Union had more men under arms and developed its nuclear, thermonuclear, and related delivery system technology. Japan, with one of the largest economies in the world, has very few men under arms. Authoritarian systems, and particularly those with planned economies, generally are able to allocate more resources to mobilized instruments for foreign policy. The political elites of all systems, however, have the task of mobilizing the resources of their countries on behalf of social goals. This task is not unrelated to foreign policy, for the development and maintenance of trading relationships in order to promote domestic development is an important part of the task of leadership in this area.

Mobilizable Resources

An effective foreign policy rests on the ability of the political elite of a country to generate economic strength and political cohesion. It is out of these factors that resources are mobilized. Normally, the full resources of a country are not mobilized on behalf of political goals, whether foreign or domestic. Consequently, in analyzing capabilities, one needs to look at what has been called, "potential,"[9] and what are here termed "mobilizable resources."

Mobilizable resources are the human and material resources which were dealt with in the chapter on domestic determinants plus available resources that might be transferred from allies or other suppliers. To do a meaningful analysis of mobilizable resources would require an understanding of the situation in which they are relevant and the purposes to which they were to be put. One can, however, identify certain factors that should be considered in such an analysis and discuss certain problems associated with such an analysis.

Two general considerations need to be kept in mind. The first is that mobilizable resources should be related to instruments and techniques of foreign policy. If the problem is the mobilization of manpower for infantry, one can examine the age cohorts appropriate for such duty, then subtract the disabled and those needed for other purposes. Since the training is relatively simple, assuming literacy, practically all such manpower represents a mobilizable resource for such a purpose. One can also project into the future simply by determining the additions to the relevant age cohort coming from younger age cohorts.

On the other hand, the development of a diplomatic corps or a fighting air capacity requires substantially more selection and more training. The educational level of at least segments of the population becomes a consideration, and training facilities and weapons become important in the generation of the air force capability. The analysis of mobilizable resources, then, needs to be a differential analysis related to the instruments that are or might be generated.

The second general consideration is to make a distinction between internally generated instruments and transfers from suppliers. Economic and military instruments are the most common resources transferred. To understand whether transferable instruments are mobilizable requires an understanding of the situation and particularly of the relationship of direct actors to peripheral actors. Second, it requires an understanding of whether the recipient country has the capacity to absorb the instruments. An example or two will illustrate this problem.

The Soviet Union in the late 1960s transferred highly sophisticated military equipment to both Egypt and North Vietnam. The North Vietnamese proved able to absorb the most advanced anti-aircraft

---

9. See Harold and Margaret Sprout, *Foundations of International Politics* (Princeton, N.J.: D. Van Nostrand Company, Inc., 1962).

equipment available. They were well disciplined and could use the equipment effectively. The Egyptians, on the other hand, were unable to make effective use of large quantities and a wide variety of modern military equipment in the 1967 war with Israel. They lacked both the skills and the discipline to employ the transferred equipment.

Internally generated instruments do not rely on allies, and analysis does not require special attention to the situation except to understand the motivations for the mobilization. Such an analysis requires rather an understanding of the domestic resources of the society in question. In addition, one can assume that a country which has the requisite skills to produce *matériel* also has the skills to employ it effectively.

There are some fifteen countries that have the technological expertise and other resources to develop nuclear weapons. Whether they do so depends on their making decisions, and these in turn depend upon the predispositions of the respective countries and upon the state of the international system.

The analysis of mobilizable resources is a difficult task, but it is also a technical and administrative one. The more important question with which we are concerned is the political question of the ability of foreign policy elites to perform acts associated with the mobilization of resources.[10] The factors which encourage the mobilization of resources and the limits on mobilization will now be examined.

Conditions of Mobilization

Three sets of factors which influence tendencies to mobilize resources for the conduct of foreign policy will be discussed. They are leadership, organization, and emotional factors, particularly fear, hatred, and anger. The first two sets of factors are largely under the control of a political elite, but the last set may also be substantially influenced by the acts of other countries.

Political Leadership

Leadership is a difficult quality to analyze, but it is a necessary component in mobilizing the resources needed to conduct foreign policy. Under various conditions, there needs to be a trained bureaucracy, in-

---

10. See the comprehensive analysis of the military component of capabilities by Knorr, *Military Power and Potential*. In addition to analyzing both what we have called mobilized instruments and mobilizable resources, Knorr discusses the political problems of mobilization and uses concepts similar to those used in this book, particularly focusing on predispositions and the importance of international situations.

Mobilization of Resources

volvement in diplomatic negotiations, budgets for cultural exhibitions, military hardware and armies, and "total" mobilization in defense of a country. Whether in a dictatorship or a democracy, whether in defense of a homeland or in pursuit of empire, there is a relationship of leaders and followers which the leaders in particular address themselves to. The fact that there are mass constituencies means that there are limits placed by them on elites, but effective leaders are able to induce their constituencies to follow them and to give them the resources necessary for effecting decisions.

Ordinary people will support a government's policy to the extent that they imagine that their own future is linked with that of the country or the regime. Some people will have an identity with the country in the sense that they feel responsible for it. The attachment of others will vary by circumstances.[11] Both to respond to and bolster the former and to generate support among the latter group, leaders may inspire their constituencies to give support to the country. In most countries where one finds that there has been a high level of mobilization of resources on behalf of national goals, there has been a man who was confident of himself and who articulated sentiments and expressed emotions and ideals that led the people to follow. Such inspiration is one of the functions of leadership.

Another function is the conceptualization of attainable goals. In any political system, but particularly in democracies, goals must be conceptualized and set in such a way that they can be attained. Otherwise, the elite will lose the confidence of constituencies who will no longer give their support. Because a political elite cannot analyze and conceptualize all of the problems of foreign policy, it must rely on bureaucracies to do so. Thus, another function of leadership is to promote morale and confidence in the bureaucracies in order to draw out of them the conceptualization and operational support that the elite needs.

Especially in a democracy, there is another function of leadership: an ability to understand what the citizenry will accept. This function may be "underplayed" or "overplayed" in the sense that leaders may go farther than or not so far as constituencies will accept. It also refers not only to the present but also to projections into the future. The development of skills in performing this function are probably possible only in political careers.

There are also longer-term leadership functions affecting the development of attachment to the country by citizens, the continued solving of the country's domestic problems which will tend to develop a propensity

---

11. See ibid., chapter 5.

to support the authoritative decisions of the country, and the maintenance of the essential goals for which the country was formed. These longer-term functions require institutions and organization.

Organization

Resources are mobilized through organization. Whatever the sentiments and aspirations of a foreign policy elite, it must rely on the organized institutions and the masses of its society for the mobilization of resources. The more highly developed economically a country is, the better equipped it will be in an organizational sense for mobilizing its resources.

The basic organization for the mobilization of resources is the educational system, in both a broad and a narrow sense. Since manpower is the most important constituent in a fund of resources, the training of that manpower in basic and more advanced skills is the most important problem in organization. It is not specific to foreign policy, except at advanced levels, and it is not specific to politics, but it is the foundation for both of these specific areas. The most important way in which education serves foreign policy is in providing training in the exercise of general intellectual skills which make people capable of learning more specific skills. To take an example, if the population of Egypt had had a higher level of general education, it is much more likely that Egyptian soldiers would have learned to use tanks and other military equipment in the 1967 war more effectively. This is why quantitative data describing the level of literacy, the incidence of scientifically-trained personnel, and so forth, provide useful information about the relative capabilities of countries.

Education also is a means for transmitting the culture of a society and for instilling the ideals and aspirations of the culture. This is done not only through formal educational institutions but also through mass media, face-to-face communications, and a variety of organizations.

The effectiveness of the mobilization of resources will also be influenced by the penetration of state organization and political party organization through the society. Thus, more highly developed countries which are characterized by such political penetration are more easily able to mobilize the resources of the society on behalf of foreign policy goals. Political organization also provides the link between foreign policy elites and economic organizations, particularly firms and industries.

Certain industries, such as aircraft industries, rely extensively on contracts for supplying government needs. Thus, both the managers and workers in such industries have a self-interest and consequently a high motivation for supporting the mobilization of resources. If a society is

Mobilization of Resources

characterized by a large segment of such industries, they may be considered to be already mobilized, but they may also be considered to have a propensity to support further mobilization. This is also true of others—such as military officers—whose careers would benefit from further mobilization.[12]

In a variety of ways, then, the organization of society influences the mobilization of resources and is a concern of political elites.

Emotional Factors

The mobilization of resources is to a large extent dependent upon emotional factors, particularly as these are channeled by political leadership. Most commonly, fear, hatred, and anger are the emotions which lead to a greater mobilization of resources. Fear can be induced by either the regime of a country or by another country. In societies where there is a government monopoly of the mass media, it is possible for the regime to generate manufactured fears and hatreds. Moreover, fear can be imposed on a population by a particularly repressive and brutal regime. Such regimes are able to mobilize almost any part of the resources of a country in the support of their foreign policies except what is necessary for domestic consumption. Where regimes do not induce fear, however, sometimes adversaries can.

Fears from outside a country are greatest in a situation in which a country is actually under military attack. In such cases, it is joined with anger, and, subject to effective leadership which gives coherence to a policy of resistance, resources can be mobilized at great sacrifices and virtually without effective imposition of many of the limits which will be dealt with below. Otherwise, fears induced from outside are greatest in the face of real, then potential, threats of military attack.

It has been stressed that these emotional factors, while important to the mobilization of resources, need to be harnessed through political leadership, for by themselves they do not lead to mobilization. They may, rather, lead people to accept occupation without resistance and to collaboration with the occupying authorities. On the other hand, political leadership without these emotional factors at work in the population may be largely ineffective, at least substantially less effective than when the emotional factors are present.

Limits on Mobilization

The above are the factors which encourage and facilitate the mobilization of resources, but they operate in the context of other factors which

---

12. See ibid., pp. 144–45.

tend to set limits on such mobilization. Three categories of limiting factors will be dealt with. They are domestic and private demands on resources, ethical considerations, and failure of will.

Domestic and Private Demands

There is a wide variety of domestic and private demands on resources. Food, clothing, shelter, health services, and tools are needed by a population to survive and produce. Because most countries most of the time are concerned for their own welfare in the first instance and the devotion to foreign policy is a secondary concern, the basic orientation is to give primacy to domestic affairs. Obviously, there is not always a sharp distinction between domestic and foreign affairs, but the basic predisposition of any society is to be concerned for its own welfare, and foreign policy is a function of this. Such a predisposition means that the demands of domestic society and of private individuals must be satisfied except under the most horrendous conditions of seige.

Just as there are industries and groups which have a propensity to support mobilization because their personal economic welfare is benefited by such mobilization, so there also are industries and groups which have a propensity to oppose mobilization because their personal economic welfare is diminished by mobilization. In addition to these groups, there are other groups—particularly in democratic societies—which have a general inclination not to support political elites on foreign policy issues.

There are cultural factors in some societies that form part of domestic demand on resources and set limits on the mobilization of resources. In Nazi Germany, for example, the status of women was regarded in such a way as to lead to continuing production in the cosmetics industry throughout World War II and to not recruiting women to work in industrial plants. In contrast, the United States employed many women in its industrial enterprises.

Mobilization is a demand for substantial sacrifice by individuals of the things that these domestic and private demands give them a propensity for. Except for those who benefit in their careers, there is economic, status, and advancement sacrifice. For manpower that might come under fire in a war, there is a demand for risking the sacrifice of sound limbs and life itself. Reverence for and jealousy of one's own life is a substantial limiting factor.

Ethical Considerations

Ethical considerations operate as limits on the mobilization of resources at three levels: in political elites; in constituencies, particularly mass constituencies; and in the international community. Each of these groups holds certain things to be right and thus to be pursued, and each designates certain things to be evil and to be avoided. In dealing with ethical considerations as limits on the mobilization of resources, the concern here is mainly with the latter: evils to be avoided.

Although members of a political elite may invoke their private conceptions of morality on occasion, the ethics of their position require them to protect the integrity of their societies.[13] This means preservation of the people, territory, and essential institutions and values of the country. Ethical considerations, then, constrain them from mobilizing resources on behalf of goals and purposes which violate any part of that meaning. If a country has a tradition of anti-militarism, for example, the elite would be constrained from mobilizing a large peacetime army. This is not to say that manpower might not be mobilized under conditions of acute fear and inspirational leadership, but it is to say that this constraint would make it more difficult to do than in its absence.

Constituencies also invoke ethical constraints. The experiences of the Boer, Algerian, and Vietnam wars indicate that democratic constituencies have a disinclination to support the evils associated with such wars. The existence of torture, dislocation of populations, killing of civilians, and so forth—inevitable consequences of involvement in such wars—are regarded as evils by mass constituencies. Large segments of democratic populations will, in such circumstances, act not to support and even to oppose mobilization in consequence of their moral revulsion.

The international community has attempted since the late nineteenth century to impose constraints on the possession and use of certain types of weapons. This movement is based on the ethical consideration of making warfare more "humane," and it makes it more difficult to mobilize these weapons. As with all of these ethical constraints, they may be overcome—as the history of international politics indicates—but they do provide obstacles to the mobilization of certain resources.

Failure of Will

Failure of will occurs after a time in which resources have been mobilized at a given level. History is replete with examples of continued resistance to military attack in which the will to resist is not diminished. Such conditions, however, offer no choice. Thus, for there to be a failure of political will, there must be an element of choice.

---

13. See a good discussion of this point and other considerations of morality in Hans J. Morgenthau, *Politics Among Nations*, 4th ed. (New York: Alfred A. Knopf, 1961), chapter 16.

Failure of will results from being tired of continued mobilization on behalf of foreign policy goals. There is a tendency in human affairs to want to bring matters to a conclusion. When continued mobilization does not promise to do so, there is an element of frustration and search for alternatives. When frustration and fatigue reach a certain level, and when alternatives are available, there is a failure of will to continue mobilizing the resources of a society.

The long neglect of domestic priorities in order to fulfill the needs of foreign policy will become evident over time and lead to pressures to reorder priorities. Shocking events and setbacks in foreign policy may also influence this failure of will. This phenomenon seems to be more characteristic of democratic societies than authoritarian ones.

When such failure reaches a certain point, there is an evident need to set different foreign policy goals. Since a failure of will occurs primarily in policies of engagement, there is likely to be a reorientation to policies of insulation. This will lead to withdrawal from situations and, if the actor in question is a direct, central actor, to a substantial restructuring of situations.

Conclusion

In this chapter, the importance of mobilizing resources has been stressed because such mobilization is a necessary condition for making and implementing decisions. There is a number of factors which promote mobilization and a number which sets limits on it.

The basic support by the population for the political elite, analyzed under the concepts of legitimacy and loyalty, is the foundation for public policy, whether domestic or foreign. This consideration shows the essential unity of national politics. The economic and political development of a country is the basis for comparing capabilities.

Beyond that, capabilities analysis can be analyzed further through power inventories and modifiers in the context of national strategy. Ultimately, however, the mobilization of resources occurs in the context of the interacting politics of political elites and masses, with a number of factors constraining and facilitating mobilization.

Let us now turn to the third category of foreign policy act: the execution of foreign policy through the application of instruments and techniques.

9

Application of Instruments and Techniques

In this chapter, we are concerned with the implementation of policies through the application of instruments and techniques. Five types of analysis will be used in this chapter. First, the instruments and techniques of foreign policy will be classified, and there will be an attempt to specify the conditions under which each will be used. Second, a catalog of bundles of instruments, in which a variety of instruments and techniques are brought to bear in the pursuit of some given goal, will be developed. Then the targets against which the instruments and techniques are applied will be specified. By identifying the targets of influence, one can then trace the paths of influence and relate these back to the processes which have been described in the foregoing chapters. In doing this, it will be possible to distinguish between the direct effects of the applications of instruments and the political influences made possible by these direct effects. Finally, an attempt will be made to analyze the predictable and unpredictable elements of the applications.

The implementation of policy relies particularly on bureaucracies. All of the personnel associated with foreign policy instruments may be considered to be bureaucratic personnel. The act of applying instruments and techniques involves particularly the relationship of the chief executive and bureaucracies. This relationship will be referred to throughout the ensuing discussion.

Classification of Instruments and Techniques

The classification of instruments and techniques which is to be used is fivefold: political, diplomatic, informational, economic, and military.

Political

The major component of political instruments is personnel, although money is an added instrument. The personnel are skilled at political organization and leadership and may be dispatched to adjacent or further countries to attempt to manipulate the political process of the target country in the direction of the given country's policies. There are many examples of such political instruments of foreign policy. In the late 1930s, Germany sent political organizers into Austria and Czechoslovakia to work with fifth columns in those countries.[1] North Vietnam sent political cadres to work in South Vietnam in 1957 after President Ngo Dinh Diem refused to engage in discussions with Ho Chi Minh concerning a plebiscite for uniting the two parts of Vietnam. China used embassy personnel in Burundi in the mid-1960s to organize political activities there. The United States Central Intelligence Agency worked in Iran in the early 1950s and in Guatemala in 1954 to lead *coups d'etat* against the incumbent governments. The political instruments of application can be used only in situations where there is a group in the target country with whom the agents can work.

Some similar activities occur that are not under the control of a political elite of a country. For example, radical leaders in the Middle East who are representatives of clandestine organizations or "out" political parties engage in political activities in foreign countries. The AFL-CIO from the United States engaged in organizational work of an anti-Communist nature in British Guiana during the struggle between Cheddi Jagan and Forbes Burnham for leadership of the impending

---

1. This example and others are discussed in Andrew M. Scott, *The Revolution in Statecraft: Informal Penetration* (New York: Random House, 1965).

The Application of Instruments and Techniques 217

independent Guyana. When such interventions occur, they may be treated by the target government as an internal problem, or that government might undertake to secure the cooperation of the government which has jurisdiction over the interventionists to help to control them and their activities. Although this uncontrolled activity is occasionally important in the foreign policies of the countries involved, normally it is not central and need not become a major part of our analysis of foreign policy.

When the political instrument is used by a neighboring country authoritatively, however, the political agents may bring to bear threats of larger interventions and can, therefore, be very important to the execution of foreign policy. The situation in Czechoslovakia in 1948 is an example. Russian political agents who advised the Czech government and who provided part of the organizational leadership for the *coup d'etat* were critical instruments for asserting Soviet control over Czechoslovakia: they had at their disposal the threat of intervention by the Soviet army.

The political instrument may sometimes be used in a supportive manner as opposed to the more common subversive manner. In either case, it is likely to be less visible than the other instruments of foreign policy and thus more difficult to research in a precise, well-documented way. In either case, also, the political instrument relates to the domestic determinants of foreign policy, and to trace the influence of such applications, we can use the framework which was used in the chapter on domestic determinants, for the precise targets and points of influence will be upon one or the other of those determinants.

Diplomatic

The second class of instruments and techniques is diplomatic. The instruments of diplomacy are skilled men who represent their own governments. The reporting function in modern states has become very specialized, with specialists in military, economic, technical, and political fields forming part of diplomatic missions. The representation function may be conducted by persuasion or negotiation. Persuasion is the attempt to convince others of one's point of view and is the task of either instructed diplomats or of persons charged with carrying out a mission, such as the United Nations Secretary General when he is heading a peace-keeping or other type of executive operation. Negotiation is an attempt to achieve agreement on a common problem or set of problems, in which the goal of achieving a solution is more important than reaching a particular solution desired by a given state.

The distinction drawn here between persuasion and negotiation rests upon a difference in approach to compromise. If a diplomat approaches a common problem with his opposite number in a spirit of reaching an acceptable solution through a compromise which takes into account each party's needs, that would be called negotiation. In contrast, the label of persuasion would be applied to the efforts of a diplomat to convince his opposite number of the need to accept a solution to the problem which his country had already adopted and upon which it was unwilling to compromise. To put the distinction in other words, persuasion is the act of selling a solution, and negotiation is the act of finding one. Thus, intermediaries would not become involved in persuasion, but both representatives of states involved in a conflict and intermediaries become involved in negotiations.

Diplomacy may be bilateral or multilateral. Bilateral diplomatic relations are the more traditional variety, although multilateral diplomacy has often been practiced in the past at peace conferences and in the coordination of alliances. Multilateral diplomacy has become more visible in the post-1918 period with the enlargement of multilateral conferences in the United Nations and other organizations. These organizations have also brought into being secretariats which, especially in the UN and the European communities and in other organizations to a lesser extent, become involved in diplomacy. These organizations have also created what Dean Rusk called "parliamentary diplomacy" but which will be excluded from the category of diplomacy here because its accomplishments and the practices associated with it are different from those involved in diplomacy.

Regardless of whether diplomacy is of the persuasive or negotiating kind, it is the coordinating instrument in foreign policy. At the disposal of diplomatic activity are the threats and promises of using or withholding the other instruments. Even when these other instruments are not explicitly invoked, their presence is normally apprehended by the diplomats. Often, the other instruments are used to make points in a negotiation which could not be made through simple verbal communication.

Because of the centrality of diplomacy to the conduct of foreign policy, it is used under all conditions except two. The first is when communications, for some reason or another, are interrupted between adversaries in a given situation. The other is when diplomacy is submerged in the use of military instruments and authorities fail to grasp the significance of diplomacy in achieving their goals.

This is not to say that diplomacy is always successful nor that it is always used wisely. In the discussion of British policy in the 1956 Suez crisis above, for example, we saw how the British failed to use their diplomatic instruments in a diplomatic campaign to neutralize possible adversaries and to gain the support of possible allies.

Informational

Whereas the diplomatic instrument is one which is used for communication with political and bureaucratic elites through formal channels, the informational instrument is one which is used for communication with masses. Although not a new instrument, it has become more prominent as a consequence of the increased importance of masses under the influence of the ideas of democracy and of the technology of communications.

The informational instruments include skilled men and the technological apparatus which is used for mass communications. The apparatus includes books, displays, libraries, radio broadcasts, pamphlets, and so forth. The skilled personnel include both those who go to other countries to engage in mass communications and the personnel associated with producing pamphlets, broadcasts, and other related activities.

Since communications consist of the interaction of the producer of the communication and the receiver, there must be groups who are receptive to given communications for them to be effective. Given receptive audiences, however, the informational instrument can be rather effective. Radio Cairo in the Middle East, for example, has been an important instrument of Egyptian influence in other Arab countries.

Economic

The economic instrument is one that is used more extensively by countries that are wealthier. It is not limited to them, however, for China, Israel, Mexico and other countries that are not among the wealthier countries in the world use economic instruments to a limited extent. Economic instruments include the factors of producing material goods except land. These are labor and capital, including technical assistance, the granting or lending of money, entrepreneurship, and so forth. It is an instrument with many manifestations and may be used either to support or to subvert incumbent regimes.

There are two essential conditions for the use of economic instruments when they are used for the conferring of economic goods by one country on another. They are (1) the availability of the goods and (2) the willingness of the receiver to accept them. They may either be requested by the receiver or offered by the donor.

Economic instruments may also be deprived in a situation where the object state is dependent upon them. These may be used in conditions wherein the deprivers—and it is usually the case that a single country is not in a position effectively to deprive another country of significant economic factors—oppose the policies of the deprived country. Economic instruments also reinforce diplomatic activities through the mechanisms of threats and promises.

Military

Finally, there are military instruments which include skilled personnel and materials which can be used to kill other personnel and to exercise force against other countries. Materials include all kinds of weapons, platforms, and conveyances which can be used for destruction. The skills involved include not only those associated with wielding weapons but also those of managing the large organizations of armed forces, procuring materials, and the strategy and tactics of using the weapons.

Military instruments may be used under a variety of conditions, but they are more likely to be used when other means of achieving goals have been exhausted. This is particularly true with respect to the major powers in the atomic age. However, the instruments of force may be used in conflict situations to take advantage of opportunities or to deprive an adversary of the advantages of attack. Under conditions of extreme fear, military instruments may be used to restore a sense of control over one's actions.

Military instruments are most often used against other military instruments, but they may also be used against civilian personnel and material resources. The use of military instruments is especially subject to the stricture that a political elite loses partial control when it assigns a mission to a bureaucracy. The military instrument may be used in ways that are not intended by the political elite and not always governed by rational objectives. Rape and looting by soldiers are the most obvious examples of how this problem manifests itself, but there are more subtle —and for purposes of policy more important—ways in which the instrument may not be subject to the control of the political elite.

Although the instruments and techniques of foreign policy may sometimes be used in isolation from one another, one may also analyze the ways in which they are orchestrated or brought together into bundles which are applied in a coherent manner.

Bundles of Instruments and Techniques

The pursuit of foreign policy objectives through the application of instruments and techniques normally occurs in circumstances which require the employment and coordination of many instruments and

The Application of Instruments and Techniques

techniques. These shall be called *bundles* of instruments and techniques. A variety of common ways in which bundles are put together will be examined.

Bundles of instruments and techniques are particularly associated with basic decisions which are usually complex and which usually initiate a complex of actions. These bundles involve activities vis-à-vis many countries, even in the situation where a country is attempting to monopoloize or duopoloize a situation. In that case, attempts are made to isolate the situation from possible outside influences.

It is difficult to develop exhaustive and mutually exclusive categories of bundles of instruments and techniques, exhaustive categories because characteristic of the human condition are the element of surprise and the exercise of imagination; mutually exclusive categories because instruments and techniques are used across a variety of foreign policy undertakings. It is nevertheless useful to treat seven categories of bundles of instruments and techniques because each has its own peculiarities and mixes of instruments. Although the instruments may be the same in each of the categories, the mix in each is different.

The categories to be used are these: (1) negotiations; (2) coalition building; (3) international community undertakings; (4) civil strife, civil order, and foreign policy; (5) international crises; (6) war; and (7) peacemaking and intermediaries. Each category has several subcategories. The instruments chosen and the skill with which they are used vary not only by the fund of resources that are available but also by the skill and imagination of the policy authorities. Therefore, it is impossible to be precise in analyzing this aspect of our subject. One can, nevertheless, say some useful things about bundles of instruments, for the idea more nearly captures the reality of foreign policy implementation than do very close analyses of the use of one or the other instruments, although close analysis is useful for some purposes.

Negotiations

The first category—negotiations—refers to diplomatic activities in which two or more countries attempt to find agreement on a given subject matter. In the classic definition of diplomatic negotiations, there is a community of interest sufficient to induce the parties to place more value on coming to an agreement than on achieving predetermined aims.[2] In the classic sense, then, diplomatic negotiations are utterly secret in order to enable the parties to compromise on their respective

---

2. A good treatment of classic diplomacy is Sir Harold Nicholson, *The Evolution of Diplomatic Method* (New York: Macmillan, 1954).

initial positions. There are many instances in the modern world in which this condition obtains: myriad bilateral negotiations in world capitals, talks like those between the United States and China in Warsaw, the strategic arms limitation talks in Vienna and Helsinki, and so forth. This condition is more likely to obtain when there are only two parties to the negotiations than when there are more.

While the community of interest in this classic sense of diplomatic negotiations is prevalent, there is also a mixture of conflict. Most states are restricted in the compromises they may make by their own countries' domestic determinants. That is, there is a linkage in the political process that occurs in diplomatic negotiations and the political process that follows in each of the states party to the negotiations. Moreover, the other instruments of each state are in the background and are kept in mind by the negotiators. If the interests of the parties are too far apart, it may be impossible to compromise and to achieve the objectives of the negotiations.

One or more of the parties may also not meet the assumption of the classical scheme: that is, they may not place a higher value on coming to an agreement than on achieving their predetermined aims. Not only may these predetermined aims be germane to the issue under discussion, but also they may include shifting the blame for not coming to agreement on to the shoulders of their negotiating partners or some other propaganda aims. They may also relate simply to achieving stature, one of the aims of Premier Khrushchev in wanting the Geneva summit conference in 1955.

Apart from the many subjects which may be negotiated through classical diplomacy, the negotiation of peace treaties is a special case of such negotiations. There is a presumed community of interest among the victors since they will have just completed a period of cooperation in defeating their enemies. However, in the absence of a powerful adversary, their particular interests and ambitions will come to the fore in peace treaty negotiations. Moreover, their postwar aims may include the extension of their influence into new areas and they may use informational instruments to seek that influence. In addition, with powerful military instruments which will be occupying territory, their diplomatic claims to territory will be stronger than equivalent claims in other kinds of diplomatic negotiations. Their different experiences in the war may have impressed memories in their consciousnesses which lead them to view desirable objectives for the postwar situation in very different terms. In such circumstances, defeated foes may be able to play a very influential role at peace conferences, as did France at the Congress of Vienna.

When the war has been indecisive, it may be impossible to come to

The Application of Instruments and Techniques

an agreement on a new status quo, as has been the case in Korea in 1953, in Indochina in 1954, and in Vietnam in the early 1970s. In other cases, the divergence of interests and the hostilities between the wartime allies may become so great that they cannot come to an agreement on a postwar settlement. This happened between the United States and the Soviet Union in Europe following World War II. In these cases, meaningful diplomatic negotiations in a classic sense are not possible, and a different kind of situation is created. Until either the situation evolves sufficiently to create a new community of interests or until the adversaries live some profound experiences that reshape their attitudes and goals, no solution will be found through diplomatic negotiations.

Successful peace negotiations have often been achieved through the transfer of territory from loser to victors or through reparations. This is the only situation in which it is likely that territory and treasure will be transferred in such large amounts and with such decisiveness in creating a new situation. On the other hand, agreements can be reached on other occasions through the transfer of territory and treasure among parties which have coincidental interests. This is particularly true in wartime, a set of circumstances which will be dealt with below.

To sum up, diplomatic negotiations are characterized by close, formal relations between two or more countries. The diplomatic instrument is the most prominent one, although the fund of resources which each of the parties has is apparent and affects the negotiations. There is a linkage of diplomatic negotiations to the domestic political structure which the respective parties must calculate in order to have the agreement accepted at home. With few exceptions, informational instruments are not employed in diplomatic negotiations. It might be mentioned that the diplomatic instrument might be employed in another way during diplomatic negotiations: that is, a country might communicate with other countries to get them to accept the existence of the negotiations and to encourage certain kinds of expectations. For example, President Nixon's trips to China and the Soviet Union in 1972 required active diplomacy to explain these initiatives to allies. On some occasions, too, a country might make a diplomatic approach to the ally of the other party to the negotiations, hoping that the ally would influence the other party to accept the proposals of the given party. One angle of the diplomacy of the United States aimed at bringing about an end to the Vietnam war was an attempt to get the Soviet Union to persuade Hanoi to negotiate on American terms.

The most important characteristic of this bundle of instruments is that it almost exclusively relies on the diplomatic instrument. The only other category in which there is such an exclusiveness of the diplomatic instrument is in peacemaking and intermediaries, with which we will deal below.

Coalition Building

The second category of bundles of instruments, coalition building, is related to the first and sometimes gives the appearance of diplomatic negotiations. However, the difference is that, in coalition building, one country attempts to persuade other countries to accept its policies. In other words, it places a higher value on achieving its goals than on the achievement of an agreement with others. In pursuing support for its goals, a country may use diplomacy, informational activities, and economic instruments. On a few occasions, which will be specified below, military instruments may be used. There is some overlap between this category of actions and the following one, but they can be differentiated on the basis of whether the purpose of the coalition building is conceived by a single country or small alliance or, alternatively, by the international community. In the category of coalition building, a distinction will be made between the more formal activities associated with alliances and more informal activities.

In treating alliances, one needs to be concerned with (1) alliance formation, (2) alliance management, (3) alliance basic decisions, and (4) withdrawal from an alliance. The central problem here is the politics of developing and keeping power in the situation of cooperation among sovereign actors.[3] The major instrument in this activity is diplomacy.

Alliances may be formed for a fixed time or indefinitely, but in either case they are motivated by interests that are thought of as relatively long term. The major motivation for forming an alliance is a common threat coming either from a single country or another coalition or alliance. In this case, there is an identical interest. But another motivation may be parallel or coincidental interests, stemming from the fact that one country may have quite different interests from another but joins together because the alliance makes it more likely that both will achieve their respective goals through the alliance. NATO is an example of an identical interest alliance, whereas Britain and Portugal's alliance is an example of the latter.

Regardless of the basis for the alliance, there must be a federator (a country which acts as the core of the alliance process) or leader. Usually,

---

3. An article which criticizes the literature that tends to reify alliances and which reminds us that "alliance behavior" is a type of national behavior by and through coalescence with other nations" is Edwin H. Fedder, "The Concept of Alliance," *International Studies Quarterly* 12 (March 1968).

The Application of Instruments and Techniques

the federator will be the country which conceives the alliance, although this is not necessarily so. The federator coordinates the initial contacts with all of the alliance partners, determines at least the broad outlines and limitations of the alliance, and plays a central role in the negotiations leading up to the initialing of the alliance document. Occasionally, there may not be a formal document, but it is the normal way in which alliances are given definition. While all of the members of the alliance need to agree to the alliance, and will consequently assist in its definition, the interests of the federator will be predominant. From this discussion, we can also infer that the federator will be a power of the first rank from among the alliance partners.

The federator, if it is a great power, may use not only its instruments of diplomatic persuasion but also promises of material aid, either economic or military, to induce its partners to join an alliance and to agree to the terms of the partnership. These instruments would be useless in the absence of a basic sympathy and receptivity on the part of the other countries involved, but they may be used marginally to get the terms desired. There are limits to the use of these instruments, particularly if they are relied on to induce support that might otherwise not be given. For, having promised materials, the federator is in a weak position in alliance management because of the commitment which it has made. If the deferential partner insists upon certain alliance policies, the federator will be subject to pressures to accede to them because of the investment it has made and because it has demonstrated the value of the alliance to it by conferring the goods.

This is a problem of alliance management. It should be clear at this point that, although the federator plays a most important role in alliance formation, the ongoing business of the alliance is not simply one of power on the side of a dominant partner and deference on the part of other countries. The complexity of patterns of influence among alliance partners is especially apparent when the partners are of relatively equal power, but it is also present in many so-called patron-client relationships. Thus, in World War II, the Grand Alliance was not marked by power and deference but rather by bargaining among relative equals. The Sino-Soviet alliance has also demonstrated vividly how a partner, when not being able to achieve its demands, can cause considerable trouble for the senior partner. The United States-South Vietnamese alliance illustrates the complexity of influence patterns in the patron-client relationship.

Alliance management is a problem akin to the domestic political process of political elites keeping power, except that the hierarchical relationships of the alliance are not so apparent and legitimate as in domestic politics. Leadership is more subject to challenge in an alliance than in domestic politics. Diplomacy reinforced with economic instruments and the transfer of military goods is the major instrument for managing the alliance. When there are immense strains in an alliance —as there were in the Sino-Soviet alliance in the 1960s—informational instruments may also be employed. The tendency in any alliance is to avoid the use of the informational instruments, however, for they tend to make management more difficult.

As domestic determinants and situations change, alliance management problems may become more difficult. Drastic changes in a situation may undermine the basis of an alliance, and it is likely in such a case to dissolve. Domestic changes, such as the economic growth of deferential partners, may lead to new demands on the alliance, particularly on the dominant partner. If these are well founded in increased domestic strength—economic wealth and political integration and security of elites —the dominant partner must accede to the demands or find its alliance subject to strains that may sever or fragment the alliance. This is what happened in NATO when the French demanded assistance with its nuclear development. When the United States refused, the strains caused by this and other reinforcing actions led to France's withdrawal from the alliance's organizational structure.

The NATO organizational structure of integration is one form by which alliances may be managed. It tends to reinforce the dominance of the major partner. The other means of management of alliances is simply coordination without integration. This form of management leaves each partner a wider freedom of determining its contributions to the alliance and more freedom of choice in pursuing its foreign policy. In the integrative form of management, only the major partner retains complete freedom of choice in determining its policies.

If the major partner exercises this freedom of choice in such a way as to be too far away from the interests of its partners, the partners will become dissatisfied and strains will be created in the alliance. If it is done in regions and with subject matter with which the partners are unconcerned, there may be no serious strain, but if it violates the interests of partners, then acute strains may develop. Let us illustrate these propositions.

The United States may pursue completely independent policies in the Western Hemisphere because its NATO allies have no interests there. On the other hand, they do have interests in the Middle East, and France has interests in Indochina. If the United States attempts to act completely independently, without taking account of its allies' interests, it will create strains in NATO. In addition, its bilateral cooperation with the Soviet Union also causes strains in the alliance because the partners are all very much interested in that relationship.

The problem of alliance management is the same for the deferent as for the dominant partners: how to retain and increase influence in the alliance. Each partner has its own ideas of what the alliance should be doing. Deferent partners are especially concerned to be consulted and to influence what might otherwise be independent decisions by the dominant partner.

Alliances are sometimes confronted with the necessity to make basic decisions. These may be generated by the alliance itself, by one of the partners, or by events outside the alliance. Essentially the same kinds of processes are involved as those involved in the domestic political process of decision making. One factor that is different is that the time needed to consult with alliance partners is longer than that required for domestic decision making. Another different factor is that the constituencies in the case of countries are entire nations with their independent resources. A third different factor may intrude in certain cases wherein there is a threat to a particular alliance partner. In such a case, and there is no equivalent in domestic politics, the influence of the threatened partner increases in influence, for it is acceded greater responsibility and perhaps greater burdens in the alliance. Alliance decisions may be typed in the same way that a single country's foreign policy decisions were typed: initiative and response. It is the decision-making *process* that is complicated by the structure of the alliance.[4]

There is an intersection of the management and basic decision functions of an alliance when a partner withdraws from an alliance. This is an occasion for a basic decision with respect to how to adjust to the departure of the partner, but it is also a problem of managing the alliance so as to retain as much of its structure and purposes as possible, given the loss of a coalition member. At such a juncture, rearrangements of the transfer of economic goods and military hardware may become particularly crucial adjuncts to skillful diplomacy.

The decision to withdraw from an alliance is by definition a national rather than an alliance decision, but alliance partners by their previous behavior will have helped to influence the decision. There will be, if the alliance partners are astute, a review of the factors that led to the withdrawal. This analysis might result in reaffirming or redefining the purposes and policies of the alliance. The process may be akin to the alliance

---

4. See Alastair Buchan, *Crisis Management: The New Diplomacy* (Boulogne-sur-Seine, France: The Atlantic Institute, 1966) for a discussion of the development of coordinating mechanisms in NATO.

formation process and conceivably can lead to the withdrawal of other partners and to the breakup of the alliance. Withdrawal, then, is an occasion of crisis proportions.

If the withdrawing partner is sufficiently weak, the other partners might even resort to invasion to forcibly keep it in the alliance, as happened with respect to Hungary in 1956. If the forcible keeping of the partner in the alliance is ruled out, there is a factor making for pressure to keep the remainder of the alliance intact. That is, withdrawal of a partner may be seen as an opportunity by an adversary to gain influence with some of the other partners to wean them away. Fear of this possibility will promote cohesion among the partners.

Withdrawal in wartime adds other complications, but the response will necessarily be the same. When Russia withdrew from World War I, its alliance partners attempted to change that decision by intervention. When Italy withdrew from the Axis partnership in World War II, Germany attempted to retain the terrntory which it held in Italy but was unable forcibly to make Italy remain. If the possibility and power are there, then, withdrawal from an alliance in wartime is highly likely to lead to the use of military instruments to coerce the partner to remain in the alliance.

Apart from alliances, there are more informal activities of coalition building. These tend to be led by single countries, although a single country may gain partners to assist it in these endeavors. One of the most important of these activities is the promotion of disintegration in an adversary alliance. The instruments that may be used are from every category, but they rely on forces of disintegration at work within the adversay partnership,

By linking with attempts at gaining independence by an ally in an adversary coalition, a country promotes disintegration. When Poland in 1956, for example, exerted some independence of the Soviet Union, the United States extended most-favored-nation trading status to Poland. In this case, as in others of this type, the United Sates was not able to initiate any action, but it was able to take actions which reinforced Poland's position vis-à-vis the Soviet Union. A variety of instruments may be used. Diplomacy may be used not only in establishing the links between the two countries involved but also in communicating with the alliance partners of the country attempting to move toward independence. Informational and economic instruments can be used, and—in the extreme—military instruments can be used.

Such activities, if pushed too hard, may be seen as a threat by the alliance partners and could lead to intervention. Thus when the Soviet Union came to the assistance of Cuba when it was trying to move away from the United States, the United States attempted to invade Cuba and topple the Castro regime. Such activities, therefore, are subject to the constraints of the alliance partners. After a time, when the new alliance is consolidated, it will be more difficult for the former alliance partners to intervene because the new situation will be seen as legitimate and because involvement in the affairs of the erstwhile partner becomes involvement in the affairs of the adversary alliance.

Another bundle of instruments in this category is the campaign to extend influence or to deprive influence to an adversary. Once again, all of the instruments may be used, but it is unlikely that the military instrument will be used in such a case. This policy can be pursued only in the case of receptive partners or political vacuums. When Yugoslavia withdrew from the Cominform in 1948, for example, the United States, by giving diplomatic and economic support to the Tito government, was able to extend its influence marginally. More important, it was able by its actions to deprive the Soviet Union of reasserting its influence in Yugoslavia.

Countries also engage in campaigns to enhance their prestige through a series of displays of one kind or another, depending upon what is admired in the age in which the display occurs. At one time in history, showing the flag is a technique. At another time, state visits and space flights may be a means. In the modern period, the most common means is through participation in international fairs and exhibitions. Such prestige is essentially an informational device, related to propaganda, and is aimed at masses of people. It is not entirely lost on elites, however.

Propaganda campaigns are also conducted, using informational activities primarily, to influence masses of people. These are often not well directed for specific purposes but are rather aimed at spreading information and an interpretation of events favorable to the broadcasting country. All forms of mass communications are used. The techniques of propaganda can also be used for more specific purposes as part of a broader diplomatic campaign. In such cases, the targets are more precisely identified and the objectives of the sending country are clearer.

Finally, in the coalition-building category, there are campaigns to take advantage of unforeseen opportunities and the mistakes of one's adversaries. All of the instruments may be used, although the lack of planning and foresight generally make informational activities the first response. These may be followed by diplomatic and other activities.

International Community Undertakings

The next category of bundles of instruments is that of international community activities. This is a coalition building process, but the impetus comes from an international organization with legal responsibility for making decisions to govern the international community. There are four important bundles of instruments which will be dealt with: diplomatic campaigns, sanctions, collective security, and multilateral program initiation.

Before proceeding to a discussion of each of the international community activities, let us distinguish between these and other foreign policy undertakings. The activities under discussion here are under the control of an authoritative decision-making body of the international community, such as the United Nations Security Council. The other foreign policy activities which are discussed in this chapter are under the control of one or more states. Although states comprise the decision-making organs of international organizations, they need to operate on a consensus principle, and they must use executive organs that are subject to the control of the body.

The first set of activities is the diplomatic campaign. This is a short-term undertaking in the neutral action category of foreign determinants. It involves the use of diplomacy to induce countries to contribute to the undertaking, negotiate the necessary local arrangements, and arrange the logistics of the operation.[5]

Sanctions aimed at isolating a country and inducing it to change its behavior in some respect is another of the bundles of instruments. Sanctions rely largely on the deprivation of instruments rather than their use. Diplomatic, informational, and economic intercourse are cut off by the international community. Military instruments may be used, but it is extraordinarily difficult to get an agreement in an international organization on their use.[6]

Collective security involves the use of all instruments, with the military one of the most important. This is largely an unpracticed bundle of policy, but the theoretical aspects are well known.[7] Since it relies so extensively on major changes in the countries of the world, it will probably be a long time before it is accepted.

---

5. The diplomatic campaign under the auspices of the United Nations Secretary General is described by Michel Virally, "The Political Role of the Secretary-General of the United Nations," mimeographed provisional translation from the French of an article in *L'Annaire Francaise de Droit International* 4 (1958).

6. A good discussion of sanctions and their limitations occurs in E. H. Carr, *The Twenty-Years Crisis, 1919–1939* (London: Macmillan and Company, 1939).

7. Excellent discussions of the theory of collective security occur in Inis L. Claude, Jr., *Swords into Plowshares: The Problems and Progress of International Organization*, 3d ed., rev. (New York: Random House, 1964), and in his *Power and International Relations* (New York: Random House, 1962).

The Application of Instruments and Techniques 231

Multilateral program initiation is the last of the bundles of instruments. This requires diplomacy in forging an initial agreement, the techniques of parliamentary diplomacy in spreading information, and the mobilization of resources from many countries in order to carry it out.

Civil Strife, Civil Order, and Foreign Policy

The fourth category of bundles of instruments is that of civil strife, civil order, and foreign policy. The instruments we are concerned with here are those associated with (1) campaigns for internal control, under both conditions of stability and of instability; (2) revolutionary campaigns; (3) civil war policies of a secessionist unit; and (4) civil war policies of the established state. Each of these sets of conditions is characterized by the use of instruments in the foreign environment even though the major purpose of each is to maintain or wrest control within a country.

Internal control is the first object of any government. Modernizing elites in underdeveloped countries base their position on achieving modernization for their people, and they rely upon outside resources. In conditions of relative stability, this may be done by the use of diplomacy within the country in dealing with donor countries. It is more difficult in conditions of relative instability because the intervention necessary to help the elite to maintain control is very great and joint decision making can overwhelm the given elite, for help comes from more powerful countries. One way of offsetting the influence of one country is through diversifying aid sources, and another is to multilateralize assistance.

If there is a major external threat to the regime, particularly if it is coupled with a major internal division, then it is more difficult (usually nearly impossible) to diversify aid resources. South Vietnam is an example of a regime which found itself in this condition in the period from the late 1950s until the early 1970s. This leads to a close alliance and problems of integration which shall be dealt with below. Informational campaigns and diplomacy are used to gain support for the embattled regime, although success depends to a large extent on the sympathy of other countries.

Revolutionary campaigns conducted by organized counter-elites also cope with the external environment. Since revolutionary elites are even weaker than the established elites against whom they are directing their resources, they rely extensively on outside help. The National Liberation Front of South Vietnam is an example of such a revolutionary elite. To gain this, they use informational and diplomatic instruments to obtain both diplomatic and material support. Their chances of success are virtually non-existent without sources of supply from outside the country. The most useful assistance in addition to resources is a contiguous sanctuary. Diplomacy is used to gain access to these contiguous territories.

Civil wars involve major divisions of countries engaged in war. The foreign policy aim of the established government is to end the secession or armed revolution by military and political means, and this entails a diplomacy which seeks to isolate the secessionist regime. The established regime will also seek arms and economic assistance from other countries and from private sources who may be motivated to assist because of the promises for future gain when the secession or revolution is needed. Nigeria in 1968 was an example.

The secessionist regime or the revolutionary movement engages in a diplomacy to seek assistance from outside resources and an informational program to gain sympathy for itself and hatred of the established government. Biafra provides an example of a particularly successful informational program. As with revolutionary movements in a lesser stage of rebellion than civil war, there is a diplomacy to seek contiguous sanctuaries.

International Crises

The next bundle of instruments category is that of international crises. The three aspects of this category which shall be treated are crisis initiation, crisis response, and crisis resolution.

Every state has, at any given time, a relationship with every other state. This relationship may be very close, as between the United States and the United Kingdom during most of the period since 1939, in an alliance. On the other hand, it can be very hostile and distant, as between the United States and China from 1953 to 1972. It may be relatively close, but hostile, as between the United States and the Soviet Union during the cold war period. It may be distant yet apathetic, as between so many countries.

Any action by any country which transforms or threatens to transform the given relationship between two countries in the direction of hostility sufficient to involve the risk of war or of increased hostilities within a short time is a crisis-initiating action. Thus, crisis involves the three dimensions of threat, urgency, and risk, and it is brought into being by an action or event which creates a situation involving all of these dimensions.

An initiating action may be any of a wide variety of actions of which a state is capable. The range of political, diplomatic, military, and economic actions which a state may take is very wide, but the number of actions which threatens war or increased hostilities is more limited. Initiating actions may not be the authoritative actions of states. They may also be events within a state which, if allowed to proceed, would threaten the relationships between that state and other states or the relationship of two other states. Initiating actions may also be undertaken by subnational groups; and, of course, they may be undertaken by a group of states.

Although the variety of discrete actions which may precipitate a crisis is very great, the actions are relevant to this analysis by reducing them to two basic categories: the effect of the action and the target of the action. As to effect, the action either has the potential for transforming relationship or it actually does transform the relationship.

Targets may either be a primary adversary or third parties. A third party may be an adversary, neutral, or ally. A target state, in the case of third parties, may be differentiated from the context in that action is taken directly upon it by an initiating state.

The initiating action in a crisis imposes on the situation a definition of the central decision to be made. It also clarifies the fundamental tensions underlying the adversary relationship. Although an initiating action may lead to confusion at first, it will become clearer who controls the central decision as the crisis unfolds. The central decision in some crises will be subject to the unilateral control of the initiating state, as it was in the Cuban missile crisis. In others, it will be subject to the unilateral control of the respondent state. More often than not, however, the central decision will come under the shared control of the adversaries.

One way of identifying who controls the central decision is to determine who owns or controls the material objects of the crisis. Control is more important in this determination than ownership, as the capture of intelligence planes indicates. When the control of the material objects of the crisis is in dispute, the control decision will be shared.

Once an initiating action occurs, it is communicated to the respondent state. The timing and nature and difficulty of this communication process have been the subject of careful studies for cases in which the initiating state has used the tactics of deception and surprise. The importance of intelligence for the respondent state is difficult to overestimate, and there are particular problems of the time sequence.

The communication process is a segmented one and one which is virtually impossible to predict. Not only are the difficulties of "noise" and verification encountered, but also there are bureaucratic problems which may interfere with the internal communication process within a government. Assuming that the initiating action is communicated to the authoritative decision-makers, they will perceive a threat, feel a sense of urgency, and recognize that risks are involved in the engagement between their state and the initiating state. They will recognize that they are faced with the occasion for a decision.

Their alternative responses were dealt with in the chapter on decisions. The alternatives are immobilism, acceptance, management, restoration, and transformation.

There are four basic ways in which an international crisis may be resolved. The first is a transformation of a situation from peace to war. Second, an extended crisis system may be established. Third, an acceptable and incremental change in relations between the crisis adversaries may be established. Fourth, a return to the pre-crisis status quo may occur.

The outcomes allow us to evaluate the success of crisis initiation and the various categories of response. This measure of success pertains only to the international aspects of crises. Their impact on the domestic scene is another problem. Success in crisis behavior can be measured by determining whether an actor has gained something it did not have before the crisis. Failure can be measured by determining whether an actor has lost something it had before the crisis. A final measure of success must be of crisis behavior itself. Was control maintained over events in such a way that the shared objectives of the adversaries—e.g., avoiding nuclear war—were accomplished?

War

The next category of bundles of instruments is that of war. Bundles of instruments are associated with war initiation, war response, and war-ending activities. The conduct of war is primarily the use of military instruments, but diplomacy, information, and economic instruments are also heavily utilized. Even when an initiating state uses surprise, it may engage in campaigns of diplomacy and informational activities designed to mislead its adversaries. Throughout the war, all of the instruments are used.

Diplomacy is used to gain allies and to transfer resources as well as to induce neutrality among countries that might be tempted to join the adversary. Diplomacy may also be used to direct communication with the adversary to limit the war or to seek war-ending negotiations.

Economic instruments are transferred among allies and there are at least attempts to deprive economic instruments from adversaries. Informational instruments are addressed to a number of audiences, in both

The Application of Instruments and Techniques

allied and friendly countries as well as in neutral countries. Even combat soldiers become targets of informational instruments.

Military instruments are the primary ones in a war, and they are used on a wide variety of targets and in many ways. There are important distinctions to be drawn among which instruments and which targets are used. In particular, the international community has norms against the use of lethal gas and biological instruments. Although it has declined in the twentieth century, the distinction between combatants and noncombatants is one that has long been held. The distinction between nuclear and "conventional" instruments continues to be a important one.

Diplomacy is the only instrument used in war-ending activities, although it may involve the use of threats of military instruments and sometimes even the use of instruments in order to demonstrate the credibility of a threat.[8]

Peacemaking and Intermediaries

The final category of bundles of instruments is that of peacemaking and intermediaries. The major instrument in these activities is diplomacy. It is one of the most difficult uses of this instrument because it works with forces not under control of the intermediaries themselves. The personal nature of diplomacy is most apparent in this kind of activity, for the intermediary diplomats must gain the trust of both parties to a conflict and help to bring them to agreement. The diplomats can invoke the threats of countries in a subtle maneuver in this kind of diplomacy, but their lack of power is generally an asset.[9]

In a few circumstances, the international community has developed more material instruments for use in neutral action campaigns. At base, these are diplomatic undertakings, but symbolic peacekeeping troops who perform watching and police functions have been useful in the Middle East, Indonesia, and Cyprus.

The point of this discussion of bundles of instruments has been to demonstrate that in a variety of circumstances countries and other organizations bring to bear a set of instruments to cope with or to draw on the international environment. Instruments are seldom used in isolation, and each instrument is used for a variety of purposes.

---

8. An excellent analysis of the use of military instruments is Thomas C. Schelling, *Arms and Influence* (New Haven and London: Yale University Press, 1965).

9. See Virally, "The Political Role of the Secretary-General," and Howard H. Lentner, "The Diplomacy of the United Nations Secretary-General," *The Western Political Quarterly* 18 (September 1965).

We now turn to an analysis of the objects or targets of the instruments and to tracing the paths of influence of the instruments, attempting to specify both the limits and the potential of the instruments.

Effects of Instruments on Targets

In analyzing the effects of instruments on targets, one cannot exhaust every nuance of each instrument, but each class of instruments can be dealt with, and some examples of direct and indirect effects can be given. In treating this subject, a type of analysis similar to the general scheme of analysis in this book will be used. That is, the application of an instrument or technique depends both on the instrument and the target, in the same way that foreign policy is dependent both on a given state and its environment. For example, we do not simply want to analyze what a diplomatic threat is; we also want to find out how it is received by the state against which it is directed. We want to know what the channel of communication is: for example, in a diplomatic threat, it is issued by a segment of the bureaucratic elite to a segment of the bureaucratic elite in another country. It is then processed and responded to. What, we ask, is the effect on the target country directly? The answer is that a threat is perceived and perhaps fears are aroused. What are the indirect effects? If the target country's elite chooses to make the threat public, perhaps, it will be a tool in their hands to mobilize resources which they otherwise could not have.

Each class of instruments will be examined, the targets against which they may be directed will be specified in terms of the variables in the domestic determinants chapter, the direct effects of the applications of instruments and techniques will be given and the probable paths of indirect influence on the politics of the situation in which they are used will be suggested. In doing this analysis, one of the major points we wish to keep in mind is that targets of political influence are not inert but are rather active participants with the wielders of the instruments in a political struggle. Thus, one cannot say that the use of this instrument will achieve that goal, for the target is an intervening variable that can make a substantial difference.

Political Instruments

The first class of instruments which was characterized above is political. As stated, the political instrument acts upon the domestic political processes of the target state. Since it is most often used as a subversive rather than a supportive instrument with respect to the regime, it may be

The Application of Instruments and Techniques

aimed against any accessible variable in the society. Its chances of success are dependent much more on the political process of the target society than on the skills and resources of the political instrument.

These skills and resources can, however, become an important marginal influence in a country that is not well-integrated. In a premobilized country, assassination and terror can undermine the legitimacy of a government unless that government is particularly adept at counter-insurgency, including not simply the repression of the interventionist political activities but also building and keeping intact the structure and programs of the society. It is the latter which are the most important. Without access to the elites of a country, there is little that can be done without adjacent territory. Consequently, it is highly improbable that countries not adjacent to countries governed by revolutionary regimes will be subject to significant political threats.

When the political activists who are intervening have direct access to some segment of the political and bureaucratic elite of the target country, they have more of a chance to be influential. There is still the process which is more direct upon the centers of power. If this activity is linked with adjacency of military forces, as in Czechoslovakia in 1948, it can have very profound effects indeed. This is an unusual case, however, and political subversion is usually marginal to the political process in which it is operating.

When political intervention is supportive, it has access to political and bureaucratic elites and essentially becomes part of the structure of authority of the target country. This condition obtains with respect to foreign aid programs and other programs of political advising. Essentially, the skills of personnel and resources of one country are incorporated into the political process of another country. This occurs only when there is an intensely shared interest between the two countries. The United Nations intervention in the Congo was an international community example of this type of intervention.

The final circumstances in which the political instrument is used, and the most effective one, is the military occupation of one country by another. The occupation is essentially a process of running the affairs of the country, although its foreign affairs cannot be said to be independent in any sense, and a process of creating a new structure of authority.

The political instrument is one which is used in several limited circumstances and does not share the broad utility of the other instruments of foreign policy. Nevertheless, it is an important one. To understand its effects, however, it is necessary to know the political processes of the target country because it is always marginal to those processes of which it becomes a part. Its effectiveness is greatest the nearer it has access to the centers of elite power in the target country.

Diplomatic Instruments

The diplomatic instrument is one which engages a segment of the bureaucracy of one country with a segment of the bureaucracy of another country. Through these segmental bureaucratic links, one political elite communicates with another political elite. The bureaucratic segment also gathers information from sources not under the control of the target country's elite. These characteristics pertain not only to foreign services but also to other segments of the bureaucratic elite which are engaged with their counterparts in other countries. In the modern period, these may include intelligence officers, military officers, agricultural specialists, information officers, commercial officers, and so forth.

Because these elite segments are professionalized, they are generally reliable with respect to conveying with skill the messages of the political elite of the given country to the elite of the target country. However, there is room for interpretation and analysis by these skilled personnel that can have an impact on how the messages are received and interpreted. Diplomacy represents, nevertheless, only slightly filtered communication with the political elite of another country whenever the subject matter is sufficient to warrant it.

The target, then, is the political elite. Diplomacy will be most effective when the political elite is most receptive. The most effective diplomacy is in the relationship between allies. That is because the perceptions and goals of the ally are most sympathetic and receptive to the advice of the country giving it. Fears and misperceptions are at a minimum.

In other circumstances, there is a need to persuade and convince, to overcome fears and to make the message which is being conveyed believable to the recipient. Moreover, to be convincing, the message must not violate the interests and the personal emotional stability of the target elite. That is not to say that diplomacy may not be used for purposes of coercion, but verbal or written communications alone then become clearly inadequate, and diplomacy must invoke the promise or threat of the other foreign policy instruments.

Diplomacy is most effective in cooperative and supportive relationships. That is, it is in such situations that diplomacy has the greatest chance of success in achieving goals. In conflict situations and on behalf of oppositional policies, it is an important instrument for conveying accurately the policy of a government, but its chances of

The Application of Instruments and Techniques 239

success are less. Apart from the situation wherein the political instrument of one country essentially becomes part of the structure of government of another country, diplomacy has the most direct access of any of the foreign policy instruments upon the target government. The variables which it attempts to manipulate are the more unstable variables in the domestic determinants category.

Informational Instruments

Informational instruments are largely directed toward mass populations and specialized interest groups, although they also have an indirect impact upon elites. It is impossible to measure the direct and indirect effects of informational policies, but some of the limits can be specified. The first limit is that informational policies are not such powerful communications media as are the more substantive acts of a country.

If informational instruments are used to explain and interpret events in a relatively nondistorted way that does not do violence to listeners' feelings about the events as they understand them from other information, it can be a very useful instrument. On the other hand, if the interpretation is not compatible with listeners' attitudes, then it may be useless.

In a conflict situation, there will be information and interpretation provided by any given country's adversaries. Thus, it is useful to attempt to gain a hearing for one's own case. Informational activities, while directed toward recipients who are already favorably inclined to listen to a particular viewpoint, can even shape the views and attitudes of constituencies in some cases. However, the general prestige of a given country among a mass audience will determine to a large extent whether the audience is receptive to messages coming from that country.

Part of the impetus for a country to use the informational instruments is the fact that adversaries also use them to provide different interpretations of events and of situations. While providing facts and interpretations, the major impact of informational instruments is upon attitudes, fears, and will. Informational policies may influence publics to be mobilized or not mobilized by their own governments. Particularly, informational policies may sustain the hopes of disaffected groups who may wish by revolution or otherwise to change the domestic regime under which they are living. While informational policies alone cannot precipitate dissident activities within another country, they can provide an important support to the morale of the dissident groups.

Economic Instruments

Economic instruments are largely channeled through authoritative regimes, either public or private. They are largely used to strengthen a government by adding to its resources or helping to solve its problems. They may also be used to induce a government to carry on a program that it would not be able to conduct without the economic resources.

It is fairly simple to calculate the direct effects of the use of economic instruments. For example, one can see a bridge or a school that has been built. However, the indirect effects are more difficult to predict. For example, the building of a school may lead to more education which may lead to more dissatisfaction which may lead to more revolutionary activities. Just what these indirect effects may be in a given country are difficult to project. On the other hand, one can say that economic progress probably leads to short-term instability but also to long-term stability within any given society.

Whether foreign economic assistance leads to political stability or political instability is dependent more upon the actions of the recipient government and the politics of the given country than upon the foreign aid. Since the recipients of foreign aid are relatively weak, however, they may be in a difficult position to strike bargains with donor countries that are to the advantage of the recipient country.

Under some conditions, it is possible that economic penetration can become so immense that the donor country controls such a large portion of the resources of the recipient country that it is difficult for the recipient to mobilize them on behalf of national policies. Moreover, donor countries are in a position to insist upon certain practices, such as adequate accounting procedures, which may have the indirect effect of helping to shape the policy of the recipient country.

Economic instruments may also be transferred as bribes or as payments to alternative elites. This is fairly marginal foreign policy, but it does give the donor country some access and influence.

Military Instruments

The last class of instruments is military. Military instruments may be displayed, demonstrated for purposes of communication, used to deter an attack by an adversary, and employed in military operations to kill and to destroy. In some periods of history, the late middle ages for instance, the military instrument represented the engagement of a segment of one country's bureaucracy with another country's. In the modern period, however, the military instruments are more versatile

The Application of Instruments and Techniques

and blunt. Modern weapons may be directed against a wide variety of targets, including populations and resources. Nuclear weapons have the capacity to wipe out western civilization in the northern hemisphere in the case of an all-out thermonuclear exchange between the United States and the Soviet Union.

While some wars in the last half of the twentieth century are characterized by the battling of one military unit with another, the more common characteristic is that the production of weapons and their supply is as important as the soldier in the field. Moreover, as in all periods of history, the significance of the military instrument lies in the political goals which it may serve. The direct effects of the military instrument lie in the destruction of lives and material goods and the control of territory. The indirect effects are the exercise of control over politics. Destruction is measurable and highly predictable, but the political impact of destruction on elites is not measurable and is less predictable.

When military weapons are displayed, the target with which they are communicating is, first of all, the population of the country and the political elites of that country where the display is occurring. Since most displays consist of parades and so forth in a given country, the military display helps to shape the attitudes of the population which views the display. There is also direct communication with the political elite who may gain confidence in seeing the military resources of their country.

Displays are also held in other areas of the world, particularly by navies. These are directed as a means of communication to the countries in the region where the navy visits as well as to interested countries from elsewhere. In addition to generating goodwill, hostility, and respect among the populace, depending upon the preconceived framework with which the members of the populace view the display, the display may be used to threaten or to reassure the elites who view it. Although primarily intended for particular elites in a region, public displays may also be viewed by others who are not intended targets. Such indirect effects are not predictable.

The existence of military instruments along with the strategy for their use may act as a deterrent to attack by another country. If the target country is convinced that the given country has the capability to inflict unacceptable damage on it, it will presumably be deterred from initiating an attack on the given country. In such a situation, each country will attempt to find ways of undermining the deterrent if only to insure that its adversary does not get ahead of it in some significant way. This has been the pattern of the modern arms race between the United States and the Soviet Union. Some of the indirect effects of this situation have been the restraint which fears of nuclear war have put on other policies, the reactions of populations to these fears, and the generation of a significant segment of the population into pacifism. This segment in the United States has been difficult to mobilize on behalf of foreign policy goals and is predisposed to receive informational messages which play on their fears.

Military instruments may be used in a very limited way in an attempt to communicate with an adversary. The use of atomic bombs on Japan in 1945 is one example. The mobilization of bombers during the Cuban missile crisis as well as the dispatch of naval vessels to uphold the blockade of Cuba and the American bombing of North Vietnamese torpedo boat bases in 1964 are other examples. Coupled with other forms of communication, these demonstrations may or may not be received accurately. There are some situations in which the psychological predispositions of the recipients make it very difficult for them to believe the communications. Several cases may be compared to illustrate this point.

In the Japanese war, the Japanese were already looking for some way to surrender. The dropping of the bombs on Hiroshima and Nagasaki reinforced these predispositions by making the problem even more urgent than it was. There was little doubt, after three and one half years of war, that the United States had the will to defeat Japan.

In the Cuban missile crisis, somewhat different conditions prevailed, but they still led to effectiveness of the communications functions of the military instruments used. The Soviet Union's attention was focused on the same problem as the United States'. The United States' action demonstrated its will in a way that helped to clear away ambiguities that were in the Soviet leadership's perceptions. Verbal communication clearly explained the use of the military instruments, and threats of further action were clearly communicated. Moreover, it was possible to meet a Soviet interest in not having Cuba invaded which provided a bargaining point to allow the Soviet Union to come to an agreement with the United States.

In Korea, there were obstacles to the Chinese effectively communicating with the United States even though they mobilized masses of troops at the North Korean border. The United States had made a public commitment to unify Korea and the verbal message came indirectly through India which was not entirely trusted. These obstacles prevented the United States from believing the demonstration, and China crossed the Yalu.

In the Tonkin Gulf incident, North Vietnam was intent upon unifying all of Vietnam. Its calculations must have been that its strategy would be successful and that perhaps American will was not great enough to commit large forces to the battle for South Vietnam. Moreover, the election campaign in the United States generated contradictory verbal messages which did not make clear the American threat to defend South Vietnam at all costs. Thus, there was a failure of the communications function of the demonstration of American bombing.

Finally, military instruments are used to kill and destroy. They are directed at people and resources. If sufficient destruction is wreaked to make it physically impossible for a country to fight back, then a military defeat will have been imposed. However, short of that, the attainment of more limited political goals is more problematical. Military instruments may be used to hurt so as to induce behavior or to stop behavior, but the amount of injury that a country is willing to sustain in order to continue what it is doing or not to comply with the will of the adversary is very difficult to calculate. In a well mobilized country, the injury will have the effect of reinforcing mobilization unless there is already a large segment of the population which is disaffected with the foreign policy of the elite.

Military instruments are used against domestic determinants. Where they enter the political process is the first thing to identify. We can then trace the probable influence in terms of the effects of that entry on the domestic political system as a whole. The direct effect is on the point of entry, while the indirect effects spread out from there in conformity with the way in which the system works, although military attack itself may induce changes in the system, as when a democracy is attacked it may reorganize its structure on a more authoritarian basis in order more effectively to resist.

Conclusion

In treating the applications of instruments and techniques, the importance of analyzing not only the instruments themselves but also the targets has been stressed. Since targets are the domestic determinants which were outlined above, the important thing to analyze is the point of entry into the domestic political system where direct effects occur and to trace from there the indirect effects which operate within the system which exists or which it may adopt in the wake of the application of instruments.

Although these processes are not well enough understood to make prediction very reliable, this type of analysis should make the problem clearer. If one knows both the given country and the target country well, he should better be able to predict both the limits and possibilities in a given interaction.

Also stressed was the observation that instruments are used in combination and that these may be thought of as bundles employed in coherent ways. A number of such bundles which use different combinations of instruments and techniques have been identified.

The applications and transfers which have been discussed, as well as the other foreign policy acts treated in previous chapters, are employed on behalf of policies, and they lead to outcomes. To these subjects we now turn.

IV

Policies and Consequences

10

Policies: Insulation, Engagement, Expansion

There is no settled way of classifying foreign policies.[1] Throughout this book, as an attempt has been made to relate variables to foreign policies, three categories—insulation, engagement, and expansion—have been referred to. These are broad and simplified categories which are based on intentions. In part, however, they refer to observable behaviors. For example, when a country joins an alliance, it is following a policy of engagement. Such a policy would not be mistakenly put into another category by any observer. Unfortunately, it is more difficult to place some other foreign policy behaviors unequivocally into one of the categories. This is a problem of operationalization. The categories are considered to be exhaustive and mutually exclusive.

---

1. For a description of the state of the discipline on this question, see Charles F. Hermann, "Policy Classification: Key to the Comparative Study of Foreign Policy," in *The Analysis of International Politics: Essays in Honor of Harold and Margaret Sprout*, ed. James N. Rosenau, Vincent Davis, and Maurice A. East (New York: The Free Press, 1972).

Before exploring each of the categories of policy and treating the more discrete actions associated with each, it will be useful to discuss the basis for the categorization. A state in its foreign policy copes with its environment, and the three categories used here represent three basic ways of coping. The distinction among the categories rest upon whether a country participates in a situation to share control of the situation with others, whether it acts to preclude the situation from its internal life and abstain from participation in it, or whether it acts unilaterally to control the situation and exclude the participation of others.

The central feature of politics—whether at the individual, group, municipal, national, or international level—is control. The distinctions among forms of government rest fundamentally on the numbers of people who exercise control over important decisions, primarily over the question of who shall rule. The development of constitutionalism is a movement to preclude government from exercising control in certain ways and to insure certain forms of shared control. Civil rights are protections for individuals to insure that they can monopolize control over certain aspects of their lives. Public calls for increased "participatory democracy" in the late 1960s sought to displace control from one locus to another.

In international politics, control is normally oligopolistic. That is, control is shared by small numbers of actors who are in both a competitive and cooperative relationship with one another. Some sovereign states choose not to participate in situations that interest them, and some do not have the capacity to participate. Still others, on occasion, choose not to share in an oligopolistic relationship, but act to monopolize a situation. These distinctions among insulation, engagement, and expansion, then rest upon two grounds. The first is whether the state acts unilaterally to control what it is interested in. The second is the arena in which it seeks control—its own country exclusively or an international situation. All three categories involve control, and all include the implication that other countries are excluded from participation in the controlling mechanisms and decisions of the situation or country at issue. Although the latter implication is obvious in the case of insulation and expansion, it is equally present in engagement policies. The fact that some states share control should not obscure the fact that other states are excluded.

Insulation is the retention of control over a country's affairs by avoiding becoming a party to a situation. A policy of insulation is one which attempts to prevent an existing or evolving situation from influencing the country which follows such a policy. Such a policy is unilateral in that, although it is necessarily dependent to some extent upon the ac-

Policies: Insulation, Engagement, Expansion 249

tions of others, it does not attempt to engage with others for its accomplishment.

Engagement is the sharing of control over a situation by joining with other countries in competition for control. Whereas unilateral policies are independent undertakings, policies of engagement are conceived as joint ventures. They may be bilateral or multilateral and vary in the same way as situations.

Expansion is the extension of control beyond what the given country at any given time already controls. Policies of expansion are unilateral in the sense that the country following them seeks to increase its monopoly of control rather than sharing it. Such policies are to some extent dependent upon what others do in response, but they do not involve engagement with others for accomplishment.

Both insulation and engagement rely upon others for support, but the nature of the relationship between the given country and other countries is substantially different in the two forms of policy. Insulation leaves the given country in control of its policies, and what it does never becomes a function of a linked situation. It is, of course, possible to miscalculate and to be drawn into a situation because of the lack of a capacity to withstand attempts by others to overwhelm the given country or to draw it into a situation. Such policies, then, involve risks and may not be successful. The history of neutrals falling before conquerors and being drawn into wars testifies to this. On the other hand, the experiences of Sweden, Burma, and others testify to the viability of this sort of policy in some situations. It might be mentioned that policies of engagement are not always successful either.

The great advantage that policies of engagement bring that policies of insulation do not is new opportunities. For example, although membership in the International Monetary Fund results in some loss of control over national currency, it also provides opportunities for increasing trade and helps to insulate members against crises in international payments. Membership in the United Nations for a small country may force it to subject its policies to the scrutiny of other members, but it also creates opportunities for a given country to attempt to influence major world problems and the policies of larger states. Although international organizations are obvious examples of policies of engagement, there are other ways of engaging, particularly through bilateral diplomatic arrangements and through participation in common actions.

Australia, for example, sent troops to fight in the Vietnam war. While there was some marginal utility from the point of view of military experience and entree to United States decision making, the major advantage for Australia was that its action tended to create an obligation by the United States to defend Australia. In the future, should Australia perceive a direct threat to itself, it can hope to engage the United States in its defense more on Australian terms than if the Commonwealth had not contributed to the defense of South Vietnam.

Policies of engagement may also be attempts to achieve other values such as an increase in a state's domain, but regardless of whether the policy is intended to achieve self-preservation or self-extension,[2] the engagement may form part of a larger situation which is threatening to an adversary coalition. This is a phenomenon that occurred when NATO was formed to protect Western Europe against the Soviet Union. The Soviet Union responded out of the fear of a revitalized Germany by forming the Warsaw Pact after German entry into NATO. In the same way, the United States expanded its engagement in the Western Pacific and Southeast Asia in 1950, but this engagement, in turn, was considered threatening by Communist China.

In this context, where conflict situations exist, the particular actions of the major parties will move the situation one way or the other; toward increasing conflict, cooperation on disengagement, competition, or a new form of coexistence until new factors lead to changes.

Turning to a more extensive analysis of each of the categories of foreign policy, some of the conditions which make it more likely that a country will adopt one kind of policy rather than another will be discussed. In addition, some of the forms which these policies take will be described.

Insulation

Policies of insulation may result from a lack of capacity to engage in a situation, from fears of the response of larger countries (particularly neighbors), from lack of interest in and identity with the situation, or from a preference based either on a genuine calculation that insulation gives the most security or the absence of threats in the environment.

The lack of capacity accounts for most policies of insulation in most situations. In contrast, countries with more developed capacities tend to be engaged in more situations. The lack of capacity must occur in the context of an absence of threats, for external threats are likely to lead a country that lacks capacity to try to mobilize resources from other countries and to engage with the threatening country. Thus, South

---

2. See Arnold Wolfers, "The Pole of Power and the Pole of Indifference," *World Politics* 4 (October 1951), for a discussion of these categories which he employs.

Policies: Insulation, Engagement, Expansion 251

Vietnam engaged the United States in an alliance for protection. It should be pointed out that South Vietnam was not entirely lacking in capacity, its strategic location from the American point of view being one of the more important factors of capacity which it brought to the alliance. If South Vietnam had been entirely lacking in this capacity to ally, it is doubtful if the United States would have been interested in the alliance.

Already cited was the example of the Soviet Union in 1918 withdrawing from World War I—a policy of insulation—because of fears of internal disintegration. The United States in the late 1930s, although not shifting from a policy of engagement, was unable to engage in the European situation except in marginal ways because the public was so cleaved.

Many countries do not engage in many situations because of a lack of identity with them or with some of their components. So long as remote situations are not threatening, there is little incentive for a country without an identity with it to become engaged. An example of a country which sought insulation in order to protect its security is Turkey during the Second World War.[3]

Policies of insulation are dependent, to a large extent, upon their acceptance by other countries. In general, other countries will respect insulation so long as they see more advantages than disadvantages flowing from that respect. At a point where they can measure opportunities in a policy of opposition to an insulated state which outweigh the costs and risks of such opposition, they will take action to invade the state or otherwise gain its commitment to their own ends. Obviously, an extraordinarily powerful state can pursue policies of insulation in a situation where there is no direct threat to it. To some extent, it relies on others, but it is also safe in the assumption that the costs of gaining its commitment will be extraordinary. Thus, the United States in the nineteenth century could safely pursue policies of insulation in a context where the British controlled the Atlantic by virtue of a continental European balance of power. Very small states, whose resources would not add much to a coalition, are usually fairly secure in pursuing policies of insulation, although their security rests almost entirely on factors which they cannot either control or influence in any significant way. States which are neither gigantic nor miniscule, however, are in a more problematic situation.

---

3. See Nuri Eren, "The Foreign Policy of Turkey," in Joseph E. Black and Kenneth W. Thompson, *Foreign Policies in a World of Change* (New York: Harper & Row, 1963).

Burma, for example, is insulated, but its insulation is almost entirely dependent upon China. Without China's acceptance, Burma could not remain in its position. This dependence, however, makes Burma vulnerable, and should China find it in its interest to take over Burma, it could probably do so, although it could be costly were Burma to adopt the Finnish response of 1939-40 to the Soviet attempt to conquer its neighbor.

Sweden, on the other hand, is heavily armed and benefits from the advantage of geographical location. In World War II, it was dependent upon the tolerance of Germany. Since then, it has been dependent upon the balance of power between the Soviet Union and the United States as well as its own armed forces. Since Sweden poses no threat to any of its neighbors, and since it is heavily armed, the costs of threatening it outweigh the advantages for any potential threatener. Moreover, Sweden—like other neutrals—can place some reliance on the international community's belief in sovereignty and self-determination.

The history of other European neutrals such as Belgium and the Netherlands in World War II, however, demonstrates how greatly policies of insulation do depend upon the international community. When the democracies were weak, they could not act to uphold that integrity of nations to which they were committed, and these small, neutral countries were overrun by superior force.

Expansion

Certain regimes seek to expand their territories. Secure in their own states and holding an ideology or set of beliefs that induce them to conquer and convert other peoples, these regimes seek, through a variety of means including military conquest, to gain dominion over additional territory. Because such attempts are threatening to others, threatened parties will generally attempt to form coalitions to resist the expansionist power. This is the familiar principle of balance of power.

Policies of expansion result from a set of domestic determinants in which the regime does not fear for its own tenure and in which the values which it wishes to transmit and is acting upon are predominant over fears. A major value that is often present in such a situation is that of rectitude. When there are doubts about what is right, it is unlikely that a regime would launch a major threat to a status quo situation. It is for this reason that democracies tend not to be so aggressive as certain dictatorships, for the very nature of democracy is that there is an absence of agreed-upon absolutes of rectitude. Rectitude is not un-

Policies: Insulation, Engagement, Expansion 253

known in democracies, but it does not play so large a part in the scheme of values there as it does in dictatorships.

Policies of expansion may be conducted with a variety of implements. Nazi Germany used—in combination with diplomacy, fifth columns, propaganda, and other tools—military force. Kwame Nkrumah of Ghana used propaganda and diplomacy to seek a Pan-African domain under his leadership. Khrushchev used diplomacy in the Berlin crisis of 1958-62. Hitler was defeated militarily as the coalition opposed to him was able to outproduce Germany while also depriving Germany of resources through bombing and battlefield slaughter. Nkrumah's foreign policies were pursued in an insecure tenure at home, and he was eventually brought down by a military takeover in his own country. Khrushchev ended his campaign for changing the status of Berlin after his defeat in the Cuban missile crisis, and because he needed to protect his regime against the internal pressures for domestic spending.

Policies of expansion are most likely to occur under each of the following sets of circumstances. The first is during a war in which a country is successful and it changes its goals to take advantage of the momentum of the crisis. The United States in Korea is an example of this circumstance. Another circumstance arises at the end of a war when the victors seek to make territorial arrangements most advantageous to themselves. The Soviet Union's activities in Eastern Europe and American actions in the Western Pacific at the end of World War II are examples of this circumstance. Another circumstance is that in which a given country feels that it can gain certain advantages by finding a solution to a particular problem in an unsettled situation. Examples of this are the Soviet pressures on Berlin and the Chinese acquisition of the Aksai Chin Plateau in its 1962 action against India. Another is the irredentist thrust into territory claimed by a given country. Egypt's attempt to recover Palestine is but one of many examples of this circumstance. Another circumstance is the political vacuum in which countries wish to deny territory to an adversary. United States' intervention in Greece and Vietnam and Soviet intervention in the Congo are examples of this circumstance at work. Finally, there is the circumstance in which the domestic determinants are structured as outlined above.

Policies of expansion result from attempts to gain power, influence, and security. They may also result from the wish for economic gain. Policies generally characterized as imperialistic have this kind of motivation, but imperialism does not exhaust the policies related to this motivation. While Japan in 1931–42 can be explained in this way, the demands of poor countries for economic assistance cannot; indeed, they cannot even be put into the category of policies of expansion.

Engagement

A state does not engage with other states for the achievement of its goals if it can reach them alone. However, since states cannot achieve their foreign policy goals alone for the most part, they engage with other states in order to achieve their goals or to prevent other states from achieving theirs at a given state's expense. How narrow or extensive goals may be can vary considerably, but states will tend to engage with as few others as are necessary to the achievement of their purposes.

Engagement is not only more common than insulation and expansion, it also tends to take forms that are more regularized. Bilateral and multilateral engagements will be dealt with. Under multilateral engagements, there will be a treatment of conferences, multilateral alliances, regional integration, and universal international organizations. The discussion will include the characteristics of each type of engagement, the problems associated with it, and the conditions under which each is created, maintained, and transformed.

Bilateral Engagements

Bilateral engagements are the most common form of transactions between countries. This is because many goals may be met through the limited cooperation or the limited conflict of a two-party interaction, and because it is easier to maintain control over a bilateral situation in many cases. Moreover, the characteristic of the small group, pointed out by Mancur Olson[4]—that both parties can rely on the mutually-shared goals, or public goods, without coercion or individual payoffs (private goods)—is most apparent in a bilateral relationship.

On the other hand, not all bilateral relationships are entered into for identical interests. They may be for mutual benefit in a way that is similar to a business transaction between buyer and seller. The interests are quite different but compatible and are served by similar means through the transaction. The alliance between Britain and Portugal is the classic example of this.

Bilateral engagements come into existence when two countries agree on a set of mutual interests (identical or parallel) or when one country makes a demand on another country and the second responds. If the engagement is of the cooperative type and the scope is limited to the two countries alone, it will tend to persist so long as the two countries agree. On the other hand, if it is conflictive and the scope of the effects is wide,

---

4. See Mancur Olson Jr., *The Logic of Collective Action: Public Goods and the Theory of Groups* (New York: Schocken Books, 1968).

other countries will attempt to gain some measure of control over the situation. As hypothesized in the chapter on situations, such situations will tend to be relatively short-lived because other countries will attempt to gain some measure of control of the situation and because the two engaged countries will either resolve their conflict or diverge in their interests.

If bilateral engagements make demands on or threaten other countries, new situations are created in which the bilateral engagement may be treated, with respect to that new situation, as a separate actor. There are separate problems involved in the relationship of the two engaged countries which will be dealt with below, and these offer further opportunities to adversaries to attempt to encourage division between the allies.

When the parties to the bilateral engagement are relatively equal with respect to skills, resources, size, and so forth, the problems associated with bilateral engagements are those of maintaining the conditions of the transaction or the implementation of the mutual goals. Unless new interests crop up or one of the parties, governed by its domestic determinants, betrays its partner, the relationship is likely to persist if it is a cooperative one. If it is conflictful, it will disappear when the conflict is resolved.

On the other hand, if the partnership is between countries that are very unequal, different problems arise. In a cooperative relationship, the larger country faces the problem of being drawn, through the actions of the smaller partner, into a conflict that does not serve its interests and goals. The smaller partner, on the other hand, is faced with the problem of making the partnership serve its interests without becoming simply a function of the interests of its partner in another situation to which its partner, but not it, is a party. The mutual interdependency of the two countries will tend to perpetuate the alliance, but this struggle over control of the direction of the alliance will be a constant problem. This is the so-called client state problem, and what this analysis suggests is that the relationship is considerably more complicated than a simple one of a puppeteer pulling strings. This is particularly true when the bilateral engagement is one side of a conflict situation with another coalition.

There may also be bilateral engagements within alliances and across alliances. Both of these tend to be disintegrating factors in the alliances. Examples of bilateral engagements within alliances are the special relationship of the United States and the United Kingdom, the French-German Treaty of 1963, the Churchill-Stalin agreements of 1944 on spheres of influence in Eastern Europe, and the United Kingdom-French invasion of Egypt in 1956. Examples of cross-alliance bilateral engagements are the United States-Soviet Union arms negotiations of the 1960s, the Cuban missile crisis, French-Rumanian trade and cultural agreements, and the American-Chinese rapprochement of the early 1970s. A multiplicity of such bilateral engagements would undermine a multilateral alliance, but few of them simply impose strains on an alliance which will most likely be able to cope with them.

Let us return to the client state problem, for it is one of the most intriguing in the analysis of foreign policy. Using traditional power theory or capabilities analysis, we should expect that as the client becomes involved in a conflict with an adversary it becomes more dependent for supplies, advice, and so forth from its benefactor. Being more dependent, the client should be under the control of the benefactor, and the benefactor, having more instruments to manipulate, should have more power over its client. We have seen in Vietnam and in the Middle East that this is not true. Empirical evidence seems to suggest that under conditions of conflict the client country increases its power vis-à-vis its benefactor and that the relationship is a very complex one, in which both countries manipulate each other at various times. What is the explanation for this?

According to the present analysis, both the situation and the domestic determinants point to this conclusion. Under conditions of conflict, a population may be mobilized more effectively than under other conditions. Even though Vietnam had a major segment of its population—the Viet Cong—actively fighting the regime, the government was at an advantage in mobilizing the population for achieving its goals. This was enhanced during the war because the population had been moved from the countryside to the cities. The channels for change and decision making were limited to the government. The United States did not have any other channel to work with. It was committed to opposition to the Viet Cong, and its dependence upon the government pressured it to accept coercive treatment of other forces in society that might offer alternatives to the incumbent elite. Both the elite and the United States were heavily dependent upon the military bureaucracy to prosecute the war. The only channel for influencing decision making, then, was the government, and the United States' position rested upon support for the government. The United States then became a factor giving cohesion and legitimacy to the government. Earlier, it was hypothesized that changes in basic decisions were most unlikely to come through an incumbent elite unless it lived through some profound experience. The United States' military commitment, however, prevented that profound experience of defeat from occurring. Because of its other alliance commitments, the United States could not betray the South Vietnamese government without

Policies: Insulation, Engagement, Expansion 257

undermining its other commitments. That is, the Vietnam situation was linked intimately with other situations through the United States. Thus, there was a relatively equal struggle for control of the partnership. Both sides had military and other instruments to use in attempting to manipulate each other, but essentially it was a diplomatic and political struggle to control the goals, strategy, and tactics of the partnership. The great strength and resources of the United States gave it close access to the Government of South Vietnam, but the situation did not allow one-sided control by the patron. Having been a two-party alliance, however, insured that both strove to achieve the mutual purposes of the alliance.

In summary, bilateral cooperative engagements are likely to find both partners cooperating to achieve the mutual purposes, but they are also characterized—like other political relationships—by a struggle to define goals, make policy decisions, and to shape the relationship. This mixture of cooperation and conflict is also characteristic of engagements of the conflict type, although different problems attend the two basic types of engagement, with different mixes of struggle and collaboration.

Multilateral Engagements

Multilateral engagements have somewhat different characteristics from bilateral engagements. Not only are there more actors, but also the patterns of collaboration, conflict, and control are different. The very existence of a multilateral engagement might be thought to imply a defeat for the objectives of monopolistic and duopolistic control.

Conferences—There arise from time to time problems that transcend the boundaries of states but do not obviously fall under the jurisdiction of the regularized procedures of alliances or international organizations. When political leaders become conscious of these problems, they sometimes feel a need for a multilateral *ad hoc* conference or at least envision some advantages in sharing information or probing for common strategies concerning the problem. Such conferences may be called under the auspices of an international organization or by a host country.

A growing consciousness of the problems of ecology in the late 1960s, for example, led the United Nations to convene a conference in Stockholm in 1972. In 1954, Indonesia hosted a conference of nonaligned countries in Bandung to bring together those states resisting great power pressures for alignment. More often, conferences are held under the auspices of established international organizations. When the problem of air piracy arose, for example, it was discussed in meetings of the International Air Transport Association.

Very large international conferences, in addition, tend to produce associated caucusing groups. These are narrower engagements to gain cooperation in putting forward the interests of the member states. The Group of 77, a caucusing group of the poorer countries, for example, was formed to protect the interests of those countries at the 1964 meeting of the United Nations Conference on Trade and Development (UNCTAD). At the United Nations itself, various caucusing groups have formed.[5]

Because of the diversity of countries, such caucuses and conferences seldom result in identical behavior. They have the advantages of exchanging information and encouraging some measure of cooperation, but such engagements fall short of the close coordination, common strategies, and joint planning that characterize multilateral alliances.

Multilateral alliances are associations of states in a coalition to oppose other states or coalitions. This means that alliances are units in conflictive situations. If the situation is transformed from conflict to another type of situation, or if the situation disappears, the alliance will dissolve. The creation, maintenance, and transformation of such situations are subject to the same processes as any other conflict.[6] We are not concerned here with the larger conflict situation to which the alliance is a party but rather with the cooperative situation of the alliance itself.

Alliances may be of a federal type or a hierarchical type. The federal type of alliance is one in which the partners are of relatively equal status; the hierarchical type is one in which there is a dominant partner and the other partners are more dependent upon it than it is upon them. The problems of management are different in each. In the federal type, policies are coordinated through diplomatic negotiations. In the hierarchical type, policies are largely determined either in the national capital of the dominant partner or through an integrated political structure.

Regardless of the type of alliance that develops, a leader or federator is necessary for a multilateral alliance to come into existence. Although the alliance serves a common or mutual purpose, the idea of an alliance must be conceived and promulgated to other prospective members. So long as the common purpose is served, the alliance will be maintained,

---

5. See Thomas Hovet Jr., *Bloc Politics at the United Nations* (Cambridge: Harvard University Press, 1960); Robert O. Keohane, "Political Influence in the General Assembly," *International Conciliation*, No. 557 (March 1966); and Hayward R. Alker and Bruce M. Russett, *World Politics in the General Assembly* (New Haven: Yale University Press, 1965).

6. For a good treatment of the dynamics of alliances, see George Liska, *Nations in Alliance* (Baltimore: The Johns Hopkins Press, 1962).

Policies: Insulation, Engagement, Expansion

and—given an organizational structure—it may persist beyond the time that the common interest is served. The most common purpose served by an alliance is to protect the members against an outside threat. Thus, alliances usually involve military coordination.

Alliances will be subject to some strains and stresses because each member will not be threatened in equal amounts. Moreover, each member will have its own interests to pursue, sometimes within the alliance and sometimes in other situations. As indicated above, alliances will tend to be transformed with the development of large numbers of significant bilateral engagements.

In the absence of coercion or inducements by the federator, an alliance will tend to have as few members as are necessary to accomplish the goals of the alliance. While alliances may add members and expand, this activity will tend to make the alliance lose focus and will become a stress on the alliance because new members bring added interests to the partnership. If members develop strong interests which are antithetical to the common purpose of the alliance, the alliance may expel the member and remain intact, provided that the truncated alliance can still serve a common purpose of the remaining members.

The larger the number of members, the more difficult will be the problem of alliance management. This is because each ally has its own interests in addition to those of the alliance. This means that it will be difficult for the partners to work out arrangements that will satisfy the national interests of its members within the context of the alliance. If there is a dominant partner, it is in a position to satisfy the national interests of smaller members by accommodating or giving the things that are desired by the smaller members, assuming a continuing commitment by the smaller member to the alliance. In the case of French demands on NATO, the insistence on a national command structure outside of NATO's integrated command, there was nothing that the dominant partner—the United States—could give except tolerance for the French position and the physical removal of resources from French soil.

The alternative for the dominant partner is to refuse demands and coerce the smaller partner to accept domination. This response to smaller partners' demands was illustrated in the cases of Hungary in 1956 and in Czechoslovakia in 1968. In these cases, demands to satisfy national interests were met by dominant partner coercion to maintain the alliance.

If there is no dominant partner, members of an alliance may make demands on each other to satisfy national interests which the other partners are unable to meet. This will lead to a breakup of the alliance. The most common condition in which this set of events occurs is the aftermath of a war when the winning alliance begins to be composed of competing demands in the peace settlement after the common purpose has been served. Other members of the winning alliance may be unable to meet these demands, and the alliance may dissolve or be transformed into an adversary relationship. This was the case with the Grand Alliance after World War II, when the Soviet Union and the western countries made demands on each other that neither could meet.

One of the problems which may arise in a hierarchical alliance comes about because the dominant partner attempts to keep control of the policies of the alliance while the deferent partners wish to gain a measure of control. The dominant partner may assist its allies in strengthening themselves, and this strength in turn may assist them in making claims for control. If the dominant partner is unwilling to accede to these claims—and it will be reluctant to do so because they are based on national as opposed to common interests—this may lead to fissures in the alliance and even to the unsatisfied member's leaving it. Before doing so, however, the challenging member will attempt to gain a share of control in the alliance on a par with the dominant partner. This was the case with both China and France in the late 1950s in their respective alliances.

The scope of alliances is determined by those who form the alliance and by the situation it is intended to address. In addition, alliances will form new threats to the adversary coalition against which they are formed. Other countries in a region will define their foreign policies to a large extent with respect to the alliances that exist. If alliances are formed around worldwide actors, all the countries in the world may define their foreign policies with respect to the major blocs. This happened in the aftermath of World War II when all the countries in the world adopted either affiliation with one of the blocs or a policy of nonalignment with respect to the blocs. Although this represented a pattern, we should not forget that each country has its own interests which are predominant but that it is obliged by the world situation to accommodate those interests.

Alliances are basically cooperative engagements. As cooperative undertakings, they are subject to the politics of coordination. They may, however, adopt an integrative type of management in which there may be a monopoly or an oligopoly of control. If there arises a major threat to the monopolistic or oligopolistic leader(s), and particularly if one of the bases of the alliance is political ideology, then the alliance relationship between certain members may become transformed into an adversary relationship. The situation thus created will be limited in scope not only to the two sides in the dispute (including whichever alliance

Policies: Insulation, Engagement, Expansion

partners align themselves with the two sides) but also the other members of the alliance. Further, the dispute may offer opportunities to other countries to engage with one or the other side in the dispute to achieve goals that would not be achievable if the alliance were solid. The disputing partners to the alliance may be receptive to such engagements because they will be able to win certain issues that they would not be able to if they kept the disputing ally. Although the winning coalition— headed by the dominant partner in the cooperative alliance—is more likely to be receptive, the disputing partner may also be in the hope of forming a new winning coalition.

The breakup of the Chinese-Soviet Union alliance illustrates these remarks. As the dispute between the Soviet Union and China grew, the Soviet Union became more receptive to a series of relationships with western countries which aimed at the enhancement of Soviet economic development and trade and at arms control. The loss of these advantages would have been the cost of maintaining the cohesion of its alliance with China. As a corollary, western countries would not have had the opportunities nor have gained the advantages of these relationships had the Soviet-Chinese alliance remained cohesive.

Although not successful, the Chinese also sought new links. These were with the underdeveloped world where China sought to promote an international organization of "new emerging forces" and a coalition of non-whites. Its ambitions were dashed by the coups in Algeria and Indonesia.

Following its "cultural revolution" in the 1960s during which China withdrew from active diplomacy, China once again in the early 1970s sought to establish new links, this time more successfully. Diplomatic relations were established with many countries, the People's Republic displaced Nationalist China as a member of the United Nations, and nearly normal relations with the United States were inaugurated.

There may be other situations that are susceptible to the development of new relationships. If a country is frustrated in its attempts to gain its goals through its old alliance, it may seek opportunities of finding other ways of achieving its goals, or it may redefine the goals in such a way that it can gain them by engaging in different situations. It may, in the face of failure of policies of engagement, turn toward policies of insulation, as China did in its cultural revolution, at least for a period of time until new resources are developed internally and/or until new opportunities present themselves in the international realm.

Regional integration—A phenomenon that has developed which is a variation on the multilateral alliance is the multilateral community organization premised on the theory of integration.[7] Through cooperative schemes and the building of common institutions, a gradual transfer of loyalties of populations is expected to occur, leading to the formation of new units which will grapple with the problems of the internal communities and their environments. These efforts are, in other words, attempts to restructure the more stable elements of domestic determinants and the creation of new ones, a process of transforming nation-states into larger entities with similar characteristics.

Some success has been achieved in Europe among the six community members in coordinating policies in the area of economic cooperation. However, each country has its own political problems which are grappled with fairly successfully by national regimes, and there has been no integration of political decision making on the domestic side. Moreover, each country has its distinct foreign policy problems both within and without the alliance. Thus, there has been no integration of foreign policy decision making. The international political situation is such that even the security community type of situation[8] has not been achieved, for there is in the divided Germany situation still a possibility that Germany might be reunited under auspices of alignment with the Soviet Union and could be threatening to France. Thus, it appears that the states will continue to dominate the situation for some time to come. As Britain becomes increasingly active in the Common Market, this probability will be reinforced.

We could demonstrate these propositions with respect to the foreign policy impact on integrating communities by charting the situations in which each of the countries are engaged. Until there is a substantial overlap in the foreign policy engagements of the individual countries, there is unlikely to be a substantial forward thrust in the direction of creating a new unit.

Universal international organization is the last category of multilateral engagements which will be discussed. Such organizations are based on a principle of voluntary association. The voluntary association is illustrated by the League of Nations and the United Nations. Just as with more limited multilateral engagements, universal organizations must have a federator which conceives and initiates the cooperative scheme.

---

7. See Ernst B. Haas, *The Uniting of Europe* (Stanford: Stanford University Press, 1958) and *Beyond the Nation-State* (Stanford: Stanford University Press, 1964) and Karl W. Deutsch, et al., *Political Community and the North Atlantic Area* (Princeton: Princeton University Press, 1957), for analyses of integration and related concepts.

8. See Deutsch, et al., *Political Community and the North Atlantic Area*.

Policies: Insulation, Engagement, Expansion 263

In the associative organization, like the United Nations, countries pursue their own interests. The politics of the organization is the politics of factions and consensus. Consensus means that, on some occasions, it may be possible to achieve common policies through the support of some factions and the toleration of others. However, there are factions which, by opposing the actions of the organization, can effectively veto those actions. The common interest of the organization is not likely to be effectively implemented except on those occasions when the most powerful members are agreed upon a course of action.

Because the organization is one in which the operating principle is struggle, it is characterized by all of the conditions of interaction. Even when conflict occurs in the organization, however, it is subject to the rules of conducting affairs and may be a substitute for conflict elsewhere.[9] Although the organization can be governed by the powerful when they agree, the smaller members can exploit the more powerful members in the same way that the smaller members of an alliance can.

International organizations come into existence when a federator is able to induce others to join as a condition of the peace settlement after a war. It will be maintained so long as it is able to deal with issues in a significant way. If the organization attempts to expand beyond what the members are willing to allow, however, it will be weakened and severely limited by the members. This happened to the United Nations in the Congo crisis and the ensuing constitutional and financial struggle between the United States and the Soviet Union. When one refers to the organization attempting to do things, it is a reference to the set of instruments which the organization embodies. If the members are unwilling to use the set of instruments available through the organization, then the organization will become irrelevant to the politics of international relations.[10]

The evolution of an international organization is subject to the same kinds of problems which international communities are in the sense that members deal with their foreign policy situations largely outside the institutions of the organization. Even where they deal with them within the institution, there is a tendency to use regional rather than global instruments. The politics of control leads countries to use those instruments which are most efficacious to their maintenance or gaining of

---

9. This point has been made by Chadwick Alger in his "Non-Resolution Consequences of the United Nations and Their Effect on International Conflict," *Journal of Conflict Resolution* 5 (1961).

10. See the analysis of this thesis by Dag Hammarskjöld in his *Introduction to the Annual Report of the Secretary-General 1960*.

control of situations, and bringing a problem into an international organization very often means a loss of control. For small countries, however, the organization may be an effective channel for attempting to gain a measure of control over situations from which they would otherwise be precluded.

Conclusion

The classification scheme for foreign policies developed in this chapter is based on the notion of whether a country acts alone or in conjunction with others and on the domain over which it seeks control. Although the scheme is a broad one, the distinctions which it makes are fundamental ones.

Less broadly conceived policies and discrete actions may be encompassed by one of the three categories of insulation, engagement, and expansion. Engagement is the most common category of policy, and the more common forms that such policies take have been discussed.

These categories relate to the question, Who controls? The foreign policy acts which have been discussed in previous chapters relate the dynamics of exercising control and wielding influence in the context of the more fundamental political question which has served as the organizing focus of this chapter.

We now turn to the final topic in this book: the consequences of foreign policy.

11

Consequences

Foreign policies have consequences for both the environment and the state. In discussing consequences, the concepts of adjustment and transformation will be used in dealing with the environment, and the concept of adaptation will be used in treating the impact of foreign policy on domestic society.

The International System

At any given time, the foreign policies of states result in a world structure. The policies of the most powerful states are the most significant factors in creating this structure. The bipolar structure that grew out of World War II and the balance of power structure that characterized world politics in the preceding period are examples. Although such structures may be relatively stable for periods of time, they are marked by a dynamic rather than a static quality. States are required to make constant adjustments to one another to maintain a rough equilibrium. Moreover, statesmen tend to be dissatisfied with one or another feature of the structure.

Such dissatisfactions are the result of changes in the domestic determinants. If, for example, a state's economy grows over a period of time, it may seek additional natural resources and markets and may seek enhanced status in the environment. Activities associated with these goals place demands on other countries which must adjust to them, either supporting or resisting the demands. This is not to suggest that we can easily classify states into those which place demands on the system and those which object to the demands. The pace of development and change does, however, vary among different countries. Thus, there is an unevenness of dissatisfactions and demands.

If a state's economy contracts through the devastation or the expenditure of its resources, its capacity is reduced, its predispositions are altered, and the demands it can make on the international system are diminished. The state may be forced to withdraw from some of the situations in which it was previously engaged.

Sometimes, the changes within a country are dramatic and radical. Although such changes do not always result in placing equally radical and dramatic demands on the international system, they sometimes do. When such demands emanate from states which are already powerful, the entire existing structure of the international system may be challenged. The challenges of Napoleonic France and Hitlerian Germany were of this order. Such profound challenges normally result in war, and, regardless of who triumphs, the structure of the international system is normally transformed in a magnitude which Kaplan refers to as a "steplevel function."[1]

The reason for the significant transformation is the alteration in both the domestic determinants of the actors and their relationships. Significantly altered or new situations interest the actors, and the capacities and predispositions are altered, sometimes fundamentally. As the aftermath of World War II so starkly illustrates, sometimes the victorious allies are unable to agree on a new world order or even on arrangements for controlling more limited situations. The transformation of the international system was particularly difficult in the aftermath of World War II for two reasons. First, there was a breakdown in the dominance of the major powers of the prewar period because their resources were diminished. Second, the newly predominant powers had particularly acute communications problems in coming to agreement on a new world order.

---

1. Morton A. Kaplan, *System and Process in International Politics* (New York: John Wiley and Sons, Inc., 1957).

Thus, a new structure arises on an informal basis, grounded in conflict and competition. Continuous adjustments are made as determinants change, and each country copes as best it can with its environment. The processes which have been described and analyzed in previous chapters go forward.

So long as states are able to adjust to the demands of the environment and those demands do not outrun the capacity of the international system to absorb whatever disruptive tendencies they contain, the international system will remain in a state of homeostatic equilibrium.[2] This state of dynamic balance refers to the pattern of relationships of the system as a whole. The foreign policies of countries very often represent demands upon other countries. Such demands may be distinguished by their effect on the international system. If the demands are responded to effectively, the pattern of relationships which consitute the international system remains essentially the same. On the other hand, if the demands cannot be absorbed, the international system may be transformed to a very different pattern of relationships. So long as the system maintains the same pattern, we can conveniently apply the term "homeostatic equilibrium."

Insofar as system equilibrium represents a form of order and the absence of war, it is a desirable state of affairs. But to the extent that it is unjust in the view of one or more states, it may be challenged. Order and justice may be incompatible, and the international system is always threatened with the inability to make them compatible by incremental adjustment.

The state of the international system as a whole is of concern not just to the countries which are dominant in shaping it. Its stability or transformation is determined by their actions, but smaller countries necessarily must take the state of the overall system into account in formulating their policies, particularly if the situations in which they are interested are linked to the dominant international system. In such cases, their maintenance of control is dependent on the insulation of the situation from the broader scope of the international system.

To attempt to generalize about adjustment and transformation in the international environment, let us return to the categories of situations analysis. They deal with the patterns and forms of interaction among states.

---

2. The categories of system capacity and disruption are those used by Kaplan, ibid., and Richard N. Rosecrance, *Action and Reaction in World Politics: International Systems in Perspective* (Boston and Toronto: Little, Brown, and Company, 1963). Homeostatic equilibrium is a concept employed by Kaplan.

Situations

Let us briefly recall the dimensions of situations described in chapter 4, for changes in those dimensions are what constitute transformation. The first dimension was boundaries. One component of boundaries is the arena, and arenas were categorized as local, regional, supraregional, and global. A second component was scope, and it was suggested that scope could be identified by examining linked situations. Objects made up the final component of boundaries, and who controls the objects at any given time was cited as an important question to be concerned with in analyzing situations.

The number and rank of the actors constitute the second dimension of situations. A distinction was drawn particularly between two-actor situations and those in which there are several actors. The relative power of the actors—both among those involved in the situation and among the whole universe of actors—is an important consideration to attend to.

The third dimension is structure. Four types of structure were identified. The two-actor or dyadic structure is one. Another is the two-coalition type. Third is the several actor with a dominant partner structure. The final type is the several actor without a dominant partner. Paths of influence vary by the type of structure.

The fourth dimension of situations was the conditions of interaction. Four categories of condition were given: conflict, competition, cooperation, and integration. It was also noted that, although situations tend to be dominated by one condition of interaction, they also are infused with other conditions. For example, predominantly conflictful situations contain elements of cooperation, and elements of conflict are present in predominantly cooperative situations.

The consequences of foreign policy in the environment are treated as the impact of policies on these dimensions of situations. These consequences, or foreign policy outcomes, may either reinforce and stabilize the dimensions of a situation, or they may transform them.

Although the contrasting categories of stability and transformation are employed to characterize the consequences of foreign policy, it is necessary to recognize variations within them. Stability and transformation are both relative. Few situations are stagnant, for change in determinants and policies occur constantly. We must expect incremental adjustments in the dimensions of situations as quite normal. For example, the predominantly conflictful situation involving Israel and the Arab states may move between periods in which their mutual hostility is expressed verbally and periods in which they are at war. We would, despite the variation in behavior which we do recognize as significant, characterize the situation as stable. It would be transformed when one of the dimensions of situations which has been identified is changed from one of the categories to another. For example, if Israel and Jordan were to change their relationship from one of predominant conflict to one of predominant cooperation by concluding a peace treaty, we would say that the situation was transformed incrementally because the number of actors in the conflict situation was diminished by one. A more significant transformation would have occurred if all of the Arab states and Israel were to conclude a peace treaty, changing the conditions of interaction of the entire situation. The situation could also be transformed significantly if either or both the United States and the Soviet Union were to be drawn into the situation as direct rather than peripheral actors. In such a case, the Middle East would become merely a function of the strategic interaction of the global situation. The scope would definitely have been changed from regional to supraregional or global, and the arena too may have changed in the same fashion.

These are broad and comprehensive categories which are used here. They are useful for analyzing situations, but they have the disability of obscuring a limited number of conceivable consequences that, although not contradictory, require further distinctions. We could agree, for example, that a thermonuclear exchange between two countries would represent significant change (perhaps transformation) from a conventional war. In the scheme here, such a change would fall within the category of stability, for the situation would remain predominantly conflictful. The elaboration of such distinctions, however, would have the disability of obscuring the comprehensive nature of the present scheme which is able to handle many more cases at a single level of analysis.[3] In this scheme, of course, the phenomenon of nuclear exchange would not be missed. It would be picked up both in the application of instruments and in consequences for the domestic determinants of a country which, in turn, would lead to transformation of the situation.

Each of the dimensions of situations may remain stable or may be transformed under varying conditions. The complexity of foreign policy activity makes it difficult to specify the conditions systematically. We can, however, discuss some of the conditions that tend to keep adjustments within the established patterns of situations and some of those that tend to produce transformations to different patterns.

---

3. For an elaboration of useful distinctions related to nuclear and thermonuclear war, see Herman Kahn, *On Escalation: Metaphors and Scenarios* (Baltimore: Penguin Books, 1968).

The boundaries and structure of situations will tend to be retained so long as the direct, central actors have the capacity to maintain control of the situation and so long as larger countries are restrained. In the case of situations which do not involve the highest ranking—or most powerful—countries in the world, the situation will remain insulated from the international system as a whole only under these conditions. If the direct, central actors lost control either through the loss of capacity or through an imminent and massive threat to some dimension of the situation, then we can expect the intervention of larger countries. Larger countries may not be restrained, thus intervening in otherwise more limited situations, if they regard the development of the situation to be threatening to themselves or their interests.

In the case of situations in which the world dominant actors are the direct, central actors, the stability of the situation is dependent upon their control alone, although changes may occur if other countries increase their capacities to the point where they can seriously challenge that control. If the condition of interaction is conflictful among the world dominant actors, and if other actors attempt to engage in the situation, the dominant actors may collaborate to exclude them or form alliances with the other actors, thus increasing the conflict by increasing the arena, scope, and number of actors.

If one of the dominant actors develops its capacity at a dramatic rate which surpasses the capacity of the other dominant partners, it may attempt to transform the situation by reducing the number of partners, seeking monopoly control over the situation. Alternatively, it may attempt to engage with one or two other partners in an alliance to achieve a smaller oligopolistic control than exists in the period before its action. The subordinate, potential partners in such an alliance might fear domination, but they might, alternatively, receive sufficient benefits to enter the engagement.

In alliances in which there is a hegemonial partner, the subordinate partners strive to develop their capacities and to seek engagements either within the alliance or across blocs in order to increase control of themselves and to gain increased freedom of action in dealing with their environments. If their capacities are sufficient, the cooperation condition that had previously existed between them and the hegemonial partner will move increasingly in the direction of conflict.

The conditions of interaction tend to be perpetuated by habits and by the achievement of interests. On the other hand, they tend to be transformed by new experiences and dissatisfactions. The condition of conflict arises when two or more countries seek the same objects which are not divisible. Competition arises when they seek similar but divisible objects. Conflict and competition produce cooperation as the conflicting countries seek support from others. Cooperation may also arise from considerations of mutual benefit, but it, in turn, gives rise to conflict and competition because cooperation among any limited set of partners excludes others. Integration may be achieved if a federator is able to persuade partners of the benefits of closer cooperation.

The dual and reciprocal relationship among the conditions of interaction suggests that the level of participation in situations may not easily be distinguished by a dichotomy of hostility and friendliness or of conflict acts and cooperative acts. Most often, conflict implies cooperation not only with other countries than the adversary but also some level of cooperation even with the adversary. Thus, the more active a country is in its environment, the more its participation is characterized by all of the conditions of interaction.[4]

Additionally, the increased participation in all conditions of interaction gives the actor the means to manipulate objects that will reinforce or change the conditions of interaction. In a conflict situation, for example, an active participant can extend threats to additional situations, thus increasing the conflict. On the other hand, the same actor may promise rewards with respect to another situation, thus emphasizing the cooperative condition present in the relationship and leading it in the direction of transformation to a predominantly cooperative set of interactions.

Countries which are involved in single situations have fewer opportunities to engage in such trade-offs. Moreover, in very tense situations, even the leaders of very active countries may have their attention focused so directly upon a single situation that it is difficult for them to imagine how they can relate other situations to the one in focus.

Apart from these considerations, there is little to be said at a generalized level about the adjustment and transformation of the conditions of interaction. The "road to theory" in this dimension of situations lies in the direction of "historical sociology," in the analysis and comparison of cases.[5]

The adjustment and transformation of situations are the outcomes of changes within the actors. These changes, as has been indicated, result from the development of capacity and from the processes of the political system in resolving its problems. In addition, there is a feedback process from action taken in the environment that results in

---

4. This interpretation is at odds with the assumptions of much of the work being done by some other scholars. See, for example, the work led by Charles McClelland in the World Events Interaction Survey at the University of Southern California.

5. See Stanley Hoffman, ed., *Contemporary Theory in International Relations* (Englewood Cliffs, N.J.: Prentice-Hall, Inc., 1960).

consequences for the state and national society. We turn to a consideration of some of these consequences, exploring the concept of national adaptation.

National Adaptation: The Impact of Foreign Policy on Domestic Society

Dealt with throughout this book has been the generation of foreign policy out of domestic society and the aspect of interaction in which the actions of other countries affect the variables of foreign policy making within the given country. In this section, an attempt will be made to answer the question of what happens to a country as a result of its own actions in the field of forcign policy.

Although foreign policy acts are largely directed toward the external environment of a country, there is also an effect on the people and resources of the country taking those acts. These consequences may be marginal or profound, long-term or short-term, temporary or permanent, adaptive or maladaptive. In terms of social systems theory, what is being talked about in this section is the learning process and the self-transformation process.

The kind of question we are concerned with is similar to the question of health, particularly of mental health. That is, what happens to the domestic determinants in terms of maintaining the ability of a country to continue to be able to choose goals and form policies to seek the values which it holds? Since foreign policy is not completely autonomous but is rather an interaction with an environment, this problem is not completely one of independence, but it is a question of being able to survive in a meaningful way in that environment. It is a question of resolving internal conflict in the same way that an individual resolves his internal conflicts so that he can deal rationally with his environment. What we are concerned with in this section, then, is the politics of national adaption.[6]

In treating this question the variables of the domestic determinants chapter will be employed, but they will be treated as dependent variables which are affected by the independent variables of decisions, mobiliza-

---

6. For a broader view of national adaptation and systematic treatments of the concept, see James N. Rosenau, *The Adaptation of National Societies: A Theory of Political System Behavior and Transformation* (New York: The McCaleb-Seiler Publishing Company, 1970), and Patrick McGowan, *Toward A Dynamic Theory of Foreign Policy* (Syracuse, N.Y.: Comparative International Studies Project, International Relations Program, Maxwell School, Syracuse University, February 1971).

tion of resources, and applications of instruments and techniques. Then these three types of acts will be treated as dependent variables which are affected by policies. The analysis will then have been completed by closing the circle of the influence of all of the variables which have been identified upon all of the others.

Very little study has been conducted of the impact of foreign policy on a country. One cannot therefore be very precise or complete. However, one can suggest a number of hypotheses about the relationship of foreign policy acts and policies and the domestic determinants of foreign policy. There is no doubt that foreign policy does have an impact on the life of a country, and that the processes of learning and of self-transformation are important processes in the maintenance of individual states and, in turn, of the nation-state system. By specifying these processes, one should also be able to find out the resiliency of states or, alternatively, the conditions under which the state system might be undermined and replaced by another system.

The effects under discussion here may be treated in two broad categories: those which stem from foreign policy acts, particularly the application of instruments and the mobilization of resources; and those which stem from policies. Some hypotheses and examples will be given.

Effects of Foreign Policy Acts

The development of political instruments—defined and discussed in chapter 9—tends to undermine democracy. This hypothesis is of little consequence in states which are not democratic. Secret police and intelligence agencies are part of the apparatus of non-democratic states. For states which are democratic, however, political instruments whether subversive or supportive are not subject to democratic controls, for by their nature they operate in secrecy. There may be adaptations of democratic controls by the use of small committees of the legislature to supervise such activities and by having the political instruments ultimately accountable to a chief executive. However, the other kinds of controls normal to a democratic state cannot operate. The creation of political instruments, thus, is an influence on the structure of the government.

The use of informational instruments produce expectations in both the purveyors and the recipients that may have to be faced. The most obvious case in which this hypothesis operated was the Hungarian revolution and counter-revolution of 1956. Having broadcasted the doctrine of liberation, the United States was faced in October 1956 with an occasion for a decision on whether to intervene. Deciding not to, some elements of American society were alienated and the credibility of the slogan of liberation was erased. It also made it impossible for the United States to use diplomatic threats in the Czechoslovak crisis of the summer of 1968.

The uses of military instruments against civilians may change the national sense of morality. Before World War II, England and the United States would have rejected in their public opinion the use of instruments of war against civilians. However, after having used aerial bombing so extensively in World War II, it was much easier to accept such actions in the future. This is a shift in national political culture.

Decisions which give tasks to the military which they cannot perform —either because of the nature of the task or because the necessary resources are denied them—lead to a sense of defeat and frustration, and this creates the conditions for a possible military threat to the state. The humiliations of the French army in World War II and in Indochina led to major frustration and a sense of defeat. When Algeria occurred, the weakness of the French political elite created the last condition for civil war and the revolt of the army which brought General DeGaulle to power. This was an impact on the structure of the government and of the political system. Probably only DeGaulle's leadership prevented a civil war which would have made it impossible for a French government to be self-controlling.

The building of a large military establishment creates particular problems of control for the political elite. These may or may not be manageable. State mastery of the instrument, however, requires adaptations of the state structure for control and a decisive and wise leadership. The creation of the instrument itself has an impact on the structure of authority. We saw above how this new bureaucracy can influence policy. On the other hand, under proper political guidance, the military may be necessary to the adaptation of the state to its environment so as to insure security and survival.[7]

The mobilization of a population tends to create new expectations and new norms of behavior in the population. This was one of the major processes at work in the movements for independence of colonial territories.[8] It also was a factor in the struggle for democracy against monarchy in the first half of the nineteenth century.[9] It was also a

---

7. See S. N. Eisenstadt, *The Political Systems of Empires* (New York: The Free Press, 1969), for an impressive analysis of the roles of bureaucracy and political leadership in historical systems.

8. See Barbara Ward, *The Rich Nations and the Poor Nations* (New York: W. W. Norton and Company, Inc., 1962).

9. See Paul Y. Hammond, "The Political Order and the Burden of External Relations," *World Politics* 19 (April 1967).

factor in bringing the Labour Government to power in England after World War II, and it was a factor in the movement of Negroes in the United States for equality.

The creation of bureaucracies of any type leads to constituency and coordination problems and has an impact on the structure of government. Although bureaucracies are important and essential instruments for conducting the affairs of large states, their creation also entails the development of new constituencies. Inertial forces in the decision-making processes tend to be strengthened, and political leaders must address new problems of coordination and control as well as new sources of demands and supports from this constituency. We saw this in the chapter on domestic determinants.

The expenditure of resources as well as the destruction of resources diminishes the capacity of a state to act in the future. In the case of Britain in World War II, for example, the expenditure of resources was so great that Britain was reduced from a position of partial dominance of the international system to a position of dependent partnership.

These are some of the hypotheses that may be examined with respect to the impact of foreign policy acts on the society which is taking them. Undoubtedly, further study of this general phenomenon will lead to the discovery of other relationships. For example, in democratic societies, decisions lead to expectations of fairly quick results and can produce fissures in a society as was the case in the United States in the Korean and Vietnamese wars. Some of these may be related to policies, to which we now turn for another set of hypotheses.

Effects of Policies

Integration leads to a loss of control over national life. If the process of integration proceeds far enough, loyalties may be shifted to a new decision-making center. In such a case, we would have the conditions for the formation of new units. Short of such a complete process of integration, to the extent that decisions are shared with allies, the state is not a self-governing entity.

Membership in alliances tends to reinforce and expand the importance of foreign policy in national life. Although alliance membership may initially be a reflection rather than a cause of concern with an international situation, it will tend to increase that concern. Foreign policy issues will become more prominent in political debate in countries which belong to alliances. This is an impact on the process of the political system.

Treaties limit freedom of action. Insofar as a country undertakes to abide by a treaty it is not free to do what it wishes in terms of the constraints of the treaty. There must be advantages to the country for it to enter into the treaty, but the cost of these advantages is a diminution of the scope of decision making.

Taking new territory creates problems of governance and integration.[10] The government which takes over a territory needs to integrate it into the social system that exists. This is a very difficult task and one that will also involve the new citizens' inputting into the political system. This will have an impact on the structure of the government and on the issues that will be faced with respect to other countries' reactions to the accession.

For democratic states, inconclusive wars in remote arenas lead to major fissures in the domestic society of the state which is projecting power. This was the case with the British in the American Revolution and in the Boer War, of France in Indochina, and of the United States in Vietnam.

Policies of expansion lead to the expenditure of resources, and success leads to further expansion, creating lines of supply problems and of the expenditure of further resources. If carried far enough, resources will not be sufficient to sustain expansion and perhaps to maintain control of the expansionary gains. This depletion of resources may make it more difficult for a country to set other policies which it might otherwise do.

Deprivation of domestic needs leads to the accumulation of demand and increases the difficulty of solving the problems created by the domestic needs. All of the countries involved in World War II—winners and losers alike—faced this problem and this phenomenon.

Policies of engagement may lead disaffected minorities to assert their claims. In a country where there are significant minorities, the involvement of the government in external engagements may be seen as an opportunity to revolt or to gain independence or make lesser claims on the government. This will especially be the case if the government is dependent upon the minority for manpower or other resources to conduct its foreign policy.

Conclusion

Foreign policy consequences are the effects of acts upon the units of analysis—the international system, situations, and actors—which were

---

10. See George F. Kennan, *Memoirs, 1925–1950* (Boston: Little, Brown and Company, 1967), who discusses this problem as applied to the German occupation of Czechoslovakia.

Consequences

discussed in the early part of the book. The full elaboration of these consequences falls into the purview of the international systems analyst rather than the foreign policy analyst. On the other hand, the foreign policy analyst could not consider his task complete without some attention to consequences.

The task of this book has now been completed by relating all of the variables with which we have been concerned to all of the others. The work of foreign policy analysis, however, is far from complete. The framework and the hypotheses of this book hopefully provide a useful approach to understanding foreign policy, but they need to be applied, tested, and then modified as elements are shown to be in error.

Selected Readings

Chapter 1—Introduction

Black, Joseph E. and Kenneth W. Thompson. *Foreign Policies in a World of Change*. New York: Harper and Row, 1963.

Farrell, Barry R., ed. *Approaches to Comparative and International Politics*. Evanston: Northwestern University Press, 1966.

Gross, Feliks. *Foreign Policy Analysis*. New York: The Philosophical Library, 1954.

Hanrieder, Wolfram F., ed. *Comparative Foreign Policy: Theoretical Essays*. New York: David McKay Company, Inc., 1971.

Herz, John. *International Politics in the Atomic Age*. New York: Columbia University Press, 1959.

──────. *Political Realism and Political Idealism: A Study in Theories and Realities*. Chicago and London: The University of Chicago Press, 1951.

Macridis, Roy C., ed. *Foreign Policy in World Politics*. 4th ed. Englewood Cliffs, N.J.: Prentice-Hall, Inc., 1972.

Marshall, Charles Burton. *The Limits of Foreign Policy*. New York: Henry Holt and Company, 1954.

Modelski, George A. *A Theory of Foreign Policy*. New York: Published for the Center of International Studies by Frederick A. Praeger, Publisher, 1962.

Rosenau, James N. *The Scientific Study of Foreign Policy*. New York: The Free Press, 1971.

──────, ed. *International Politics and Foreign Policy: A Reader in Research and Theory*. New York: Free Press of Glencoe, 1961.

──────, ed. *International Politics and Foreign Policy: A Reader in Research and Theory*. Rev. ed. New York: The Free Press, 1969.

Singer, J. David, ed. *Human Behavior and International Politics: Contributions From the Social–Psychological Sciences*. Chicago: Rand McNally and Company, 1965.

──────, ed. *Quantitative International Politics: Insights and Evidence*. New York: The Free Press, 1968.

Wilkinson, David O. *Comparative Foreign Relations: Framework and Methods*. Belmont, Calif.: Dickenson Publishing Company, Inc., 1969.

Chapter 2—Actors

Almond, Gabriel A. and G. Bingham Powell. *Comparative Politics: A Developmental Approach*. Boston and Toronto: Little, Brown and Company, 1966.

Claude, Inis L., Jr. *Swords into Plowshares: The Problems and Progress of International Organization*. 3d ed., rev. New York: Random House, 1964.

Connor, Walker, "Nation-Building or Nation-Destroying?" *World Politics* 24 (April 1972).

Elkind, David. "Erik Erikson's Eight Ages of Man." *The New York Times Magazine*, 5 April 1970.

Erikson, Erik. *Gandhi's Truth: On the Origins of Militant Nonviolence*. New York: W. W. Norton and Company, 1969.

Graymer, LeRoy, ed. *Systems and Actors in International Politics*. Scranton/London/Toronto: Chandler Publishing Company, 1971.

Holsti, K. J. "National Role Conceptions in the Study of Foreign Policy." *International Studies Quarterly* 14 (September 1970).

Mitrany, David. *A Working Peace System*. London and New York: Royal Institute of International Affairs, 1946.

Nye, Joseph S. and Robert O. Keohane. *Transnational Relations and World Politics*. Cambridge, Massachusetts: Harvard University Press, 1972.

Riggs, Robert E. "The United Nations as an Influence on United States Policy." *International Studies Quarterly* 11 (March 1967).

Russett, Bruce M., et. al. *World Handbook of Social and Political Indicators*. New Haven: Yale University Press, 1964.

Servan-Schreiber, Jean-Jacques. *The American Challenge*. Translated by Ronald Steel. New York: Atheneum, 1969.

Vernon, Raymond. *Sovereignty at Bay: The Multinational Spread of U.S. Enterprises*. New York and London: Basic Books, Inc., 1971.

Chapter 3—The International Environment

Aron, Raymond. *Peace and War: A Theory of International Relations*. Translated by Richard Howard and Annette Baker Fox. New York, Washington: Frederick A. Praeger, Publishers, 1967.

Hoffmann, Stanley. *Contemporary Theory in International Relations*. Englewood Cliffs, N.J.: Prentice-Hall, Inc., 1960.

Kaplan, Morton A. *System and Process in International Politics*. New York: John Wiley and Sons, Inc., 1957.

Knorr, Klaus and Sidney Verba. *The International System: Theoretical Essays*. Princeton: Princeton University Press, 1961.

McClelland, Charles. *Theory and the International System*. New York: The Macmillan Company, 1966.

Rosecrance, Richard N. *Action and Reaction in World Politics: International Systems in Perspective*. Boston and Toronto: Little, Brown and Company, 1963.

Wright, Quincey. *The Study of International Relations*. New York: Appleton–Century–Crofts, 1955.

Chapter 4—Situations

Binder, Leonard. "The Middle East as a Subordinate International System." *World Politics* 10 (April 1959).

Brecher, Michael. "International Relations and Asian Studies: The Subordinate State System of Asia." *World Politics* 15 (January 1963).

Cantori, Louis J. and Steven J. Spiegel. *The International Politics of Regions: A Comparative Approach*. Englewood Cliffs, N.J.: Prentice-Hall, Inc., 1970.

Riker, William H. *The Theory of Political Coalitions*. New Haven and London: Yale University Press, 1962.

Russett, Bruce M. *International Regions and the International System: A Study of Political Ecology*. Chicago: Rand McNally and Company, 1967.

Sprout, Harold and Margaret Sprout. "Environmental Factors in the Study of International Politics." *The Journal of Conflict Resolution* 1 (1957).

Young, Oran R. *The Intermediaries: Third Parties in International Crises*. Princeton: Princeton University Press, 1967.

Chapter 5—Foreign Determinants

Carr, E. H. *The Twenty Years Crisis, 1919–1939*. 2d ed. New York and Evanston: Harper and Row, 1964.

Morgenthau, Hans J. *Politics Among Nations: The Struggle for Power and Peace*. 4th ed. New York: Alfred A. Knopf, 1967.

Schelling, Thomas C. *Arms and Influence*. New Haven and London: Yale University Press, 1966.

Scott, Andrew M. *The Revolution in Statecraft: Informal Penetration*. New York: Random House, 1965.

Sprout, Harold and Margaret Sprout. *The Ecological Perspective on Human Affairs with Special Reference to International Politics*. Princeton: Princeton University Press, 1965.

Wohlstetter, Roberta. "Cuba and Pearl Harbor: Hindsight and Foresight." *Foreign Affairs* 43 (July 1965).

Chapter 6—Domestic Determinants

Almond, Gabriel A. and James S. Coleman, eds. *The Politics of Developing Areas*. Princeton: Princeton University Press, 1960.

Almond, Gabriel A. and Sidney Verba. *The Civic Culture: Political Attitudes and Democracy in Five Nations*. Boston and Toronto: Little, Brown and Company, 1965.

De Rivera, Joseph. *The Psychological Dimension of Foreign Policy*. Columbus, Ohio: Charles E. Merrill Publishing Company, 1968.

Lowi, Theodore J. *The End of Liberalism*. New York: W. W. Norton and Company, 1969.

Pye, Lucian W. and Sidney Verba, eds. *Political Culture and Political Development*. Princeton: Princeton University Press, 1965.

Rosenau, James N., ed. *Domestic Sources of Foreign Policy*. New York: The Free Press, 1967.

Waltz, Kenneth N. *Foreign Policy and Democratic Politics: The American and British Experience*. Boston and Toronto: Little, Brown and Company, 1967.

Chapter 7—Decisions

Allison, Graham T. "Conceptual Models and the Cuban Missile Crisis." *The American Political Science Review* 62 (September 1969).

_____. *Essence of Decision: Explaining the Cuban Missile Crisis*. Boston: Little, Brown and Company, 1971.

Almond, Gabriel A. *The American People and Foreign Policy*. New York: Frederick A. Praeger, Publisher, 1960.

Braybrooke, David and Charles E. Lindblom. *A Strategy of Decision: Policy Evaluation as a Social Process*. New York: The Free Press, 1963.

Cohen, Bernard C. *The Political Process and Foreign Policy: The Making of of the Japanese Peace Settlement*. Princeton: Princeton University Press, 1957.

_____. *The Press and Foreign Policy*. Princeton: Princeton University Press, 1963.

Frankel, Joseph. *The Making of Foreign Policy: An Analysis of Decision-Making*. London: Oxford University Press, 1963.

George, Alexander L. and Juliette L. *Woodrow Wilson and Colonel House: A Personality Study*. New York: Dover Publications, Inc., 1956.

Janowitz, Morris. *The Military in the Political Development of New Nations*. Chicago and London: The University of Chicago Press, 1964.

March, James G. and Herbert Simon. *Organizations*. New York: John Wiley and Sons, Inc., 1958.

Neustadt, Richard E. *Presidential Power: The Politics of Leadership.* New York: John Wiley and Sons, 1960.

Robinson, James A. *Congress and Foreign Policy-Making: A Study in Legislative Influence and Initiative.* Homewood, Ill.: The Dorsey Press, Inc., 1962.

Scott, Andrew M. and Raymond H. Dawson. *Readings in the Making of American Foreign Policy.* New York: The Macmillan Company, 1965.

Snyder, Richard C., H. W. Bruck, and Burton Sapin, eds. *Foreign Policy Decision-Making: An Approach to the Study of International Politics.* New York: The Free Press of Glencoe, 1962.

Chapter 8—Mobilization of Resources

Deutsch, Karl W. *Nationalism and Social Communication: An Inquiry into the Foundations of Nationality.* 2d ed. Cambridge, Massachusetts and London: The M.I.T. Press, 1966.

——————. *The Nerves of Government: Models of Political Communication and Control.* New York: The Free Press, 1963.

Gurr, Ted Robert. *Why Men Rebel.* Princeton: Princeton University Press, 1970.

Knorr, Klaus. *Military Power and Potential.* Lexington, Massachusetts: D.C. Heath and Company, 1970.

Sprout, Harold and Margaret Sprout. *Foundations of International Politics.* Princeton: D. Van Nostrand Company, Inc., 1962.

Wohlstetter, Albert. "Illusions of Distance." *Foreign Affairs* 46 (January 1968).

Chapter 9—Application of Instruments and Techniques

Buchan, Alastair. *Crisis Management: The New Diplomacy.* Boulogne-sur-Seine, France: The Atlantic Institute, 1966.

Hermann, Charles F., ed. *International Crises: Insights and Evidence.* New York: The Free Press, 1972.

Nicholson, Sir Harold. *The Evolution of Diplomatic Method.* New York: The Macmillan Company, 1954.

Rosenau, James N., ed. *Linkage Politics: Essays on the Convergence of National and International Systems.* New York: The Free Press, 1969.

Schelling, Thomas C. *The Strategy of Conflict.* New York: Oxford University Press, 1963.

Chapter 10—Policies

Alker, Hayward R. and Bruce M. Russett. *World Politics in the General Assembly.* New Haven: Yale University Press, 1965.

Claude, Inis L., Jr. *Power and International Relations.* New York: Random House, 1962.

Deutsch, Karl W., et al. *Political Community and the North Atlantic Area.* Princeton: Princeton University Press, 1957.

Fedder, Edwin H. "The Concept of Alliance." *International Studies Quarterly* 12 (March 1968).

Friedman, Julian R., Christopher Bladen, and Steven Rosen. *Alliance in International Politics.* Boston: Allyn and Bacon, Inc., 1970.

Haas, Ernst B. *Beyond the Nation-State.* Stanford: Stanford University Press, 1964.

———. *The Uniting of Europe.* Stanford: Stanford University Press, 1958.

Hovet, Thomas, Jr. *Bloc Politics at the United Nations.* Cambridge, Mass.: Harvard University Press, 1960.

Liska, George. *Nations in Alliance.* Baltimore: The Johns Hopkins Press, 1962.

Olson, Mancur, Jr. *The Logic of Collective Action: Public Goods and the Theory of Groups.* New York: Schocken Books, 1968.

Rosenau, James N., Vincent Davis, and Maurice A. East, eds. *The Analysis of International Politics: Essays in Honor of Harold and Margaret Sprout.* New York: The Free Press, 1972.

Wolfers, Arnold. *Discord and Collaboration: Essays on International Politics.* Baltimore: The Johns Hopkins Press, 1962.

Chapter 11—Consequences

Hammond, Paul Y. "The Political Order and the Burden of External Relations." *World Politics* 19 (April 1967).

McGowan, Patrick. *Toward a Dynamic Theory of Foreign Policy.* Syracuse, N.Y.: Comparative International Studies Project, International Relations Program, Maxwell School, Syracuse University. February 1971.

Rosenau, James N. *The Adaptation of National Societies: A Theory of Political System Behavior and Transformation.* New York: The McCaleb-Seiler Publishing Company, 1970.

Index

Actors, 5, 6, 11, 12, 17, 19, 22, 24, 37; intergovernmental organizations, 21; states, 17, 24–37; transnational, 12, 19, 22–24, 37
Adaptation, 7, 13, 272–77; effects of foreign policy acts, 273–75; effects of policies, 275
Adjustment, 9, 13, 265, 267–72
Adjustment process, 6, 7
Adversaries, 10, 111–12, 183, 222, 239
Afghanistan: regime type, 42; size, 39
AFL-CIO, 18, 216
Africa, 20, 35, 61, 62, 138; French-speaking, 18; west, 35, 137
Albania, 106; regime type, 42; size, 39
Al Fatah, 18, 94
Algeria, 124; political identity, 45; regime type, 42; role of French army, 188; size, 39
Alienation, 57, 144, 181
Alliances, 4, 9, 29, 30, 36, 68, 78–79, 91, 105, 106, 107, 158, 185, 187, 224–29, 231, 254–64, 270; anti-Communist, 54; basic decisions, 227; federal type, 258; formation, 224–25; hierarchical type, 258; impact on domestic politics, 275; management, 225–27; multilateral, 258–61; withdrawal from, 227–29
Allies, 111–12, 208, 223, 238, 266
Angola: regime type, 42; size, 39
Application of instruments and techniques, 17–18, 215–46
Arab-Israeli dispute, 18
Arabs, 22, 64
Arab states, 94, 102
Area rank, 39–41
Argentina: political identity, 45; rank, 27; regime type, 42; size, 39
Arms race, 241–42
Asia, 61–62
Atomic bomb. See Nuclear weapons
Attitudes, 60–64, 107, 137, 140, 155–56, 186, 239

Australia: political identity, 45; rank, 27; regime type, 42; size, 39; in Vietnam war, 96, 249–50
Austria, 137; German intervention, 216; rank, 27; regime type, 42; size, 39
Authoritarianism. See Political systems: authoritarian

Balance of power, 3, 7, 55, 81, 106, 149, 150, 252, 265
Bandung Conference, 54, 125, 257
Bangladesh, 52–57, 63, 138, 202; regime type, 42; size, 39
Bay of Pigs, 192
Belgium, 252; rank, 27; regime type, 42; responsibility, 36; size, 39
Bengalis, 63
Berlin crisis, 150, 175, 253
Bhutto, Zulfiqar Ali, 52
Biafra, 61, 138, 139, 202, 232; French support, 153
Bipolarity, 5, 7, 55, 102, 105, 106, 153, 265
Boer War, 213; effect on United Kingdom, 276
Bolivia: regime type, 42; size, 39
Brazil, 126, 139; characteristics, 26; political identity, 45; rank, 27; regime type, 42; size, 39
British Guiana, 216
Brussels Pact, 106
Bulgaria: regime type, 42; size, 39
Bureaucracies, 13, 33, 162–68, 178, 180, 185, 205, 209, 237, 238, 240, 275; military, 177; in sequential and basic decisions, 174; special problems, 188–90
Burma, 202, 249, 252; regime type, 42; security dilemma, 2; size, 39
Burundi, 21; Chinese intervention, 216; regime type, 42; size, 39

Cambodia, 96, 148, 150; regime type, 42; security dilemma, 2; size, 39

285

Cameroon: regime type, 42; size, 39
Canada, 18, 20, 195, 201; as ally of United States, 29; characteristics, 28; in Middle East situation in 1956, 126–32; and multinational corporations, 23; perception of threat, 147; political identity, 45; rank, 27; regime type, 42; relations with United States, 96; responsibility, 36; size, 39; in Vietnam situation, 96
Capabilities, 59, 170, 200, 204, 210
Capabilities analysis, 67–68, 205–7
Capacity, 12, 18, 20, 22, 25–32, 33, 38, 68, 73, 75, 107, 112, 135, 137, 138, 141, 203, 249, 250, 270, 275
Central African Republic: regime type, 42; size, 39
Ceylon. *See* Sri Lanka
Chad: regime type, 42; size, 39
Chief executive, 13, 31, 187; relations with constituencies, 188–97; relations with mass public, 199–214
Chile, 61; regime type, 42; size, 39
China, People's Republic, 32, 72, 138, 250; alliance behavior, 260; alliance with USSR, 106; cultural revolution, 181, 191; goals, 152; intervention in Burundi, 216; in Kashmir dispute, 97; in Korean war, 242; nuclear weapons, 60, 76; perception of threats, 147; political culture, 144; political identity, 45; President Nixon's visit, 175; rank, 27; regime type, 42; relations with Burma, 252; relations with India and Pakistan, 54; relations with United States, 222, 232; 1949 revolution, 178; Sino-Soviet dispute, 99–101; size, 39; support of Pakistan, 53; use of economic instruments, 219; in Vietnam situation, 96; war against India, 253; in Western Pacific and East Asia, 99
China, Republic of. *See* Taiwan
Churchill, Winston, 86
Civil-military relations, 224
Civil order, 231–32
Civil war, 162, 194, 232
Client state problem, 256–57
Climate, 58, 137, 138
Coalition building, 224–29
Cold war, 36, 232
Colombia: regime type, 42; size, 39
Common Market. *See* European Economic Community
Communism, 61
Communist bloc, 99, 106
Communist countries, 37

Communist parties, 24, 146
Competition, 84–90; definition, 87
Conditions of interaction, 84–90
Conferences, international, 257–58
Conflict, 84–90, 122, 263; definition, 86
Congo (Kinshasa), 18, 20; Soviet intervention, 253; United Nations intervention, 237. *See also* Zaire
Congo crisis, 36, 263
Congress of Vienna, 222
Consensus (in international organizations), 263
Consequences, 13, 265–77
Constituencies, 13, 161–68, 178, 209, 213, 239; relations with elites, 187–97
Constraining forces, 12, 57–66
Control, 6, 13, 18, 19, 23, 68, 73, 75, 77–84, 86–87, 188, 189, 191, 248, 263–64, 270, 274
Cooperation, 84–90; definition, 87
Costa Rica; regime type, 42; size, 39
Coup d'état, 8, 162, 192
Crisis, international, 8, 10, 68, 184–85, 186, 194, 232–34; initiation, 232–33; resolution, 234; response, 234
Cuba, 115; in Cuban missile crisis, 91; help from USSR, 228–29; political identity, 45; regime type, 42; 1959 revolution, 178; shift of alignment, 106; size, 39
Cuban missile crisis, 77, 90–91, 92, 148, 150, 154, 185, 233, 242, 253
Culture, 23, 57, 61, 64, 138, 143–60, 170, 210
"Cultural revolution," 181, 261
Cyprus, 20, 29, 96; peacekeeping troops, 235; regime type, 42; size, 39
Czechoslovakia, 259; as ally of USSR, 29; 1948 coup, 217, 237; German intervention, 216; goals, 151; 1968 invasion, 25, 147, 150, 184, 274; political identity, 46; rank, 27; regime type, 42; size, 39

Dahomey; regime type, 42; size, 39
Decisions, 8, 10, 12, 13, 17, 18, 208, 248; basic, 174–75, 221; classification, 12, 173–76; conditions for making, 12, 181–82, 186; drift, 175; external pressures for, 182, 186; initiative, 175; internal pressures for, 176–81; political process, 12, 167; response 175; sequential, 174–75
Decision channels: change in government structures, 196–97; change in personnel, 192–94; change in policy by

Decision channels (Cont.)
  incumbent elite, 194–95; dominant coalition change, 195–96
Decision making process, 8, 186–97
Decision making: approach to study, 3; elites, 10; in international organizations, 22; in multinational corporations, 22
Decisional phase, 110–12
DeGaulle, Charles, 169; coming to power, 274; control of French army, 189; establishment of Fifth Republic, 181; foreign policy, 153; reaction to Cuban missile crisis, 91
Democracy, 61, 274
Denmark: political identity, 46; rank, 27; regime type, 42; size, 39
Destroyers-for-bases deal, 138
Determinants, 7; domestic, 8, 12, 24, 31, 135–70; foreign, 12, 105–34; 136; highly stable, 136–43; moderately stable, 143–68; unstable, 136, 168–70
Deterrence, 117, 241
Diem, Ngo Dinh, 216
Diplomacy, 18, 64, 70, 217–19, 253
Diplomatic campaign, 230
Disintegration, 79, 138, 149, 150, 181, 185, 194, 228, 255
Dissent, 33; in United States, 57
Domestic politics (compared with international politics), 2
Dominican Republic: regime type, 42; size, 39; United States' intervention, 25, 150

Eastern Europe, 21, 72, 75, 94, 106, 146, 255
Economic assistance, 240, 253
Economic development, 19, 53, 59
Economic growth, 33, 53
Ecuador: regime type, 42; size, 39
Effectiveness, 9, 13. See also Success
Effects of foreign policy acts, 273–75
Egypt, 9, 22, 29, 65, 94, 102, 115, 141, 152; attempt to recover Palestine, 253; form of government, 196; level of education, 210; 1956 invasion, 255; non-alignment, 106; political identity, 46; regime type, 42; relations with Jordan, 193; security dilemma, 2; situation in Middle East in 1956, 123–33; size, 39; use of Soviet military equipment, 207–8
Eisenhower, Dwight D., 86, 125, 126, 133; peace in Korea, 192; 1956 presidential election, 169

Elections, 8, 192; in Pakistan, 53
Electorate, 167
Elites, 13, 139, 145–50, 160, 162–68, 178, 180, 182, 186, 187, 209, 210, 219, 225–26, 231, 237–39, 241; in basic decisions, 174; conceptions of morality, 213; relations with constituencies, 187–97; relations with mass publics, 199
El Salvadore: regime type, 42; size, 39
Emotions, 33; as factors in mobilizing resources, 211
Enemy, 30. See also Adversary
Engagement, policy of, 6, 254–64
English-Speaking Union, 19
Environment, 5, 7, 11, 12, 17, 18, 30, 34, 35, 38, 51–65, 67, 105, 107, 136, 159, 170, 177, 186, 194, 197, 205, 235, 248, 262, 272; constraining and facilitating factors, 57–65
Equilibrium, 56, 265
Ethics: as limit on mobilization of resources, 212–13
Ethiopia, 62; regime type, 42; size, 39
Ethnic groups, 33, 53, 61, 140
Europe, 29, 34, 36, 77. See also Eastern Europe; Western Europe
European Economic Community, 5, 19, 20, 64, 94, 99, 145, 262
Execution phase, 110–12
Expansion, policy of, 6, 252–53
Expectations, 119, 127, 191, 192, 203, 273–75
Experiences, 35, 37, 45–50, 139, 148, 170, 194, 222

Facilitating forces, 12, 57–65
Failure, 179; in crises, 234
Failure of will: as limit on mobilization of resources, 213–14
Fears, 8, 24, 140, 144, 147, 149–51, 168, 179, 186, 191, 211, 213, 228, 238, 239
Federator, 87, 224–25, 259, 263
Finland: regime type, 42; size, 39
Food and Agricultural Organization, 64
Foreign aid, 9, 33, 113–14
Foreign policies, 6, 13; classification, 247–50; consequences, 13, 265–77; engagement, 13, 32, 147, 179, 183, 194, 214, 249, 254–64; expansion, 13, 152, 249, 252–53; insulation, 6, 13, 22, 147, 179, 183, 193, 214, 248–49, 250–52
Foreign policy: analysis as science, 10; channels of change, 8, 192–97; choice, 8–9; costs, 10; distinction from domestic policy, 4–5; and domestic life, 11;

Foreign policy (Cont.)
  effect of size, 138; environment, 51–65; errors in analysis, 37; features of approach to study, 6; as focus of study, 3; impact of technology, 59–60; influence of wealth, 142; implementation, 12, 215–44; initiatives, 183; objectives, 204; planning, 107; and political process, 13; requirements for adjustment, 7; and situations, 67; study of, 3–10; theory of, 13, and time, 9
Foreign policy acts, 12, 17; application of instruments and techniques, 215–44; decisions, 173–97; mobilization of resources, 199–214; related to political process, 167–68; instruments and techniques, 12, 18, 84, 121, 132, 139, 140, 207; bundles of, 220–36; classification, 216–20; diplomatic, 114–15, 217–19, 238–40; economic, 115–17, 219–20, 240; effects on targets, 236–43; informational, 115, 219, 239; military, 117, 220, 240–43; mobilized, 204; political, 113–14, 216–17, 236–38
Fortune, 169–70, 188
France, 18, 34, 37, 58, 152; alliance behavior, 259–60; at Congress of Vienna, 222; end of Fourth Republic, 188; Fifth Republic, 181; foreign policy under DeGaulle, 153; Fourth Republic, 181; goals, 151; interest in Indochina, 226; 1956 invasion of Egypt, 109, 169, 225; as invasion route in World War II, 174; in Middle East, 94; and nuclear weapons, 60; nuclear weapons development, 76; political identity, 46; policy toward NATO, 226; rank, 27; reaction to Cuban missile crisis, 91; regime type, 42; responsibility, 36; situation in Middle East in 1956, 123–33; size, 39; treaty with West Germany, 96; in Vietnam situation, 96
France, Napoleanic: challenge to international system, 266
Freedom of action, 275–76
Freedom of choice, 9, 226
French army, 188, 274

Game theory, 86, 195
Gandhi, Indira, 202
Gandhi, Mahatma, 34–35
Geneva Disarmament Conference, 120
Genotypes, 24, 31
Geographical area, 27–29

Geography, 53
Germany, 28, 201; divided, 262; response to defeat, 145; reunification, 146, 152, 169; Soviet fear of, 250; unification, 168
Germany, East, 74; rank, 27; regime type, 42; size, 39
Germany, Nazi, 76, 85, 149, 150, 174, 180, 252, 253; alliances, 228; annexation of Austria, 137; challenge to international system, 266; declaration of war against United States, 182; mobilization in World War II, 212; political intervention, 216; security dilemma, 2; in World War II, 109, 141, 206
Germany, West, 20; 74; access to nuclear weapons, 156; goals, 151; political identity, 46; rank, 27; regime type, 42; size, 39; treaty with France, 96
Ghana, 34, 35, 36, 137, 253; political identity, 47; regime type, 42; size, 39
Goals: alliance, 259; state, 8, 19, 29, 31, 32, 35, 58, 59, 84, 106, 116, 151–53, 177, 179, 192, 194, 214, 254
Grand Alliance, 225, 260
Great powers: definition, 26–27
Greece, 96; regime type, 42; size, 39; United States' intervention, 253
GNP, 26, 27, 37, 59–60, 112, 142
Group of, 77, 63, 258
Guatemala: CIA intervention, 216; regime type, 42; size, 39
Guerrillas, 54, 187, 193
Guinea: political identity, 47; size, 39

Haiti, 138; regime type, 42; size, 39
Hammarskjöld, Dag, 125, 147, 263
Hanoi, 223
Hatred, 211
Hegemony, 70, 79, 151
Hitler, Adolf, 77, 116, 125, 137, 149, 175, 253
Ho Chi Minh, 216
Honduras: regime type, 42; size, 39
Hong Kong: regime type, 42; size, 39
Human resources, 58–59
Hungarian revolution, 273
Hungary, 228, 259; political identity, 47; regime type, 42; size, 40; Soviet invasion, 4, 105
Hussein, King, 193

Ibo Tribe, 202
Ideas, 33, 60, 61, 170; association of countries with, 34, 37, 45–50

Index

Identity: countries', 32, 33–37, 38, 45–50, 144, 148, 250; personal, 34–35, 57, 209; as used by Erik H. Erikson, 34–35
Ideology, 58, 178, 252; of United Nations, 20
Inaction: definition, 109
Independence movements, 274
India, 54, 57, 58; characteristics, 26; creation of Bangladesh, 52; in ICC, 96; Kashmir dispute, 97; in Korean war, 242; intervention in Pakistan, 25; nonalignment, 106; nuclear potential, 76; particularistic loyalties, 202; partition, 54; perception of threats, 147; political identity, 47; rank, 27; regime type, 42; responsibility, 36; size, 40; support by USSR, 53; Tashkent settlement, 72; treaty with USSR, 52; war against China, 253
Indochina, 21, 99; French interest, 226
Indochina war: effect on France, 276; settlement, 223
Indonesia, 183, 196; conference host, 257; nonalignment, 106; nuclear potential, 76; political identity, 47; peacekeeping troops, 235; rank, 27; regime type, 42; size, 40
Inequality, 63
Influence, 9, 19, 60, 76, 77–84, 86–87, 183, 191, 193, 203
Information, 111, 179, 180, 190, 192, 238, 239
Instability, 203, 231
Institute for Defense Analysis, 178
Institute for Strategic Studies, 205
Institutions, 87, 165, 262; economic, 65–65; political, 64–65
Insulation, policy of, 6, 250–52
Integration, 28, 56, 61, 85, 116, 226, 276; definition, 87; of population, 139, 140; regional, 261–62; in Western Europe, 169
Intelligence agencies, 189
Intentions, 110
Interest articulation functions, 163
Interest groups, 239
Interests, 30, 73, 76, 106, 222, 223, 224, 250, 254, 259, 270
Intermediaries, 218
Internal control, 231
International actors. *See* Actors
IATA, 19, 257
International community, 130, 213, 252
International community undertakings, 229–31
International conferences, 257–58

International Control Commission (ICC), 96
International environment, 51–65. *See also* Environment
International Federation of Trade Unions, 19
International law, 58, 64
International Monetary Fund (IMF), 19, 20, 64, 110, 127–28, 142, 249
International organizations, 12, 19, 37, 64, 230–31, 249, 262–64; intergovernmental organizations, 19, 20, 22; nongovernmental international organizations, 22
International Political Science Association, 19
International system, 5, 6, 12, 21, 22, 24, 32, 37, 55, 61, 68, 69, 72, 76, 105, 106, 107, 187, 208, 270; consequences of foreign policy for, 265–67; disturbance and regulation, 56; structure, 59
Inter-University Consortium for Political Research, 26
Intervention, 22, 63, 73, 142, 217, 231, 237, 270
Invasion, 32, 146
Iran, 62; CIA intervention, 216; regime type, 42; size, 39
Iraq, 125, 133; regime type, 42; size, 40
Ireland: regime type, 42; size, 40
Irredenta, 146
Islands, 28
Isolation, 123
Israel, 22, 29, 65, 73, 93, 94, 102, 141, 150; 1956 invasion of Egypt, 109, 169; political identity, 47; regime type, 42; relations with Jordan, 269; security dilemma, 2; situation in Middle East in 1956, 123–33; size, 40; use of economic instruments, 219; 1967 war, 208
Italy, 137; political identity, 47; rank, 27; regime type, 42; size, 40; withdrawal from Axis, 228
Ivory Coast: political identity, 47; regime type, 42; size, 40

Jamaica: regime type, 43; size, 40
Japan, 20, 60, 201, 206; atomic attack, 242; 1941 attack on United States, 4, 116; nuclear potential, 76; policies in 1931-1942, 253; political identity, 47; rank, 27; regime type, 43; relations with United States, 175; response to defeat, 145; size, 40; in Western Pacific and East Asia, 99
Johnson, Lyndon B., 75

Jordan, 62, 94, 109, 133, 193; political identity, 48; regime type, 43; relations with Israel, 269; size, 40
Journalists, 178
Justice, 58

Kashmir dispute, 54, 72, 90, 97–99
Kennedy, John F.: Bay of Pigs, 192–93
Kenya: regime type, 43; size, 40
Khan, Yahya, 52, 53
Khrushchev, Nikita, 101, 150, 175; attainment of leadership, 193; Berlin crisis, 253; Geneva summit conference, 222; political fortunes, 196
Korea, North, 106; regime type, 43; seizure of U.S.S. *Pueblo*, 184; size, 40
Korean war, 70, 86, 180, 188, 194, 242, 253; effect in United States, 182; truce, 223
Korea, South: regime type, 43; size, 40; in Vietnam war, 96

Language, 64, 145
Laos, 71, 96; regime type, 43; size, 40
Latin America, 29, 36, 62
Latin America Free Trading Area, 20
Lebanon, 130; regime type, 43; size, 40; United States' intervention, 183
Leader, death of, 192
Leaders, 13, 137, 146, 179, 187, 257, 275
Leadership, 35, 139, 145, 160, 193, 204, 213; as factor in mobilization of resources, 208–10, 211
League of Nations, 262
Legislatures, 178, 273
Legitimacy, 10, 53, 144, 149, 163, 170, 181, 186, 191, 200–204, 237
Lenin, 150
Level of analysis, 11, 35, 56
Liberia: regime type, 43; size, 40
Libya, 9; regime type, 43; size, 40
Location, 28–30, 138–39
Location indexes, 39–41
Loyalties, 262; conflicts in, 201
Loyalty, 24, 57, 113, 144, 200–4; generational, 62; instrumental sources, 201–4; sentimental sources, 201–4

MacArthur, Douglas, 188
Malagsy: regime type, 43; size, 40
Malawi: regime type, 43; size, 40
Malaysia, 64: political identity, 48; regime type, 43; size, 40
Mali: regime type, 43; size, 40
Marshall Plan, 116, 174
Marx, Karl, 62

Mass media, 107, 115, 210
Mass public, 13, 162–68, 187; relations with political elites, 199–214
Master race, 180
Mauritania: regime type, 43; size, 40
Maximum goals, 152–53
Mediterranean, 94, 148
Memories, 139, 146, 148, 153–55, 222
Mexico, 37; political identity, 48; rank, 27; regime type, 43; size, 40; use of economic instruments, 219
Middle East, 22, 58, 65, 73, 90–94, 102, 110; Canadian participation, 147; 1956 crisis, 20, 123–33, 218; NATO interest, 226; peacekeeping troops, 235; potential for transformation, 269; radical leaders, 216; Radio Cairo, 219
Middle powers: definition, 26–27
Military, 189–90
Military establishment: effect on political elite, 274
Minimum goals, 152–53
Minorities, 276
Misperceptions, 238
Mobilization of resources, 12, 17, 18; conditions, 208–11; limits, 211–14; related to political process, 167; mobilized instruments, 204–6
Modernization, 53, 141
"Modifiers of power inventories," 204–5
Molotov-Ribbentrop agreement, 77, 152
Monarchy, 62
Mongolia: regime type, 43; size, 40
Money, 63
Monroe Doctrine, 144
Morality, 274
Morocco: regime type, 43; size, 40
Motivations, 25
Mozambique: regime type, 43; size, 40
MLF, 74, 75, 154, 156
Multi-national corporations, 18, 22, 23, 62
Munich, 154

Nasser, Gamal Abdel, 125, 129, 130, 150, 196
Nation, 201; distinction from state, 34
National boundaries, 18
Nationalism, 53, 116, 202, 203; national consciousness, 34
National Security Council, 163, 178
Natural disasters, 146
Natural resources, 29, 58
Nazi ideology, 150
Negotiations, 217–18, 221–24
Nepal: regime type, 43; size, 40

Index

Netherlands: as neutral, 252; rank, 27; regime type, 43; size, 40
Neutral action: definition, 109
Neutrals, 112, 137
"New emerging forces," 261
New Zealand: regime type, 43; size, 40; in Vietnam war, 96
Nicaragua: regime type, 43; size, 40
Niger: regime type, 43; size, 40
Nigeria, 35, 36, 61, 137, 139, 232; civil war, 138; particularistic loyalties, 202; political identity, 48; regime type, 43; size, 40; structural changes in government, 196
Nixon, Richard M., 150; Vietnam policy, 182; visit to China, 175; visits to China and Soviet Union, 223
Nixon doctrine, 144
Nkrumah, Kwame, 35, 202, 253
"Noise," 233
Nonaligned countries, 120
Nonalignment, 54
Nongovernmental groups, 13, 162–68
Nongovernmental international organizations, 19
Norms, 107
NATO, 19, 74, 90, 94–96, 106, 120, 130, 151, 153, 224, 250, 258; French withdrawal, 226; linked to Cuban missile crisis, 91; reaction to Soviet invasion of Hungary, 105; reduction of Canadian forces, 147
"Northern tier," 125
Norway: regime type, 43; size, 40
Nuclear Nonproliferation Treaty, 74–76
Nuclear proliferation, 156
Nuclear Test Ban Treaty, 76
Nuclear war, 146, 147, 269
Nuclear weapons, 60, 69, 76, 117, 130, 140, 195, 206, 208, 241

Objects, 74; in a situation, 68
Occupation (of a country), 237
Operational definitions, 11, 26, 31, 135
Operational environment, 110–11
Opportunities, 182–83, 186, 251
Oppositional action: definition, 109
Organization: as factor in mobilizing resources, 210–11
Organization of African Unity, 19, 20, 21
Organization of American States, 64; linked to Cuban missile crisis, 91

Pacifism, 242
Pakistan, 58, 63, 138; Awami League, 51, 52; creation of Bangladesh, 51–55; Kashmir dispute, 97; Indian interven-

Pakistan (Cont.)
tion, 25; National Assembly, 51, 52; People's Party, 52; political identity, 48; rank, 27; regime type, 43; size, 40; Tashkent settlement, 72
Palestine, 253
Panama: regime type, 43; size, 40
Pan-Africa, 253
Pan-German, 180
Paraguay: regime type, 43; size, 40
"Parliamentary diplomacy," 218
Parsons, Talcott, 55, 143
"Participatory democracy," 248
Patron-client relationship, 225
Peace, 69–70, 73
Peace groups, 140
Peacemaking and intermediaries, 235–36
Peace negotiations, 223
Peace settlements, 185–86
Pearl Harbor, 116, 182
Penetrated political system, 114
Perceptions, 8, 111, 112, 144, 156–59, 168, 177, 179, 192, 194
Personality, 203; as factor in decision making, 176–77
Persuasion, 217–18
Peru: regime type, 43; size, 40
Philippines: regime type, 43; size, 40
Poland, 58, 175, 228; German invasion, 77; goals, 151; in ICC, 96; rank, 27; regime type, 43; size, 28, 40
Policy: definition, 3–4
Political executive, 160–68
Political leadership, 160–68. *See also* Leadership
Political process, 160–68
Political systems, 17, 35, 37, 160–68; authoritarian, 8, 9, 30, 31, 160–68, 175, 190, 191, 199, 206, 214; democratic, 8, 9, 30, 31, 160–68, 175, 190, 191, 199, 209, 214, 252–53, 273; dictatorships, 160–68, 196, 252–53; domestic, 8; juntas, 160–68; mobilized, 204; mobilized modern, 30, 31, 166, 201–4; modern, 30; monarchy, 274; parliamentary, 160–68; presidential, 160–68; premobilized, 237; premobilized modern, 30, 31, 201–4; primitive, 30; regime types, 62; traditional, 30, 201
Population, 27, 28, 29, 53, 59, 139–41, 240; age distribution, 139; geographical distribution, 139–40; productive, 28; rank, 39–41
Portugal: alliance with United Kingdom, 224, 254; regime type, 43; size, 40

"Potential," 207
Power, 60, 224
Power inventories, 204
Predisposition, 12, 25, 32–37, 38, 75, 105, 107, 112, 137, 141, 144, 208, 212, 242
Press, 190
Press leaks, 166, 191
Prestige, 150, 239
Preventive war, 29
Propaganda, 63, 229, 253
Psychological environment, 108, 110–11
Psychoanalytic theory, 34–35
Public opinion, 190, 274
Pueblo, U.S.S., 184

Quebec, 18
"Quebec Libre," 153

Race, 64
Rahman, Sheikh Mujibur, 51, 52, 53
Rand Corporation, 178
Ranks of countries, 26–27, 37, 112
Rationality, 111
Rectitude, 252–53
Refugees, 18
Regime change, 180
Regime types, 30, 31, 42–44
Regions, 36, 68, 137, 226
Reification, 35, 57
Religion, 54, 57–58, 61, 64, 145
Resources, 9, 17, 30, 142, 241; domestic and private demands on, 212; expenditure, 275; material, 141–43; mobilizable, 206–8
Responsibility of states, 45–50
Revolution, 11, 33, 34, 62, 142, 178, 187, 196, 203, 231, 240
Revolutionary regimes, 11, 33
Rhodesia, 116; regime type, 43; size, 40
Risks, 232, 251
Roles: individual, 203; state, 35, 36, 69, 70, 71, 84, 137, 225
Roosevelt, Franklin D., 114
Rule application functions, 163, 188
Rule making functions, 163
Rumania, 105; regime type, 43; size, 40
Rusk, Dean, 218
Russia, 137, 149, 194; 1917 revolution, 178, 191
Rwanda: regime type, 43; size, 40

Sanctions, international, 230
Saudi Arabia: regime type, 43; size, 40
Secret police, 189
Security, 27, 28, 137, 146–49, 250
Security dilemma, 1–2

Self-determination, 53
Senegal: regime type, 43; size, 40
Separation of powers, 165
Sèvres, 125
Siberia, 139
Sierra Leone: regime type, 43; size, 40
Sihanouk, Norodom, 148, 202
Sinai Desert, 126
Singapore: regime type, 43; size, 40
Sino-Soviet alliance, 226
Sino-Soviet dispute, 54, 91, 99–101, 145, 261
Situations, 3, 5, 6, 7, 8, 10, 12, 17, 18, 19, 21, 25, 26, 31, 32, 33, 37, 38, 60, 61, 67–102, 107, 112, 133, 136, 146, 147, 204, 207, 214, 238, 239, 248, 250, 255, 258, 268–72; boundaries, 71–75; conditions of interaction, 84–90; linked, 74; number and rank of actors, 75–77; perceptions of, 158; structures, 77–84; transformation, 7, 8
Size, 137–38
Size index, 28, 29, 39–41, 42–44, 45–50
Small powers, 26–27
Social cleavages, 60–64
Socialist states, 61
Society, 34, 37; cohesion, 32
Somalia: regime type, 43; size, 41
South Africa, 58, 61, 64; political identity, 48; rank, 27; regime type, 43; size, 41
Southeast Asia, 148, 250
Sovereign equality, 64
Sovereignty, 58, 62, 146
Soviet bloc, 105
Spain: political identity, 49; rank, 27; regime type, 43; size, 41
Specialized agencies, 21
Sri Lanka: regime type, 43; size, 41
Stability, 36, 231, 267
Stalin, Joseph, 86, 161, 165
States, 12, 19; as actors, 24, 38; location, 26; distinction from nation, 34; size, 24, 26; types of political regimes, 24, 26; wealth, 24, 26
"Step-level function," 266
Stockholm Conference, 257
Strategic arms limitation talks, 222
Strategic location, 32
Strategic theory, 204
State system, 22
Stimson doctrine, 144
Structural differentiation, 30
Structures, governmental, 8
Student movement, 62

Style, national, 143–60
Subrahmanyam, K., 54
Sudan: regime type, 43; size, 41
Success, 77, 107, 134, 179; in crises, 234
Succession, 203
Succession processes, 192
Suez Canal, 124
Sukarno, 192, 202
Summit conference, 168
Superpowers, 73; definition, 26–27
Supportive action: definition, 109
Sweden, 154, 249, 252; rank, 27; regime type, 43; size, 41
Switzerland, 201; political identity, 49; rank, 27; regime type, 43; size, 41
Syria, 94, 126, 131–33; regime type, 43; size, 41
Systems analysis, 55–57

Taiwan, 32, 147; regime type, 43; size, 41
Tashkent settlement, 72
Tanzania: political identity, 49; regime type, 43; size, 41
Targets, 84, 120, 121, 132, 183, 234–35, 236–43
Technical assistance, 19, 20, 200, 203
Technological innovation, 194–95
Technology, 23, 24, 57, 58–60, 76, 137, 138–39, 140, 141, 177–78
Terrain, 137, 138
Territorial state, 59, 61
Territory, 34, 68, 137, 146, 222, 223, 237, 252; effect of conquest, 276
Tet offensive, 169
Thailand: political identity, 49; regime type, 43; size, 41; in Vietnam war, 96
Thermonuclear war, 68
Third world, 53
Threats, 24, 146, 147, 151, 182–83, 186, 194, 217, 218, 231, 232, 236, 250, 251; perceptions of, 156–57
Time, 9, 10, 69, 157, 190, 192; critical, 169, 184; natural, 184
Tito, 202, 229
Togo: regime type, 43; size, 41
Tonkin Gulf incident, 242
Transformation, 7, 13, 56, 266
Transnational forces, 55
Treaties, 64, 275–76
Tribe, 61
Trinidad: regime type, 43; size, 41
Trinidad and Tobago, 138
Truman doctrine, 144
Truman, Harry S, 188
Tunisia: regime type, 43; size, 41

Turkey, 96, 251; as ally of United States, 29; political identity, 49; rank, 27; regime type, 44; size, 41
Tylor's definition of culture, 143

Uganda, 169; regime type, 44; size, 41
Underdeveloped countries, 19, 37, 166, 180, 231; and multinational corporations, 23
USSR, 21, 28, 29, 58, 72, 73, 77, 201, 206, 223, 260; aid to North Vietnam, 145; alliances, 106; arms negotiations, 256; arms race, 242; basis of political support for elites, 166; control of Eastern Europe, 61; Czechoslovak coup, 217; in Cuban missile crisis, 77, 91, 185, 242; in Eastern Europe, 253; effect of memories, 154; emigration tax, 5; empire, 61; European policy, 146; intervention in Congo, 253; intervention in Hungary, 105; intervention in Czechoslovakia, 25, 150; goals, 151, 152–53; in Kashmir dispute, 97; leadership struggle, 193; in Middle East, 94, 110, 269; military aid to Egypt and North Vietnam, 207; and nuclear nonproliferation treaty, 74; nuclear war, 241; nuclear weapons, 60; perception of nuclear proliferation, 156; perception of threats, 147; policy after Cuban missile crisis, 148; political identity, 49; position on United States' nuclear monopoly, 76; rank, 27; regime type, 44; relations with allies, 228; relations with India, 54; relations with United States, 227, 232, 252; responsibility, 36; security dilemma, 1; Sino-Soviet dispute, 99–101; size, 41; support of India in 1971, 53; Tashkent agreement, 72, 109; treaty with India, 52; United Nations policy, 20; in Vietnam situation, 96; in Western Pacific and East Asia, 99; withdrawal from World War I, 251; in World War II, 85, 109
United Arab Republic. See Egypt
United Kingdom, 29, 58, 152, 201; alliance with Portugal, 224, 254; American Revolution, 276; arms to Jordan, 193; British empire, 35; decision making process, 164; invasion of Egypt, 109, 169, 255; Labour Government, 275; in Middle East, 94, 110; public opinion, 274; political identity, 50; rank, 27; relations with United States,

United Kingdom (Cont.)
232; regime type, 44; responsibility, 36; size, 41; special relationship with United States, 255; in Western Pacific and East Asia, 99; in World War II, 85–86, 141, 145, 275

United Nations, 3, 18, 19, 20, 21, 64, 65, 203, 218, 262–63; advantages of membership, 62; Chinese seat, 261; Congo operation, 36; General Assembly, 53, 61, 126; implications of membership, 249; intervention in Congo, 237; in Kashmir dispute, 98; in Middle East, 22, 70, 102; Secretary-General, 20, 109, 125, 130, 217; Security Council, 53, 107, 230; specialized agencies, 20, 64; Stockholm conference, 257; UNCTAD, 63, 258; UNEF, 22

United States, 29, 37, 58, 72, 73, 74, 96, 206, 223; aid to Britain, 145; aid to Pakistan, 54; Air Force, 193; alliance policies, 226; alliance system, 106; alliance with South Vietnam, 225, 251; alliance with Taiwan, 32; arms to Jordan, 193; arms negotiations, 256; arms race, 242; 1941 attack by Japan, 4; before World War II, 182; bipartisanship, 182; bombing North Vietnam, 242; CIA, 192; Congress, 166, 190; in Cuban missile crisis, 77, 91, 185; and 1968 Czechoslovak crisis, 274; definition of security interests, 144; decision making process, 164; dissent, 57; 1971 economic policies, 175; economic policy, 20; effect of memories, 154; entry into World War II, 182; expansion, 250; Far East policy, 116; goal of integration, 153; and Hungarian revolution, 273; influence in Western Europe, 146; intervention, 253; intervention in Dominican Republic, 25, 150; intervention in Lebanon, 183; Joint Chiefs of Staff, 195; in Kashmir dispute, 97; in Korean War, 242, 253; in Middle East, 94, 102, 109, 110, 269; military constituency, 190; mobilization in World War II, 212; monopoly of nuclear weapons, 60, 76; and multinational corporations, 23; National Security Council, 197; Negroes, 275; and nonproliferation treaty, 74; in NATO, 94; nuclear war, 241; opportunities in Indonesia, 183; perception of nuclear proliferation, 156; perception of threats, 147; policy, 10; political identity, 50; political style, 144;

United States (Cont.)
promotion of disintegration, 228–29; *Pueblo* crisis, 184; policy after Cuban missile crisis, 148; public opinion, 274; rank, 27; regime type, 44; relations with Australia, 249–50; relations with China, 222, 232; relations with South Vietnam, 256–57; relations with USSR, 4, 232, 252; relations with United Kingdom, 232; relations with West Germany, 151; response to Czech invasion, 184; responsibility, 36; security dilemma, 1, 2; Senate, 176, 187, 196; shifts in attitudes, 169; size, 41; special relationship with United Kingdom, 255; support of Pakistan, 53; structural change in government, 196–97; in Vietnam war, 61, 96, 109, 187; war with Germany, 174; in Western Pacific and East Asia, 99, 253; withdrawal from Vietnam, 150; in World War II, 85–86, 109, 141

Upper Volta: regime type, 44; size, 41
Urgency, 232
Uruguay: regime type, 44; size, 41
U Thant (in Cuban missile crisis), 91

Values, 35, 191; common, 145–49
Venezuela: regime type, 44; size, 41
Viet Cong, 18, 96, 148, 231
Vienna, 222
Vietnam, 242; United States' intervention, 154
Vietnam, North, 73, 96, 106, 109, 145, 148, 150; intervention in South Vietnam, 216; regime type, 44; resistance to United States' attacks, 61; size, 41; Tonkin Gulf incident, 242; United States' bombing, 242; use of Soviet military equipment, 207–8
Vietnam, South, 18, 73, 96, 109, 137, 150, 242; alliance with United States, 225, 250–51; intervention by North Vietnam, 216; regime subject to threat, 231; regime type, 44; relations with United States, 256–57; size, 41
Vietnam war, 10, 57, 61, 71, 73, 86, 90, 96–97, 109, 150, 187, 213; effect on United States, 182, 276; settlement, 223

War, 10, 30, 64, 70, 73, 137, 140, 174, 185, 186, 187, 222, 234–35, 241, 266; effects of inconclusive wars, 276; risk, 232
War criminals, 145

Index

Warsaw (US-China talks), 222
Warsaw Pact, 20, 120; formation, 250; invasion of Czechoslovakia, 184
Wealth, 142–43, 145
Western Europe, 21, 28, 72, 75, 94, 125, 145, 146, 152–53, 250; dependence on oil, 58; integration, 61; perception of threats, 147; recovery from World War II, 116
Western European Union, 106
Western Hemisphere, 21, 226
Western Pacific, 250
Western Pacific and East Asia, 90, 99–100
Winning coalition, 8

World Bank, 19, 64, 142
World Health Organization, 19
World order, 61, 62
World War II, 28; alliance behavior, 85–86; cause, 150; decisions, 174

Yalu, 242
Yemen: regime type, 44; size, 41
Yugoslavia, 126, 229; regime type, 44; size, 41

Zaire: regime type, 44; size, 41
Zambia, 58; regime type, 44; size, 41
Zero-sum condition, 86, 87

Augsburg College
WITHDRAWN
Minneapolis, Minnesota 55454